FRENCH LEAVE

JOHN BURTON RACE

Photography by

PIA TRYDE

Ⓔⓟ

EBURY PRESS

CONTENTS

Aut

As I stood on the deck of the ferry on that chilly August morning, I felt a sense of relief. After all the months of planning, phone calls and complicated arrangements, we were finally on the first leg of our journey to France, where we were going to be spending the next year.

I'd had a difficult three years, going through the upheaval of leaving my successful Berkshire restaurant, opening a new one in London, and working hard to regain my previously established two Michelin star status. It had been an exciting and successful time. We got our Michelin stars back, but I had begun to realise that London was no different from Berkshire. There were the same pressures, only more so, and something was definitely missing. I was fed up with spending four hours a day in a car commuting up and down from Oxfordshire, and, more importantly, I wasn't enjoying the job as much as I used to. The business side had completely taken over, and the one thing I loved more than anything else, the thing I had a real passion for – the cooking – had gone onto the back burner. I wanted to get that passion back. I wanted to change my life.

Like many chefs, perhaps, I'd spent so long thinking about how to create spectacular dishes that somewhere along the line I'd lost the plot – I had lost sight of the very thing that is at the heart of all good food: superb ingredients. I wanted to start again, at the beginning. My plan was to write a book that would go back to basics and rediscover the pleasures of simple food. I wanted to find out more about fine ingredients at their source, and the people who produced them – and I needed to go where the textures and flavours of the food conformed to my high ideals.

France was the obvious choice. Not only did it have the world's finest cuisine, but my training as a chef had been primarily French-influenced, so moving there would be a return to my culinary roots. Also, and perhaps more importantly, I had always loved the place with a passion – its landscape, its people and their wonderful *joie de vivre* (it's no coincidence that the French invented the term). This was a country where I had always felt at home – a place where good food and wines were not just designer accessories, but an integral part of life; where the textures and flavours of food were what they should be. What better place to study ingredients at their best?

And then the doubts had set in – you know, those niggling doubts you sometimes have in the small hours of the morning. Taking a year off was all very well, but what if it didn't work? What if Kim (my wife) hated it? What if the kids hated it? I so much wanted to introduce them to a new way of life.

But what if the whole enterprise was a complete disaster? It was something we had discussed endlessly as a family over the whole of the previous year. Kim was totally supportive, and selling the idea to the younger children – Eliza (7), Charles (5) and Amelia (affectionately known as Millie, 3) – had been relatively easy. They were young enough to see the whole thing as an adventure. But we'd met a lot of opposition from the older girls. Eve (16), Olivia (13) and Martha Daisy (12) were, understandably, apprehensive – upset at leaving their friends, and scared at the thought of leaving home and moving to a new country and new schools. After months of heated rows, they had gradually come round to the idea, but then, about two months before leaving England, Eve had fallen in love – with Tom, a 19-year-old builder's apprentice she'd met in Reading. As far as she was concerned, this was the real thing – and she wasn't about to let it go. As the time to leave drew nearer, she got sulkier and sulkier, constantly trying to muster more support from Olivia and Martha.

Faced with the possibility of an all-out rebellion on our hands, Kim and I had decided we all needed a holiday. So we booked a villa for two weeks in Biarritz, on the French Basque coast. It had sun, sea and sand, and would be a gentle introduction to our final move to France – a soothing transitional period where we could forget all our worries and just enjoy ourselves. And now here we were, on the Plymouth to Santander ferry – a leisurely, comfortable 26-hour crossing that we had hoped would take the edge off things – and Eve had gone AWOL.

I looked for her frantically for an hour, and eventually found her, huddled in the corner of an observation deck. Her face was streaked with tears and she was staring out of the window looking utterly miserable. (I thank God every day that I'm not a teenager, or in love for the first time any more.) We had a long talk, and she seemed to cheer up a bit. I thought about how I could make things better for her. Maybe I could involve her in the book in some way – say, by asking her to type up some of the manuscript? It was worth a try. We called a truce and somehow got through the rest of the crossing.

The next day, which dawned bright and sunny, I looked out of the cabin window and caught my first glimpse of the Spanish coastline, shimmering in the morning sun. The sea was a beautiful turquoise colour and the sky was clear blue, with not a cloud in sight. It already felt much warmer than England. Things were looking up. We docked at 8.15 a.m. and made for the French border, driving past magnificent mountain ranges and stunning beaches on the way. It was wonderful to see the burnt orange roof tiles and the whitewashed walls of Spanish houses again. By the time we hit Biarritz, three and a half hours later, we were in real holiday mood.

The plan was to stay there for two weeks, then go to Toulouse, spend the night there, and, on 15 September, take the motorway down to our new house. But until then, we had a fortnight of relaxation ahead of us. I still remember those two wonderful weeks – the swimming, the lazing in the sun, the sightseeing, the visits to local markets, the seafood meals, the breathtaking views from our villa, the mountains silhouetted by the moon at night, throwing a diffused light onto the Atlantic. But most of all I remember the fun we had, joking around with each other. For two weeks at least, all our differences were forgotten and we were a family again…

It was 15 September – the day we were leaving for our new home. D-Day. Strangely, now that the time had finally come, all my earlier doubts had gone, and I was bursting with excitement, adrenalin pumping at the thought of what lay ahead. This was an adventure, and I was a teenager again. It was the same for Kim. But as we all met up at the cars that morning, it was pretty clear that not everyone felt the same way. Eliza, Charles and Millie were, as always, fine, but one look at the sulky expressions on Olivia, Martha and Eve's faces told me we had problems again.

It was with battle lines drawn, then, and both cars stuffed to the gills with suitcases, that we set off from Toulouse in convoy – me in front with Eve, Olivia, Charles and Millie, and Kim behind with Martha and Eliza. It was 7 a.m. and the weather looked ominously bad. The day before had been perfect – blue skies and not a cloud to be seen. Now it was overcast, with a heavy mist that virtually obliterated the sky and seemed to add to the children's feelings of gloom. By 9 o'clock we were on the A61 motorway, heading frustratingly slowly towards Montpellier and Carcassonne. Our ultimate destination was the Aude – a *département* of the region of

Languedoc Roussillon in south-west France. This is the 'other' south of France – the one that rarely gets a mention, having long been eclipsed by her more famous, more chic and more ostentatious cousin, Provence. For me, that had been its appeal. Kim and I had been frequent visitors to France; over the years we'd been to Provence, Loire, Burgundy, Normandy and Brittany, and I knew the food of these regions very well. But the Aude was *La France profonde* – a truly traditional and rural area that had been relatively untainted by tourism and modern cooking trends. I found the thought of that exciting.

We drove past spectacular countryside – the Pyrenees on one side and the great parallel stretch of peaks known as the Montagne Noire (Black Mountain) on the other – and finally reached the Aude at around lunchtime. The moment we got there I was struck by the change in scenery. The snow-capped mountains and green hills had given way to a flatter, more agricultural landscape. Dusty and parched in the sun, the sand-coloured clay soil, dotted with red-roofed houses and single cypress trees sticking out of the ground like needles, looked more like Tuscany than France. Apart, that is, from the sunflowers, which were everywhere. The sun, which throughout the journey had been desperately trying to break through the mist, now finally came out, bursting gloriously through the clouds and bathing the countryside in light. This was no mellow English autumn day, but the blazing heat of full summer. We all instantly cheered up.

The house we were making for was in a tiny hamlet called Montferrand. It had been a last-minute choice – the tail end of a protracted and messy period of house-hunting. We (Kim and I, that is) had fallen in love with a fabulous place near the Black Mountain. And then, at the last minute, it had fallen through. This had coincided with a 'bad' family patch, when the kids were depressed about the move, and Kim and I had just got back to England after one of our many recce trips for the children's schools. We had to make a decision – fast – and, in a rare moment of weakness, Kim (no doubt feeling she had enough on her plate dealing with the girls) suggested that I go out and try to find somewhere. If it didn't work out, we could always move, she reasoned. After looking at scores of places on my own, I began to feel pretty fed up, but finally – pressurised, time-wise, into making a choice – had opted for a 19th-century *mas*, or farmhouse, in Montferrand. My visit to the house had been so rushed that I could barely remember it. I seemed to recall that the house itself hadn't impressed me much, but the location was fantastic. Perched on top of a hill, overlooking fields, it was quiet and remote – perfect for all my writing, I thought.

But now, as we all looked out for the Montferrand signpost, I began to have second thoughts. Knowing we were very near our destination, everyone in the car was beginning to get really excited. But not me. Suddenly, my doubts came creeping back, and I began to feel panicky, overwhelmed at a sense of driving into the unknown. I'd done lots of background reading about the Aude, of course, but, apart from our short recce trips, I didn't know it at all. So I had committed my family to moving to a new country for a year, into a house they'd never seen, on the basis of a choice I'd made after only one brief visit. It wasn't a great start, considering that half of them hadn't wanted to come in the first place. What the hell am I going to do, I was thinking to myself, if they don't like this house? And, worse still, what the hell am I going to do if they really hate France? This could be the end of my marriage, and my family, I suddenly thought in a panic.

As we took the Montferrand turning, I gabbled on like a madman, trying to hide my nervousness, but everyone else in the car was quiet. Very quiet. Flanked by sunflowers on the left and a carpet of golden rapeseed on the right, we passed the signs for Montmaur, Soupex, then a large crucifix – you know, the sort you often see in Catholic countries (all the kids were hanging out of the car windows now, looking around and wondering which of the houses in the distance was ours). High up in the sky a buzzard flew past. After twisting and turning down the lanes, I finally hit the approach to the house: an avenue of trees – oak, more of those Tuscan cypresses, and flashes of grey and silver leaves. And then, right at the back, there it was – the house, half-hidden by the tree canopy, and glinting in the sun like a piece of beautifully hidden treasure.

We sped on through the trees, approaching the house from the back, then took a long sweeping curve around the driveway towards the front, and I took it all in properly – I think for the first time. There was a chestnut tree in full fruit, and then the house itself – the same as I remembered, yet different. The

BELOW: *Our new home for a year. Built in the 19th century as a* mas, *or farmhouse, the house had certainly seen better days – but I fell in love with it just the same.*

walls, which before had seemed a dull brown were now, in the sun, ochre-coloured and magnificent, and there was a heavy wooden rustic door that I hadn't recalled seeing before. It was glorious, and, oh, so unmistakably French. Kim looked delighted. We all fell out of the cars, the kids squealing in their excitement and running all over the garden. Only Eve let the side down, with the immortal words, 'Aw, Dad, what a dump!'

I knew the house was scruffy round the edges, but I could now see it had masses of character to make up for that, and I was angry that Eve hadn't been able to see it too. But I wasn't going to let anything take away my excitement, so I swallowed my irritation and went to the outbuilding where Paul, the owner of the house, lived, to get the key. The door was opened by a middle-aged man who looked the spitting image of Jean-Paul Belmondo. He stood there for a second, smoking a cheroot, then broke into a smile, welcomed me

in and went off to get the key. As I stood there waiting I couldn't help but notice the paintings on his wall − fantastic seascapes, vibrant, exciting and colourful − I loved them. 'So you like the paintings,' Paul said, handing me the key on his return. 'They're done by a local painter, Michel Calvet. He lives on that hill over there (pointing at the next hill along)… You should go and visit him some time. He always likes visitors.' I made a mental note of this and went back to Kim, and we began to explore the house together.

After the bright sunshine outside, the interior looked dark, but I could now see there was nothing a lick of paint wouldn't sort out, and that the house clearly had more potential than I'd remembered. There were fantastic original features, such as a wrought-iron staircase and beautiful patterned floor tiles, and the views from every window were breathtaking. It was a massive place: six bedrooms, two enormous reception rooms − one of them oak-beamed with a huge fireplace − and a large kitchen-cum-dining-room. But only one bathroom. Why hadn't that registered with me before? 'One bathroom?' shrieked Kim. 'One bathroom − between eight of us? That's the last time I let you do any house-hunting.' But the way I was feeling right then, I honestly don't think anything could have fazed me.

We went outside to join the children, and this time I explored the garden properly. It was about half an acre in size and had pots of lavender, laurel bushes, some unusual conifers, a fig tree (green figs, unfortunately, not black, but beautiful nevertheless) and, at the back, a magnificent cedar tree with a rope swing. On the far right was a large stone-paved terrace.

Beyond the garden were about 300 hectares of fields, partly given over to sunflowers and wheat: some of the land looked as if it had been ploughed and cut within the last few weeks. The views from the garden, as from the house, were magnificent. We were at the top of a hill, a valley in front of us and a valley behind, and could even make out the contours of the snow-capped Pyrenees. But it was the smells that we were instantly struck by − a heady mixture of lavender, newly cut wheat and flowers, and dusty straw.

We spent the rest of that day unpacking and shopping for basic foodstuffs, and generally picking Paul's brains about the area. I was interested mainly in

OPPOSITE: *The medieval town of Revel, with its fantastic food and flower market, colourful houses and fine arcades, was a regular family haunt.*

food markets, of course, and was delighted to hear there was a good weekly one nearby, in Revel. It was held on Saturdays and was not only the best in the area, but had recently been designated one of the best in France. Thankfully, we only had two days to wait before the next one, but to me it seemed like a lifetime.

The furniture removal van arrived the next day, so we had plenty of unpacking and sorting out to keep us busy. And, of course, there was always the happy prospect of sitting outside in the sunshine. I think Kim and I were in a perpetual daze for those first couple of days, and had to keep pinching ourselves to make sure it was all real. I remember constantly going out to the bench in the garden, needing to stare at the view and take in those wonderful smells, like a drug addict wanting a fix.

That Saturday dawned bright and sunny, and we set off to Revel market early (we knew it closed at 12.30 p.m. and I was determined not to miss one second). I still remember that first visit. I had been to hundreds of French markets before, but this rated as one of the best, and still does. Not just for its produce, but also because of its appearance. What I really liked about it was the fact that it was so traditional. When country towns originally developed in France, they tended to be built around a central square that was either arcaded to offer protection from extremes of weather, or had a covered area with a market hall, or *halle de marchés*. A 14th-century town, Revel is one of the few places that still retains its *halle*, and, with its clock tower and red-tiled roof supported by ancient wooden pillars, was one of the nicest I'd ever seen. I was especially struck by the brightly canopied stalls outside the covered areas, and by the fine 17th- and 18th-century houses with their beautiful arcades.

The market itself was everything I'd hoped for – teeming with food, people and atmosphere. It was more like a Harrods sale than the lacklustre shopping you see in British supermarkets. Here people were craning their necks to look at the stalls with – something I've always loved about the French – their eyes lighting up at the sight of particular foodstuffs they were interested in. And the produce itself was, of course, fantastic. My eyes roamed greedily over the Pêches de Vigne (massive golden peaches with burgundy- and purple-

veined flesh), the fat purple figs, the plump grapes looking fit to burst, the specialist stalls with ducks, quails, honey, Foie gras, chestnuts, and cheeses from the Auvergne, and the neatly laid-out rows of perfect vegetables. Then there were the local specialities, the *pain de seigle* (rye bread) that was such a perfect match with the oysters that would come in a month later; the hot and peppery *radis noir* (black radishes), delicious when finely grated and cooked in a port syrup, with some gently fried Foie gras on top; and finally the fabulous plump *pruneaux d'Agen* – a particular favourite (the Lot-et-Garonne produces thousands of tonnes of these wonderful prunes each year). And everywhere I looked there were those fat, glorious ceps, fried by the locals with garlic and parsley in their traditional *poêles* (long-handled frying pans), or simply served in omelettes. Even the take-away food was out of the ordinary – chicken and quails spit-roasted over potatoes, and cartwheel-sized pans with steaming Moules à la crème. (Which must have been good because the local women were queuing up holding plastic containers waiting to be filled.) We moved on to where a young man in a blue-and-white-striped sweatshirt was making Aligot – that five-star, 3,000 calories a smell, headily

delicious combination of garlic, mashed potato, Cantal cheese and crème fraîche. I watched, mesmerised, as he mixed the ingredients with a long paddle, then lifted the mixture up high, and swirled it around. In the end, it all became too much; I caved in and bought some for lunch. I also bought some bread to have with it, along with masses of other provisions, including some *saucissons* that I thought I might cook with potatoes – a kind of French bangers and mash that I hoped would break the children into French food gently.

I thought about the market all the way home. Seeing those wonderful ingredients had made me excited about food all over again, and I wanted to learn exactly why they were so fantastic. I really felt I needed to talk to the people who grew or produced this stuff and made it so special, but didn't know how to go about it. This was partly due to the language problem. My French wasn't as good as I hoped, and I was having a lot of difficulty understanding the local dialect – derived from the medieval language known as *langue d'Oc*. Apart from that, the stall-holders seemed friendly enough, though I couldn't help feeling there was a kind of invisible barrier between

RIGHT: *Charles, Eliza*
and I look on,
mesmerised, as a man
makes Aligot in Revel
Market.

us. I needed them to let me into their world, but would they do it?

There were torrential rains that night and we woke up to grey skies – not what you expect from the south of France at all, but the up side was that we were able to get down to yet more unpacking without being tempted outside by the hot weather. Kim spent most of that Sunday sorting out the children's school bags, and there was a general feeling of gloom and doom about the place because the next day was the first day of school.

That first Monday is not a day I care to remember. The school was in the nearby town of Castelnaudary, probably best known for being home to the French Foreign Legion, and as we drove through, it seemed to look far grimmer than I'd remembered from our recce trips. The girls had been holding back their tears from the moment we'd set off. When we got there, the headmistress and teachers couldn't have been more enthusiastic, and everything seemed fine until the time came for Eve to go into her class. She refused to go, turned her face to the wall and started to cry, shrugging off any attempts by the headmistress to reassure her. I finally managed to persuade her to go in, and then had to face the same thing all over again with Olivia and Martha. Eventually, they both went in crying. Eliza seemed to be fine until the last minute, and then she stiffened up and began to look terribly nervous. Kim began to cry, and it wasn't long before I was at it too. It was

Charles who saved the day. He said he was Spiderman, and that the French teachers and children were like green goblins and he was going to zap them all. I think it was probably at that point that Kim and I realised he'd never get a job in the Diplomatic Service, but at least it worked. Reassured by his jokes, Millie went in without a struggle.

Kim and I spent all day worrying about the girls and wondering how they'd got on. The full horror emerged that evening, when we went to pick them up. They'd had a terrible day. They hated the school and there was no way they were going back. There were the usual outbursts – Eve swearing, Olivia and Martha crying and shouting, and me, in the middle, trying to be rational, trying to explain that sometimes life was about facing and getting through difficult situations. Kim was understandably depressed because they were depressed. I was depressed because they were all depressed, and eventually I gave in. It was no good – we would just have to find another school. I went outside and stared at the big sky and the views. Somehow even the cedar tree in the garden didn't look quite so magnificent any more.

It was the following week that I met Michel Calvet for the first time. Kim and I were waiting to hear from a school in Toulouse that might take the girls, and were both feeling a bit twitchy. I was bored with sitting and doing nothing, and wanted to cook. We had so many eggs in the fridge that I had decided on a Crème brûlée, but I couldn't get the damned thing to work. I soon realised what was wrong. The eggs were far richer and better than those in England, and I'd used too many. In fact, I'd now used them all. Frustrated, I left it and started working on some recipes, but couldn't settle. Eventually, I became so restless that I decided to go out. I remembered the painter that Paul had mentioned – Michel Calvet – and suddenly thought I'd pay him a visit.

Driving up the hill to Michel's house on that beautiful September day, I was struck yet again by the beauty of the landscape. As I stopped to let a hare cross the path, I looked at the fields of sunflowers around me and thought, 'Maybe I'll get bored with all this one day. But not just yet…'

Michel's house was beautiful, with magnificent views of the Pyrenees and a garden full of olive trees, some of them very old. There was no reply when I rang the doorbell, but I could hear music blaring out of a radio, so I followed the sound and ran into a blonde woman in her early forties, who was picking vervain. She greeted me charmingly – to my surprise she was English – and introduced herself as Michel's wife Lesley. He was working in his studio, she explained. 'Just follow the sound of the Cuban music.' I did, and was drawn to a small outbuilding, where I found him smoking a cigar while working on a brightly coloured seascape.

Michel seemed delighted to see me. He had heard that Kim and I were renting the house in Montferrand, and had been meaning to call in, but he'd been very busy finishing some paintings for an exhibition. He was from Toulouse, it turned out, and had been living in the Aude for six years. He loved the Aude, he said – it was so much nicer than Provence, which was *trop touristique*. This region was more rustic and authentic, and the people were more genuine – not as money-minded. No, the Aude was definitely the place, he pronounced enthusiastically. The countryside was beautiful and calm, the skies big and fantastic, and the burnished gold of the vineyards in autumn was *magnifique*. It was only here that he had found true *paix d'esprit* (it sounded so much better than the English 'peace of mind').

He warmed to his theme, extolling the pleasures of the countryside in the autumn and the smell of ceps in the woods. He had discovered some fantastic ones in woodland that formed part of an estate in the Black Mountain. The owner's name was Madame de Lassus, and she was always happy for him to pick them. He would introduce me to her, he continued enthusiastically. At that point, Lesley joined us, and when I mentioned how much work we needed to do on the house, she kindly offered to help with recommendations for tradesmen. I left two hours later, pleased with having made new friends.

Lesley was as good as her word, and over the next few days plied us with the names of painters, decorators, upholsterers and interior designers. It was great to watch the house finally start to take shape. The news from the Toulouse school, meanwhile, wasn't good, and Kim and I were plunged into the whole business of school-searching again. We were dreading the thought of reaching half-term with the older girls, Eve, Martha and Olivia, still not placed, but fortunately, within a few weeks they were accepted at a school in

Revel, where, to our relief, they seemed very happy.

By now we'd slipped into a very pleasant routine of sitting in the garden under the cedar tree on hot days, and, as the weather cooled down, going out on shopping trips, visiting local markets and restaurants, and exploring the countryside with Lesley and Michel. I had got my bearings now and realised that the house straddled several different regions: the Aude, the Tarn and the Haute-Garonne. There was masses to see, and we crammed in a lot of local sights: the beautiful city of Toulouse, with its attractive pink buildings, wonderful shops and bustling nightlife, Carcassonne, the Canal du Midi (France's oldest working waterway, built during the reign of Louis XIV), and the many lovely medieval villages in the area, of which Sorèze, with its 17th-century Abbaye-Ecole, was my favourite. Charles especially loved the Cathar castles – no fairytale castles of the Loire, these, but grim, rather forbidding affairs perched on the top of hills. Charles loved exploring and running around in them, imagining he was a knight on horseback.

In the late afternoons, I would take the younger children out for walks, and we had great fun exploring the local wildlife together. We often saw hares, partridges, buzzards and red kites, and on one memorable occasion our first sighting of a deer. I idly wondered if we'd ever see one of the famous wild boars that roamed the area and were hunted in the traditional *chasse*. After supper (invariably eaten outside), when the younger children were in bed and the older ones were inside watching TV, Kim and I would sit out and watch the *Coucher du soleil* – the glorious sunsets that we never tired of.

In early October, our family was complete when our five-month-old Labrador pup, Fendi, was air-freighted out from England. I went to the airport to pick her up, and after supper, I sat under the cedar tree, throwing pine cones for her to fetch. The sunset had left crimson streaks on the contours of the Pyrenees, and I thought, 'It doesn't get much better than this.'

Things couldn't have been better from a personal point of view. But work was quite another matter. I'd been in France for nearly a month now, and still hadn't met any local food producers. I knew it was early days, but I was starting to get impatient – itching to get out there to talk to those people, and

RIGHT: *Eliza and Fendi, our pet Labrador, having a snooze. From the day that Fendi arrived, she and Eliza were inseparable.*

frustrated that I hadn't really met anyone who could help me. I was just beginning to wonder how long it might take – and then I got the phone call…

The fig tree was full of fruit – groaning from the weight – and the figs were over-ripe. I was angry with myself that I hadn't made use of the past fortnight and picked them. They were only green figs, admittedly, not purple ones, but I could have made jam if only I'd organised myself properly. There'd been a dramatic thunderstorm the night before, and it was now a ridiculously hot October day. I was just wondering how it was that I'd managed to spend a whole afternoon doing nothing but watch the local farmer plough his fields when the phone rang. It was a Madame de Lassus. Lost in that heat haze, I racked my brains trying to remember who it was, though her name sounded familiar. And then she mentioned Michel Calvet and I remembered. It was the ceps lady. She had heard I was in the area, she said, and would I like to come to her farm? I was over the moon. Yes, I said excitedly. Could I come over straight away, or was that too soon?

It took me about 20 minutes to find a pair of shoes (Fendi had an annoying habit of making off with every shoe she saw and hiding it – she cost us a fortune that first year!), then, suitably shod, I turned up at Madame de Lassus's house – a beautiful old-style farmhouse in the Black Mountain. Madame de Lassus (for some reason, we never did get on first-name terms) took me around her wonderful 100-hectare farm. Some of the land had been dug out to form a beautiful man-made lake, which was full of trout; the rest was partly cultivated with sunflowers (for oil) and organic maize (to feed the farm ducks), but most of it consisted of the deciduous oak and fern woods that I knew were the best habitat for ceps.

Naturally, I had come completely unprepared, but thankfully Madame de Lassus, a handsome, early middle-aged woman with fantastic cheekbones and wise grey eyes, immediately took over. With a Gallic equivalent of 'tut-tut', she armed me with a wicker basket and a stout stick – a basic tool for finding ceps. They favoured half-shaded conditions, she explained, and were often hidden by fern leaves. Their reddish-brown colouring also meant that they were often mistaken for dead leaves themselves. So you needed the stick to poke about.

As we walked into the woods, I was instantly struck by the mossy, mushroomy smell where the just-fallen rain had hit the earth, and felt really exhilarated at this, my first mushroom hunt. Mushroom hunting is a favourite pastime all over France, though with the large variety of poisonous mushrooms around, it's not something that's taken lightly. There isn't a pharmacy in France, however small, where the chemist won't know which are poisonous and which not, so he knows what medicine to offer in the event of poisoning. There are hundreds of varieties of mushroom in France, but the cep – found in most sauces in the region and in the ubiquitous Omelette aux cèpes – is the one that's most closely associated with the south-west. The cep looks quite different from the other edible varieties of mushroom you're likely to come across around here. For a start, there are no gills underneath the cap, as you would expect, but a mass of spongey spores. The cap itself can be any shade of brown (usually, it's reddish-brown), but it's the stems that are really distinctive. They are fat and bulbous, and get thicker towards the foot.

As we moved around the woods, Madame de Lassus made encouraging noises as she told me where to look. 'La fougère,' she kept saying, instructing me to look under the ferns, and I would gingerly move the fern leaves with my stick, peering at the ground. The classic tell-tale sign, she said, was the sight of small white mushrooms. They tasted like flour and weren't worth eating themselves, but you always found ceps near them. After spending about an hour bashing the undergrowth, beating the ferns and sniffing around the oak trees, I began to see that you needed a lot of patience to find ceps. Perhaps we were too late in the year, I suggested to Madame de Lassus. She assured me otherwise, explaining that although ceps were theoretically found from spring to autumn, autumn was *sans doute* the best time. The sun had to get through the leaf cover to heat the ground in July, she said. Spring ceps were fine, but they simply didn't keep – you had to eat them straight away… No, no, autumn was just fine.

We carried on for another hour, and just as I was really beginning to give up, I found one – a massive brute of a thing, more than 15cm across. I leapt about like a mad dervish in excitement, but on looking closer it turned out to be crawling with maggots. This was often the case, Madame de Lassus declared philosophically. When big ceps like that were found, they were often past their best. I was crestfallen, but she was not to be deterred. 'Courage!' she said. Ceps were never found on their own. If you found one, there was sure to be another nearby. So we went into battle again.

She was right, of course. I found them five minutes later – three medium-sized beauties – firm, completely maggot-free and easily enough to go with the roast chicken dish I planned to make that night. We swapped ideas about what to do with them, and her views were quite clear. You should never wash ceps – or any mushrooms for that matter. She simply brushed them, and fried them with oil, garlic, salt and pepper, then added some parsley (to make persillade) and served them with sautéed potatoes in a dish called Pommes sarladaises. She loved them as a garnish with duck breasts, or simply filled them with garlic butter and put them under the grill. I told her about my idea for a Roast chicken dish with cep fricassée and she nodded approvingly.

I went home with my ceps that day, triumphant. At last, I'd had my first real experience with food at its source. It was a great feeling. When I told the younger children about my day, they were all really excited, and that evening, as I went out for my walk with Charles, Millie and Eliza, we all took sticks and pushed back ferns whenever we saw them, pretending to find ceps. That evening, I cooked my finds accompanied by roast chicken, followed by Apple

crêpe. The children are normally my harshest critics, but this time everyone was happy.

By the end of October, it was still hot enough to sit out during the day, though the evenings were getting chillier and we began to have our meals inside. The children were all happy now. Their French was coming on in leaps and bounds, and they seemed to have really settled in. There was the odd moan from Eve, of course, but even she had cheered up – partly because she'd had a weekend visit from Tom, but mostly because she'd struck up a friendship with Michel and Lesley's 16-year-old daughter, Tatjana. They became inseparable.

The house was looking fantastic now – completely transformed with a coat of whitewash and some delicate white linens that Kim had cleverly chosen, which made it a brighter and altogether happier place to live, though the walls still looked rather bare. As a sort of house-warming, and a thank you to Lesley for all her help, we invited her and Michel for supper – and I was touched when Michel turned up with some of his paintings under his arm. A house-warming present, he said shyly. They looked fantastic set against the white walls.

It was one of many evenings we spent together, either at each other's houses, or in restaurants, where we sampled the local food – hearty vegetable soups, rabbit and hare stews, and duck, duck, duck everywhere. I became excited at the thought of maintaining the character of these regional dishes, while adapting them to a more modern style of cooking. The more I got to know about the local cuisine, the more I found that in every restaurant, from the humblest brasserie to the grandest Michelin-starred venue, one dish featured more than any other, and would almost come to haunt me in a way I could never have imagined. That dish was cassoulet.

I've always been fascinated by the way food develops in different countries, and particularly with the dishes that become part of a nation's folklore. In a country as big as France you can't really talk about a single national dish – rather, about regional specialities. But every so often a region will come up with a dish that transcends its own geographical limits, and reaches national iconic status, becoming an identifiable symbol of its country. There are many such dishes in the pantheon of local French cuisine. In Burgundy it's Boeuf bourguignon, in Marseille it's Bouillabaisse, and in south-western France it's that hearty concoction of beans, duck fat and pork known as Cassoulet.

The dish is said to have originated in Castelnaudary, though you try telling that to the people of Toulouse. For the truth is that this humble dish is a bit of a political hot potato, with people claiming its origins pretty much everywhere from the Pyrenees to Carcassonne. Cassoulet is big business here – not only because it is served in virtually every restaurant in the region, but because it's France's main tinned food: at least six varieties of the stuff are sold in any good local supermarket.

Local legend has it that Cassoulet originated in the 14th century, during the Hundred Years War, when Castelnaudary was under siege from the English army led by Edward, the Black Prince. The people of the town, the story goes, gathered their last provisions – beans and scraps of meat – cooked them all together and ate them. You've got to hand it to the French – if I'd just eaten a hearty bowl of Cassoulet, I wouldn't be able to move for at least three hours, but the brave citizens of Castelnaudary were so fortified by the dish that they defeated the weedy, ill-nourished English troops, who promptly legged it all the way back to the Channel.

Well, that's the story, anyway. Naturally, everyone in the area has their own personal recipe for Cassoulet, and the variations are legion. But to the purist, a Cassoulet, for it to be worthy of the name, has four basic requirements. It must be (1) made from white beans from the Lauragais (an area to the west of Carcassonne and the Black Mountain), prepared and cooked in (2) a *cassole* (the glazed terracotta bowl that gives the dish its name) that's been made in the village of Issel, and (3) water from Castelnaudary, over (4) a fire of furze taken from the Black Mountain.

I can't believe anyone actually goes that far, but Cassoulet is certainly taken very seriously here. Even so, when Lesley told me there was actually a Grande Confrérie du Cassoulet (Grand Brotherhood of the Cassoulet) with its own grand master, I thought she was joking. Were they like freemasons?

I wondered. Was there a special oath and a special Cassoulet handshake? I had to check it out. A few phone calls later, it was all arranged. Monsieur Jean-Louis Malé, a vice-president of the society, would be happy to see me.

Monsieur Malé lived in Villasavary, just outside Castelnaudary. I pulled up outside his home, an attractive white house in a pleasant, tree-lined street, rang the doorbell and waited. No response. Maybe he was out, or had forgotten our appointment. I tried again. Nothing. I put my ear to the door to see if I could hear any signs of life. There was a sound I couldn't quite place – a sort of rustling noise, interspersed with what sounded like flapping. Maybe Monsieur Malé had a pet bird that had got loose, and he was trying to capture it before opening the door. It was getting louder and louder now. It must be a pretty massive bird, I thought. And then the door opened to reveal the most extraordinary sight.

There stood Jean-Louis Malé, over 6 feet tall, spectacles gleaming in the sunlight, and wearing what looked like an upturned bowl on his head. As I stood there momentarily transfixed, my eyes moved further down to the rest of his outfit: thin, bedraggled yellow ribbons trailed down the sides of the bowl to meet a long, russet brown gown with huge sleeves that flopped about all over the place. The overall effect was a cross between a Sister of Charity and Widow Twanky.

As I stood there looking embarrassed, he clearly saw the humour of the occasion and laughed, welcoming me into his house, full of apologies. Anxious not to be late, he explained, he had hurried back from a meeting with the Confrérie and hadn't had time to change. As he flitted to the end of the room, he gestured for me to sit down, waving his arms. (Aha! That's where the flapping sound came from: it was those huge sleeves.)

The strangeness of our encounter over, Jean-Louis, as he insisted I call him – went into more details about the Confrérie. It had been set up by ten chefs in around 1940, with the sole aim of maintaining the traditional qualities of the Cassoulet in the canton of Castelnaudary. Today there were about 1,000 people in the Confrérie, each charged with the task of overseeing the quality of the dish for an area of 20 km around the town.

The Confrérie had a strict hierarchy, Jean-Louis explained. You started out as a *dignitaire*, then, after one or two years, you became a *chevalier*. That's when you got to wear the hat (made in the shape of an upturned Cassoulet bowl, it turned out), the clothes and a huge medal bearing the words *Grande Confrérie du Cassoulet*. Higher up were two vice-presidents, of which he was one, and a grand master, who directed the whole thing. There was a Cassoulet festival in Castelnaudary every year, he said. It went on for two or three days and attracted about 80,000 people. I must be sure to go.

Jean-Louis was hugely entertaining company. Three hours – and endless cups of coffee – later, I reluctantly took my leave, on his insistence that Kim and I go round to his house for supper. He would cook me 'something special' he promised. It had been the strangest of first encounters, but Jean-Louis would turn out to be one of my greatest friends. The 'something special' materialised just two weeks later when Jean-Louis and his wife Marie invited us for a delicious four-course meal of fresh oysters, fillet of beef in truffle sauce, profiteroles and a mouth-watering array of local cheeses. Jean-Louis

was certainly serious about food. Inspired (and intrigued) by his insistence
that I join the Confrérie myself, I resolved to include a Cassoulet recipe in
this book.

The rest of November passed uneventfully. I imagined we would now drift
into winter, with nothing much happening, but then came the real highlight
of my first few months in France – my first truffle-hunting expedition.

When Paul, the owner of the house, first said he knew a local man who could
take me out truffle-hunting, I was sceptical. After all, I thought, everyone
knows Périgord is the truffle area of France, not the Aude. But according to
Paul and his friend Claude, there were truffles all round the Aude, Tarn and
Haute-Garonne. I ran the idea past Jean-Louis and Michel, and their
reaction was both instant and unanimous: 'Impossible!' they both said.

They didn't believe it, and I didn't believe it, but I had to find out, so a few
days later I took Paul up on his offer. After a quick phone call, everything was
arranged, and minutes later we were in the car and on the road.

As we drove up to Claude's ivy-covered house on that drizzly November
afternoon, our eyes were drawn to a wired enclosure in the small wooded
garden. Inside were several dogs, wagging their tails and barking. They were
pointers – the kind of dogs the French love to use for hunting. No doubt one
of these would be coming out with us, I thought, as we rang the doorbell and
waited for Claude. The door opened, and, as if fired from a catapult, the
family pet – a tiny black and white dog, a Jack Russell cross – shot out and
sprang up and down, squealing. All smiles, Claude followed, apologising
profusely for the dog's excesses, and he warmly welcomed us inside while he
got ready. As he put his jacket on and picked up a plastic bag containing
pieces of saucisson, I looked in the general direction of the enclosure and
asked him which of the dogs would be coming with us. 'Non, monsieur,'
Claude said, tapping my arm and pointing down at the little dog that had
greeted us so effusively. 'Ici. Voici Moustique.'

I looked down again at the tiny dog with its, dainty paws, curly white tail and
ridiculously small nose – surely far too delicate to be of any use – and

thought, you must be joking. Not this dog – please. This was a family pet, that definitely had a rather pampered look. This certainly did not look like a master of the rustic rough-and-tumble world of truffle-hunting. Moustique (the name means 'mosquito' in French) looked up at me haughtily, as if somehow aware of the important weight that was being placed on his shoulders. And I looked at him. I know what I do to mosquitoes, I thought.

Much against my better judgement, we started out with a turn around Claude's garden. As we walked along, I looked at this silly little dog skipping in front of us, and, to be honest, I felt a bit of a prat. I thought about what Michel and Jean-Louis had said, and began to have the feeling that my leg was being pulled – just *ever* so slightly.

I couldn't have been more wrong. Within minutes, Moustique started scratching away at the ground under a tree. Claude immediately bent down

and began cutting away the grass with a bent screwdriver (the standard tool of all truffle-hunters) and unearthed – a mushroom. Moustique sat back as Claude rewarded him with a piece of saucisson and a pat on the head, and we moved on. Seconds later, the same thing happened, but this time, to my amazement, Claude dug out a truffle. Yes, it really *was* a truffle – a walnut-sized one. I took it gingerly as he handed it to me.

The truffle is not, I have to say, one of nature's most beautiful creations. Dark, warty and irregular in shape, to the untrained eye it can look a bit like a clod of earth. Even after all my years as a chef, it still seems incredible to me that something that can look so, well, frankly, vile, can taste so sublime, but it does. Truffles in prime condition are miraculous things – ingredients that cooks swoon over. They are the crowning glory of *haute cuisine*, where they're used in sauces and an endless array of sophisticated fish, chicken and veal dishes, but, oh, the joy of this magical food is that it works just as well when added to basic ingredients, transforming a simple dish, such as scrambled eggs, into a meal fit for the gods. What makes truffles so desirable, of course, is their rarity value, which has come about because they're so difficult to find. These *grande dames* of the mushroom family are so rare and highly prized that they're treated – and weighed – like gold, with prices for the world-famous Périgord truffles (known as 'black diamonds') reaching as high as 450 euros a kilo (£300 a pound) for high-quality specimens.

Could Claude's truffle possibly match up? I had to find out. There are three things to look for when deciding if a truffle is ripe: its appearance, feel and smell. A cardinal rule when buying a truffle is to remove the earth, which can often hide the flaws. Not only that, but some unscrupulous sellers will actually put mud around the truffle to improve the weight. And why pay 450 euros a kilo for a lump of mud?

Once you've got rid of the earth, your truffle, if it's in prime condition, should be black and firm. Sometimes the only way to tell is to cut off a slice and look inside. This isn't normally possible when buying one, as most truffle-sellers are unwilling to put their wares to the test. But I didn't have to worry about that, so I simply broke off a bit and looked. The results were disappointing. Instead of being black and firm, with delicate white marbling inside, Claude's truffle was grey and crumbly, with creamy-coloured flecks.

Next came the smell test. A ripe truffle has a strong, earthy, pungent aroma that can make a fully grown man reel at ten paces. I closed my eyes and took a whiff... Nothing. As far I was concerned, these were old summer truffles. But Claude said no, they were autumn truffles. Well, I've never heard of autumn truffles, and to me they had all the characteristics of summer ones that had been left in the ground for too long. Claude could see I didn't really believe him and, helpful chap that he is, offered to take us to the estate of his employer, Monsieur Rive, who ran a *truffetière*, or truffle plantation, a few miles away, in the Tarn region. We got in the car and set off.

As we hit the Tarn, signs sprouted along the roadside reminding us that this was the Pays de Cocagne, the 'Land of Milk and Honey', named after the *cocagnes*, or balls of locally produced woad flat brought the area untold wealth during the 16th century.

Monsieur Rive's estate consisted of a magnificent 18th-century house set on a hill overlooking 10 hectares of woods. The skyline on the hillside opposite was dominated by the 11th-century Château Magrin, which now houses a woad museum. Bathed in golden sunshine, it made me think that perhaps winter was still some time away after all. As Paul, Claude, Moustique and I walked along a tree-lined path on the estate, we met Monsieur Rive, a rotund, moustachioed man with a twinkle in his eye and a definite *joie de vivre*. This was a man who clearly loved life, food – and talking. And truffles were his chosen subject. Moustique – now on his home territory – positively swaggered with confidence, his position as Truffle King unchallenged. The small steps had given way to a purposeful stride as he set about his business, sniffing importantly at trees and occasionally scratching around. As he dug, so Claude bent down with his screwdriver. Out came one truffle, then another. It seemed barely possible. In the few minutes it took Claude and Monsieur Rive to explain that this was the end of the season and there were absolutely no more truffles left in the ground the amazing Moustique had unearthed four, each the size of a lump of coal.

As Rive talked about the prices he could get for his truffles – 100 euros (£60) per kilo for the summer truffle, 200 euros (£120) for the Bourgogne truffle –

I began to see the financial value of dogs like Moustique. I wondered idly if his nose could be insured, like Betty Grable's legs. It was then that I started plotting his abduction. These Aude truffles were all very well, but what if I took Moustique to Périgord? I could be set up for life. I've got to nick that dog, I thought.

I was brought down to earth by Monsieur Rive's story of what happened when he had bought the house in 1961. The local mayor had told him everyone knew he was buying the estate because there were truffles there. Naturally excited, Rive had asked where they were. 'Ah!' the mayor had said slyly. 'C'est un secret'.

'Secret' was a word I often came across with truffles, as I attempted to enter this complex and mysterious world. Even on the brief car journey to the Tarn, I had tried to quiz Claude about how he knew where to take the dog, or how much he knew about cultivating these rare culinary gems – only to be met with reticence: 'It's all to do with the spores,' he had said darkly. 'But all that is secret – and very complicated.' Monsieur Rive was not about to give away any trade secrets, but he nevertheless spent some time telling us about the background to his *truffetière*.

Intrigued by the mayor's comments, he had joined a syndicate of around 100 people, which was devoted to cultivating truffles. He learnt that they were often found around the base of oak and lime trees, and how to look for other tell-tale signs, such as *brûlée* (burnt grass) and stones that had turned white, both caused by chemicals given off by the truffles underground. Within two months, he had found his first truffle.

The truffle syndicate that Monsieur Rive joined started cultivating acorns found at the base of trees where truffles had been discovered before, with surprising results. As the oak trees matured, they too produced truffles. Although the experiment was completely unscientific, it seemed to work, and Monsieur Rive's estate now produces 30 kg of truffles a year. One of his biggest customers is an Englishman, once *sous-chef* at the London Savoy, who has opened up a local gastronomic restaurant.

OPPOSITE: *Claude and I examining truffles, under the watchful supervision of the Truffle King himself – the inimitable Moustique.*

OPPOSITE: *Me giving Charles cookery lessons – a potential recipe for disaster.*

As Monsieur Rive showed us his small plantation of oak trees, he explained the crucial role of dogs in truffle-hunting. Pigs were traditionally used, he said, but they love truffles so much that they simply eat them. Dogs are much more reliable, he went on, and relatively easy to train. It's simply a matter of burying a truffle with a treat that the dog likes. Gradually, the dog comes to associate the truffle with the treat and, in time, the treat can be left out and used as a reward. The dog will only sniff out a truffle when it's ripe, so everyone is happy. 'How long does it take to train them?' I asked. 'Anything from one month to nine months,' he replied. At which point Claude intervened. 'Moustique took only six weeks,' he said, and Moustique pricked up his ears as if to say 'That's me!'

As we took our leave, the sun disappeared and there was suddenly a distinct chill in the air, but I felt warmed by the charm and simple generosity of these men who had been prepared to give up an entire afternoon to share their great knowledge and passion of food with me.

It had been a funny sort of a day. We had gone out with the wrong sort of dog to the wrong part of France at the wrong time of the year, but we had found truffles, and I had held them in my hand. And, what's more, I had a great story to tell in the local bars. What a fantastic end to my first autumn in France. I'd had a wonderful three months. But now the nights were drawing in, the trees were bare and the skies were the colour of lead. Winter was definitely coming.

Autumn Recipes

TRUFFLED SCRAMBLED EGGS

The best truffles available are black ones called *Tuber melanosporum*, and the wonderful Italian white ones *Tuber magnatum*. Summer truffles which are brown in colour are available from May through to mid-July. They have a woody flavour, but not the pungent smell that I prefer and that you get with the Périgord truffle, but they do cost a fraction of the price.

Try this scrambled egg dish when you are looking for something different for breakfast. Take a large black truffle and place it in a plastic airtight container with 8 free-range eggs for 2–3 days. During this time the truffle will impart its flavour to the eggs. Alternatively, try a tiny amount of truffle shaved into a tasty breakfast omelette – delicious.

Serves 4

4 LARGE SLICES BRIOCHE (SEE
   PAGE 222) OR SOUR DOUGH
   BREAD
50 G UNSALTED BUTTER
8 EGGS
125 ML MILK
SALT AND PEPPER
1 LARGE TRUFFLE

1. Toast the brioche. Place on 4 individual plates for serving.

2. Melt the butter in a large saucepan.

3. Crack the eggs into a bowl, add the milk and, with a whisk, beat together until smooth.

4. Pour the mixture into the butter and, with a wooden spoon, continuously stir the beaten egg over a moderate heat to scramble. Season with salt and pepper.

5. As soon as the eggs start to scramble, spoon them on to the brioche toast. Grate the fresh truffle over the eggs and serve immediately.

C E L E R I A C   S O U P

The truffle oil used here is purely a personal preference. It adds not just flavour and richness to the taste of the soup, but also gives it a lightness of texture. If you don't like truffle oil, however, just add a knob of butter to enrich the soup. You can also enhance the flavour of the soup by adding parsley, for instance.

Serves 8

2 CELERIAC BULBS, TOTAL
   WEIGHT 800 G
125 G UNSALTED BUTTER
1 SPRIG FRESH THYME
1 BAY LEAF
1 GARLIC CLOVE, PEELED AND
   CHOPPED
750 ML CHICKEN STOCK (SEE
   PAGE 293)
250 ML DOUBLE CREAM
2 DESSERTSPOONS TRUFFLE OIL
   OR A KNOB OF BUTTER
   (OPTIONAL)
JUICE OF $\frac{1}{2}$ LEMON
SALT AND PEPPER

1. Cut the celeriac bulbs into manageable chunks and peel. Roughly chop them into pieces of about 1cm each.

2. Melt the butter in a large saucepan, then add the celeriac, herbs and garlic and cook gently on a low heat for about 20 minutes, until soft but not browned in colour.

3. Add the chicken stock and bring the soup to the boil, skimming off with a slotted spoon any sediment and froth that rise to the surface. Turn the heat down to a gentle simmer and cook the soup for a further 40 minutes.

4. Add the cream and bring the soup back to the boil. Take the saucepan off the stove and ladle the celeriac and stock into a liquidiser. Blend the soup until smooth, which will take about 2 minutes on maximum speed.

5. Stop the liquidiser and add the truffle oil, lemon juice and salt and pepper to taste. Blend again for a further 30 seconds. Pour into bowls. Serve immediately.

SALTED COD CROQUETTES

The thing to remember about salt cod is to soak the fish in water that is changed regularly over 24-hours. When poaching the fish remember not to boil it or it will become tough.

Serves 6

300 G POTATO, COOKED AND
    MASHED
2 DESSERTSPOON FLAT-LEAF
    PARSLEY, FINELY CHOPPED
400 G SALTED COD, SOAKED AS
    DESCRIBED ABOVE
I GARLIC CLOVE, PEELED AND
    FINELY CHOPPED
150 ML MILK, BOILED
150 ML OLIVE OIL
JUICE OF $\frac{1}{2}$ LEMON
CAYENNE PEPPER
OIL FOR DEEP-FRYING
    (GROUNDNUT IS BEST)

COATING

100 G PLAIN FLOUR, SIEVED
2 EGGS, BEATEN
200 G FRESH WHITE
    BREADCRUMBS

1. When the potato is cool, stir in the parsley.

2. Half fill a roasting tin with water. Bring to the boil, turn down the heat and add the cod. Cook gently for 15 minutes, remembering not to boil. Drain, then cool, then skin the fish and remove all the bones. Flake the fish into a bowl.

3. Put the potato and fish into a food processor, along with the garlic. With the machine on, pour some milk in, then some olive oil and then more milk. Repeat until all the milk and oil have been used. Add the lemon juice and cayenne to taste.

4. For the coating, put the flour onto one plate, pour the egg onto a second and sprinkle the breadcrumbs onto a third. Dust your hands with flour, pinch off some of the cod mixture and roll it to form a cylinder about 5cm long and 4cm in diameter. Repeat.

5. Roll each croquette first in the flour, then in the egg, shaking off any excess, then roll in the breadcrumbs to coat. Chill to 'set' the coating.

6. Pour some oil to a level of no more than a third of the depth of a large saucepan. When the oil is hot (about 190°C/375°F), gently lower in the croquettes. Fry until golden and, with a slotted spoon, transfer to kitchen paper. Place the croquettes in the oven, at about 160°C /325°F / Gas 3, and fry some more. Do this in at least two batches. If you cook them all at once they will go soggy. Serve.

A Salad of Scallops with Hazelnuts and Apples

Scallops, which are in season from October to March, should always be undercooked: very pink is best. This recipe uses raw, marinated scallops.

Serves 4

24 LARGE SCALLOPS, IN THEIR
   SHELLS

100 ML HAZELNUT OIL

2 SHALLOTS, PEELED AND
   CHOPPED

2 GARLIC CLOVES, PEELED AND
   CHOPPED

2 SPRIGS FRESH THYME

$^{1}/_{2}$ BAY LEAF

RIND OF 1 LEMON

SALAD

$^{1}/_{2}$ CURLY ENDIVE

1 RADICCHIO HEAD

2 HANDFULS LAMB'S LETTUCE

2 HANDFULS ROCKET LEAVES

1 SHALLOT, PEELED AND
   CHOPPED

125 G SHELLED HAZELNUTS,
   ROASTED AND SKINNED
   (SEE PAGE 279)

40 ML HAZELNUT VINAIGRETTE
   (SEE PAGE 295)

1 FIRM GREEN APPLE, E.G.
   GRANNY SMITH

$^{1}/_{2}$ TEASPOON CASTER SUGAR

SALT AND PEPPER

JUICE OF 1 LEMON (SEE ABOVE)

6 NEW POTATOES, COOKED
SKINNED AND SLICED

1. First open the scallops. Hold the shell between your forefinger and thumb. Insert a small, strong palette knife into the pointed end of the shell and in one action with a movement of your wrist, prise the two halves of the shell apart. Alternatively ask your fishmonger to open them. Remove the top shell, then insert a palette knife underneath the white scallop flesh, cutting through the connecting ligament, but being careful not to damage the flesh. With a sharp knife, cut the white and the orange-coloured flesh – the coral – from the remaining 'beard'. Wash the flesh under cold running water and dry.

2. Put the scallop pieces into a shallow dish, pour over the oil and add the shallots, garlic, thyme and bay leaf. Peel the rind from the lemon, then cut away any white pith. Put the rind into a small pan of boiling water and cook for 5 minutes. Strain and refresh under cold running water until cool. Dry on a piece of kitchen paper and add to the scallops. Store in the refrigerator overnight.

3. Just before serving, wash and dry all the lettuce leaves. Place these in a large bowl, then add the chopped shallot and toasted hazelnuts. Sprinkle over the hazelnut vinaigrette and toss the salad.

4. Quarter, core and peel the apple. Slice finely, then cut into matchsticks. Put into a bowl, sprinkle with the sugar and squeeze the juice of half the lemon over them. Turn them over, so that they are

covered with the juice. Spoon a little apple onto the middle of 6 x 26cm plates to form a tall mound and cover with the lettuce leaves. Pick out the hazelnuts from the vinaigrette and arrange, about 5-6 per plate, around the salad. Arrange the potato slices around, 5-6 per plate.

5. Remove the scallops from the oil and transfer them to a plate. Put 2 large frying pans on the stove to heat. Pour a dessertspoon of the oil from the marinade into each of the pans. As the oil begins to smoke, add the scallops, fry on one side for about 2 minutes to brown slightly, then turn over and cook for a further 2 minutes.

6. Transfer the scallops to the potato slices. Season each scallop with a little salt and pepper and lemon juice. Serve.

GRILLED MUSSELS WITH GARLIC AND ALMOND BUTTER

I first ate this dish in a little brasserie overlooking the port in St Jean-de-Luz. Adding ground almonds to the butter creates a rich, bubbling crust.

Serves 8 as a main course

3 KG LARGE, LIVE MUSSELS

30 G UNSALTED BUTTER

I ONION, PEELED AND CHOPPED

I LEEK, WASHED AND CHOPPED

I CARROT, PEELED AND CHOPPED

I CELERY STICK, FINELY CHOPPED

I GARLIC CLOVE, PEELED AND
   FINELY CHOPPED

I SPRIG FRESH THYME

2 SPRIGS FLAT-LEAF PARSLEY

I TEASPOON BLACK
   PEPPERCORNS, CRACKED

375 ML DRY WHITE WINE

GARLIC AND ALMOND BUTTER

250 G UNSALTED BUTTER, DICED

3 GARLIC CLOVES, PEELED AND
   VERY FINELY CHOPPED

100 G WHITE BREADCRUMBS

100 ML DRY WHITE WINE

125 G BLANCHED ALMONDS,
   CHOPPED OR GROUND

2 LARGE SPRIGS FLAT-LEAF
   PARSLEY, LEAVES PICKED OFF
   AND FINELY CHOPPED

SALT AND PEPPER

LEMON JUICE

1. Wash, clean and scrape the mussels. If any remain open and do not close when you tap them against the side of the sink, throw them away.

2. In a large, lidded pan, melt the butter, then add the chopped vegetables, garlic, herbs and peppercorns. Pour in the wine and bring to the boil. Tip in the mussels, cover with the lid and immediately return to the boil. Steaming the mussels with the lid onto open them should take about 5 minutes.

3. Strain the mussels into a colander. Discard any that remain closed and separate the mussels from their shells by cutting the membrane that attaches each mussel to its shell. Place each mussel into a half-shell (discarding the empty half-shells) and arrange on a baking sheet.

4. Preheat the grill to a medium-to-high setting.

5. Next make the garlic and almond butter. Put the diced butter into a mixer and beat it until it is soft and pale in colour, then add the garlic. Place the breadcrumbs in a bowl and pour over the wine, letting it soak in until the crumbs are just moist. Add the almonds and then add this mixture to the butter. Add the parsley, with salt, pepper and lemon juice to taste.

6. Top each mussel with a teaspoon of the savoury butter and place them under the preheated grill for 5 minutes until crisp-looking and golden.

ROASTED SKATE WINGS WITH CAPERS AND PARSLEY

This recipe is based on the classic French dish *Raie au beurre noir*, except that no 'black' butter is used and I have added capers to the finished sauce.

Serves 6

6 SKATE WINGS, 1.5 KG IN TOTAL,
 OR APPROX. 250 G EACH

SALT AND PEPPER

100 ML OLIVE OIL

125 G UNSALTED BUTTER

125 ML CHICKEN STOCK (SEE
 PAGE 293)

JUICE OF 1 LEMON

2 DESSERTSPOONS CAPERS IN
 BRINE, RINSED

1 DESSERTSPOON FLAT-LEAF
 PARSLEY, CHOPPED

1. Wash the skate wings under cold running water. With a pair of sharp scissors, cut around the thin part of the wing, about 1cm from the edge, and discard it, then dry the fish on some kitchen paper and season each side.

2. Preheat the oven to 220°C/425°F/Gas 7. Place a large, ovenproof pan on the stove to heat. Add the olive oil, and just as it starts to smoke, put in the skate wings, dark side down first. Fry the fish for 3 minutes on each side, then turn them over.

3. Place the pan in the hot oven and roast the skate for 10 minutes or until just cooked. Using a fish slice, remove the skate wings, dark side up, and lay them on a board. Insert a fish filleting knife into the skin and carefully peel it away from the succulent white flesh. You can also remove the softer white under skin in this way, if you prefer not to leave it on. Place the wings in a flat serving dish and keep warm in the oven, on the lowest setting, while you quickly prepare the sauce.

4. Add the butter to the pan and heat. As it starts to bubble and turn nut-brown, pour in the stock. Boil and reduce the sauce until it becomes syrupy. Squeeze in the lemon juice, add the capers and parsley.

5. Immediately pour the sauce over the skate and serve with mashed potatoes and a green salad.

SOLE POACHED WITH MUSSELS AND PRAWNS

When buying sole, choose the fish that look the most shiny, are firm to the touch and that do not contain roe, as these fish always taste better.

Serves 6

6 X 500 G DOVER SOLE

MUSSEL AND PRAWN SAUCE

I KG LIVE MUSSELS (SMALL ONES
  ARE THE SWEETEST IN
  FLAVOUR)

450 ML DRY WHITE WINE

I LEEK, WASHED AND FINELY
  CHOPPED

I CELERY STICK, TRIMMED AND
  FINELY CHOPPED

I CARROT, PEELED AND FINELY
  CHOPPED

4 SHALLOTS, PEELED AND FINELY
  CHOPPED

2 GARLIC CLOVES, PEELED AND
  FINELY CHOPPED

I BAY LEAF

I SPRIG FRESH THYME

200 ML FISH STOCK
  (SEE PAGE 294)

200 ML DOUBLE CREAM

50 G UNSALTED BUTTER, DICED

JUICE OF ¼ LEMON

I DESSERTSPOON CHOPPED
  FLAT-LEAF PARSLEY

24 COOKED PRAWNS OR 500 G
  GREY SHRIMPS, PEELED

SALT AND PEPPER

CAYENNE PEPPER

1. First wash the mussels and remove the 'beards', then put them in a colander to drain. Discard any that remain open and do not close when tapped.

2. Bring the wine to the boil in a large, lidded saucepan. Add the chopped vegetables and garlic, along with the bay leaf, thyme, a little black pepper and the mussels. Place the lid on the saucepan and cook the mussels for at least 5 minutes on maximum heat, or until they open.

3. As soon as the mussels have opened, turn them out of the pan into a colander with a bowl underneath to catch the cooking juices. Separate the mussels from their shells and keep them in another bowl. Discard any that remain closed.

4. Strain the mussel cooking juices through a fine sieve or muslin cloth into a roasting tin large enough to accommodate all 6 fish.

5. Ask your fishmonger to remove the dark skin from each sole. Leave the head on but, with a pair of sharp scissors, remove the gills yourself.

6. Preheat the oven to 220°C/425°F/Gas 7.

7. Lay the sole in the roasting tin and cover with the cooking juices from the mussels. Pour in the fish stock and put the tin on the stove, bringing the liquid to the boil. Cover the fish with greaseproof paper and place in the preheated oven to cook for about 12 minutes.

8. Remove the soles from the oven and carefully place in a suitable serving dish. Again, cover them with the greaseproof paper to keep warm.

9. Strain all the cooking juices into a saucepan and bring to the boil so that the liquid reduces by half. Add the cream and bring it back up to the boil. Whisk the butter, piece by piece, into the sauce. When this has become incorporated into the sauce, squeeze in the lemon juice.

10. Reduce the heat so that the sauce is just simmering and add the chopped parsley, mussels and prawns or shrimps. Add a little salt and a pinch of cayenne pepper to taste.

11. Arrange the fish on 6 plates and cover each one with liberal amounts of the finished sauce.

DUCK À L'ORANGE

Like Onion soup (see page 114), this classic French dish is one that was badly cooked in most restaurants in England during the 1980s. Prepared properly, however, it is delicious.

Serves 8

2 X 2 KG BARBARY DUCKS

SALT AND PEPPER

100 G UNSALTED BUTTER

2 DESSERTSPOONS OLIVE OIL

200 ML GRAND MARNIER

100 G CASTER SUGAR

150 ML CIDER VINEGAR

9 ORANGES

A LARGE BUNCH OF FLAT
   LEAF PARSLEY

1. Preheat the oven to 220°C/425°F/Gas 7.

2. Season the ducks. Heat half the butter and all the oil in a roasting tin ontop of the stove. When the butter and oil start to smoke, brown the birds on all sides. Roast in the preheated hot oven for about 50 minutes.

3. Remove the ducks to a chopping board. Pour the liquid fat that has accumulated in the tin during cooking into a bowl, and keep for the next recipe!

4. Put the roasting tin coated in fats and juices back on the stove. Pour in half the Grand Marnier, set light to it and deglaze the pan. Add the sugar. Pour in the vinegar. Boil and reduce the liquid until syrupy.

5. Remove the peel from 3 of the oranges with a zester and set aside. Divide 2 of the oranges into segments and again set aside. Squeeze the juice from the 7 whole oranges.

6. Pour the orange juice through a sieve into the roasting tin and boil to reduce. Add the segments of orange, orange zest and remaining Grand Marnier to the sauce. Cut the remaining butter into small pieces and, piece by piece, whisk and dissolve it into the sauce.

7. Turn the birds in the orange sauce to coat them. Transfer to a warm serving dish and garnish with the watercress. Mashed potatoes go well with this.

CASSOULET

Cassoulet is a very heavy dish and lengthy to prepare, so always start the day before!

Serves 8

STOCK

1 KG PORK BONES (FROM THE
     LOIN, BELLY OR CHEST)

2 PIG'S TROTTERS

1 KG SHIN OF VEAL

1 KG CHICKEN PIECES

3 LITRES WATER

1 ONION, PEELED AND CHOPPED

1 CARROT, PEELED AND CHOPPED

2 CELERY STICKS, PEELED AND
     ROUGHLY CHOPPED

1 LEEK, WASHED AND CHOPPED

1 GARLIC BULB, PEELED AND
     CHOPPED

1 BAY LEAF

2 SPRIGS FRESH THYME

2 SPRIGS FLAT-LEAF PARSLEY

1 TEASPOON BLACK PEPPERCORNS

BEANS

750 G DRIED WHITE KIDNEY
     BEANS, SOAKED OVERNIGHT

100 G PORK LOIN FAT, CUT INTO
     STRIPS

1.5 LITRES WATER

2 SPRIGS FRESH THYME

1 BAY LEAF

1/2 GARLIC BULB, HALVED

MEATS

4 SMALL DUCK LEGS

1 KG PIECE OF PORK (LOIN, BELLY
     OR CHEST)

1. For the stock, ask your butcher to chop the pork bones into small pieces. Put the trotters, veal, chicken and all the bones into a large, lidded saucepan. Cover them with cold water and bring to the boil. Add the vegetables, garlic, herbs and peppercorns, and bring back to the boil. Skim off any fat that rises to the surface and turn the stock down to a simmer. Cook, covered, for at least 4 hours, until the meat starts to fall off the shin.

2. Strain the stock into another saucepan and boil to reduce the liquid by half. You need 1.5 litres of finished stock for 8 people.

3. Wash the beans and strain, then place in a saucepan, cover with more water and bring to the boil. Cook at a rapid boil for 5 minutes, then strain again.

4. Put the beans back into the pan, add the pork fat and cover with water. Add the thyme, bay leaf and garlic, and bring to the boil. Turn down to a simmer, cover and cook for about 1½ hours, until tender and nearly all the water has evaporated. Most of the fat will have been absorbed into the beans: remove what's left. Pick out the bay leaf, thyme and garlic, and discard. Set the beans aside.

5. Put the duck legs in a deep roasting tin. With a knife, remove the rind from the pork and add the meat to the tin. Mix the salt, juniper berries, thyme, bay leaf, garlic and peppercorns, and sprinkle over the duck and pork. Cover the tin with clingfilm and put in the fridge overnight.

150 G COARSE SEA SALT

3 JUNIPER BERRIES, CRUSHED

1 SPRIG FRESH THYME, LEAVES
   PICKED FROM THE STALKS

1 BAY LEAF

2 GARLIC CLOVES, PEELED AND
   CRUSHED

1 DESSERTSPOON BLACK
   PEPPERCORNS, CRUSHED

8 TOULOUSE SAUSAGES

SAUTÉ

2 TABLESPOONS COOKING FAT,
   FROM THE PORK AND DUCK

1 ONION, PEELED AND CHOPPED

3 LARGE TOMATOES, SKINNED,
   SEEDED AND CHOPPED

2 GARLIC CLOVES, PEELED AND
   FINELY CHOPPED

1 SPRIG FRESH THYME

2 BAY LEAVES

175 G WHITE BREADCRUMBS

6. In the morning, remove the bay leaf and thyme and, under cold running water, wash all the salt from the duck and pork. Dry the meat on a clean tea-towel.

7. Meanwhile, preheat the oven to 180°C/350°F/ Gas 4, then roast the duck and pork for 1½ hours. Remove the meat from the oven, cut the duck legs in half and slice the pork into 8 pieces roughly 1cm thick, then set aside on a plate.

8. For the sauté, heat the fat in a frying pan, add the onion and fry until golden. Add the tomatoes, garlic, thyme and bay leaves, and cook for 5 minutes. Tip the mixture into a large casserole dish.

9. Preheat the oven to 200°C/400°F/Gas 6.

10. In a frying pan, brown the sausages in some more of the fat and place them in the casserole.

11. Pour in the stock, then place the pork and duck in the casserole, and sprinkle in the beans. Cover with the breadcrumbs and cook in the oven for about an hour until crisp and golden. Serve.

Roast Duck with Prunes

Agen, a small medieval town situated between Toulouse and Bordeaux, produces about 65 per cent of all the plums grown in France, most of which are dried and known as pruneaux d'Agen.

Serves 4

2 SMALL ORGANIC OR FREE-
　RANGE BARBARY DUCKS, 4–5 KG
　TOTAL WEIGHT

SALT AND PEPPER

I ONION, PEELED AND CHOPPED

I LARGE CARROT, PEELED AND
　CHOPPED

2 CELERY STICKS, TRIMMED AND
　CHOPPED

2 DESSERTSPOONS DUCK FAT OR
　CLARIFIED BUTTER

I BAY LEAF

I SPRIG FRESH THYME

2 GARLIC CLOVES, PEELED

400 ML RED WINE (E.G.
　MINERVOIS, CORBIÈRES OR
　MADIRAN)

250 G PITTED, READY-TO-EAT
　AGEN PRUNES

750 ML CHICKEN STOCK
　(SEE PAGE 293)

100 ML ARMAGNAC

I DESSERTSPOON CASTER SUGAR

1. Preheat the oven to 230°C/450°F/Gas 8.

2. Season the ducks, and roast in the oven for 50 minutes. Take them out and place on a rack to cool.

3. Dry the vegetables on kitchen paper. In a large saucepan, melt the fat or butter until it starts to smoke, then add the vegetables and cook until golden. Add the bay leaf, thyme and garlic.

4. Cut and remove the duck legs from the birds, then carefully remove the breasts. Put the pieces in a roasting tin. They will still be very pink.

5. Chop up the carcasses and add these to the vegetables. Pour in the wine, add half the prunes and boil to reduce the wine until it evaporates. Pour in the chicken stock, bring the sauce to the boil and skim off any sediment or froth that rises to the surface. Turn the sauce down to a rapid simmer and allow to cook for about 45 minutes until reduced by half. Pass the sauce through a fine sieve into another saucepan and gently simmer on the stove.

6. Warm the remaining prunes in a pan with the Armagnac and sugar. Heat until the liquid evaporates and the prunes look glazed and sticky.

7. Sprinkle the prunes over the duck and return to the oven to warm for 10 minutes. Pour the reduced sauce over the duck and serve immediately with sauté potatoes and French beans.

ROAST FARM CHICKEN WITH CEP FRICASSÉE

I asked the butcher in the market to chop the heads off the chickens and singe all the stubble, and he obliged. When you buy them in England, I am sure they will be oven-ready!

Serves 8

2 X 1.5 KG CHICKENS (E.G. BLACK-
    LEGGED CHICKEN OR
    POULETS DES LANDES)
FINE SEA SALT AND PEPPER
30 ML VEGETABLE OIL
1 KG FRESH CEPS
1 SMALL ONION, PEELED AND
    ROUGHLY CHOPPED
2 GARLIC CLOVES, PEELED AND
    CHOPPED
1 SPRIG FRESH THYME
1 SPRIG FRESH TARRAGON
A HANDFUL OF PARSLEY STALKS
500 ML CHICKEN STOCK (SEE
    PAGE 293)
50 ML DOUBLE CREAM
JUICE OF ½ LEMON
2 SHALLOTS, PEELED AND FINELY
    CHOPPED
30 G UNSALTED BUTTER
2 SPRIGS FLAT-LEAF PARSLEY,
    FINELY CHOPPED

1. Preheat the oven to 180°C/350°F/Gas 4.

2. Season the chickens. Place in a roasting tin and pour most of the vegetable oil over them. Cook in the oven for about 40 minutes.

3. Wipe the ceps thoroughly with damp kitchen paper. Scrape out the gills. Separate the heads for garnishing and the stalks for the sauce. Dry both thoroughly on kitchen paper. Slice the stalks.

4. Remove the chickens from the oven. With a fork, lift each of them from the roasting tin. Tip the onion, half the garlic, the thyme, tarragon, cep and parsley stalks into the tin. Place the chickens on top and return them to the oven for another 30 minutes, basting occasionally. (In all, they should take 1 hour 10 minutes to cook.) The cep stalks will absorb all the fat and juices from the birds.

5. When the chickens are cooked (pierce to check that the juices run clear), transfer them to a board to cool before dividing them into portions.

6. Put the roasting tin with the cooked cep stalks and its other ingredients on the stove and add the chicken stock. Bring to the boil, reduce the heat and gently simmer for a further 10 minutes.

7. Strain the liquid through a very fine sieve into a smaller pan and bring to the boil. Add the cream, squeeze in the lemon juice and check the seasoning.

8. Heat a small frying pan with the remaining oil.
When the oil begins to smoke, tip in the cep
caps, shallots and remaining garlic in one go.
Add the butter and, when melted, cook for 2–3
minutes, stirring continuously. Sprinkle the
parsley over the ceps.

9. Divide the chicken into portions (4 legs,
4 breasts) and cover each portion with some of the
fricassée. Pour a little of the sauce around the
chicken and serve. Good accompaniments are
steamed French beans and some thick, fresh pasta.

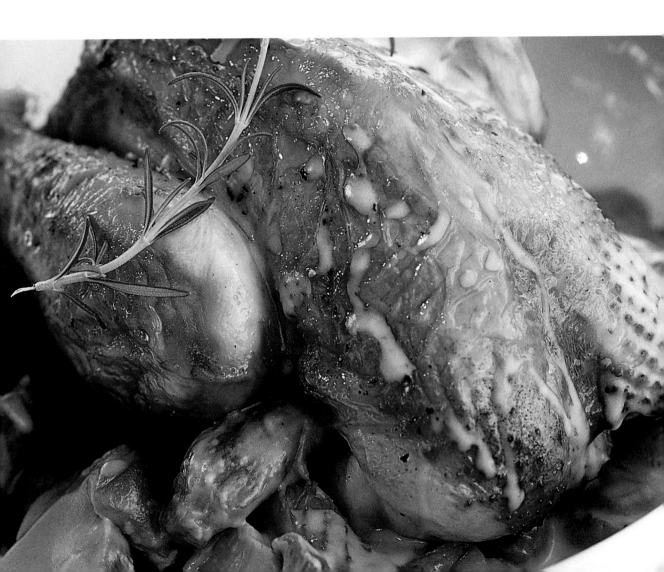

PHEASANT WITH PUY LENTILS

It is very difficult to specify an exact length of time for hanging game birds, but for pheasants, about 3 days in a cool, dry area with plenty of fresh air should be counted as minimum amount of time.

Serves 6

3 X 1 KG PHEASANTS, PLUCKED
 (YOUNG HENS ARE THE BEST)

3 X 50 G SLICES FAT OR STREAKY
 BACON OR SALT PORK

SALT AND PEPPER

6–8 JUNIPER BERRIES, OR TO
 TASTE, CRUSHED

75 ML CORN OIL

2 ONIONS, PEELED AND CHOPPED

1 CARROT, PEELED AND CHOPPED

1 CELERY STICK, TRIMMED AND
 CHOPPED

1 LEEK, WASHED AND CHOPPED

2 GARLIC CLOVES, PEELED

300 ML CHICKEN STOCK (SEE
 PAGE 293)

LENTILS

100 G PUY LENTILS

1 LARGE BACON BONE
 OR A 50 G PIECE OF BACON

1 GARLIC CLOVE, PEELED

2 SPRIGS FRESH THYME

$^{1}/_{2}$ BAY LEAF

500 ML CHICKEN STOCK (SEE
 PAGE 293)

25 BACON LARDONS, FRIED

1. Soak the lentils under cold running water for about 10 minutes. Preheat the oven to 200°C/400°F/Gas 6.

2. Cover each pheasant with a thin slice of bacon fat or pork and tie on. Season the birds with salt and pepper and the juniper berries (crushed with the back of a knife or in a spice or coffee grinder).

3. Heat the oil in a roasting tin. When it starts to smoke, brown the birds on all sides. Add the onion, carrot, celery, leek and garlic to the tin, then put it into the oven. Roast for about 35 minutes, basting the birds regularly.

4. Meanwhile, strain the lentils in a sieve, place them in a large, lidded saucepan with the bacon bone, garlic, thyme and bay leaf, and cover with the 500ml chicken stock. Bring the stock to the boil, cover with the lid and reduce the heat to a simmer. Cook the lentils until tender – about the same length of time as the pheasants. Mix in the fried bacon lardons.

5. Take the pheasants out of the oven, and leave to relax for at least 10 minutes.

6. Meanwhile, put the stock on the stove to boil and reduce by about half. Strain the contents of the pan into a small saucepan. Bring the gravy back to the boil, skimming any sediment that rises to the

surface. Turn the heat right down and keep warm.

7. Present the pheasants to your guests, then divide them into portions by first removing the legs and then the breasts.

8. Spoon 2 dessertspoonfuls of lentils onto the middle of 6 dinner plates, and arrange 1 leg and 1 breast of pheasant on top. Ladle a little of the hot gravy over the top. Serve this dish with roast potatoes and roasted shallots .

Fricassée of Rabbit in a Mustard Velouté

Ask your butcher to joint the rabbits and chop the remaining bones into small pieces for the stock.

Serves 4

2 RABBITS (APPROX. 1.5 KG EACH),
    SKINNED AND JOINTED

40 G PLAIN FLOUR

SALT AND PEPPER

2 DESSERTSPOONS DUCK FAT

110 ML DOUBLE CREAM

1 DESSERTSPOON CHIVES, CHOPPED

1 DESSERTSPOON CHAMPAGNE
    SEED MUSTARD

LEMON JUICE

RABBIT STOCK

750 G RABBIT BONES, CHOPPED

1 ONION, PEELED AND DICED

1 CARROT, PEELED AND DICED

1 LEEK, WASHED AND DICED

1 CELERY STICK, DICED

1 SPRIG FRESH THYME

1 BAY LEAF

1 PARSLEY STALK

1 SPRIG FRESH TARRAGON

4 GARLIC CLOVES, PEELED AND
    FINELY CHOPPED

200 G TOMATOES, HALVED AND
    DESEEDED

250 ML WHITE WINE

750 ML CHICKEN STOCK
    (SEE PAGE 293)

LEMON JUICE

1. For the stock, place the chopped rabbit bones in a saucepan. Add the vegetable dice, along with the herbs, garlic and tomatoes, and pour in the wine. Cook and reduce the wine until it has evaporated.

2. Pour in the chicken stock and bring to the boil, skimming off any sediment. Turn it down to a rapid simmer, cook and reduce the liquid by half, down to about 500 ml. Strain the stock through a sieve.

3. Preheat the oven to 220°C/425°F/Gas 7.

4. Place the rabbit joints in a roasting tin, sieve the flour over and season. In a frying pan, heat the fat until it starts to smoke. Dust off the excess flour from the joints and place them in the pan. Fry each piece until it is sealed and golden brown on one side, then turn it over and fry the other.

5. Put the joints in the roasting tin and roast in the oven for about 10 minutes, turning the pieces over at regular intervals. When the flesh is firm to the touch, it is cooked. Take the tin out of the oven and place the joints on a dish to rest.

6. Tip off the excess fat in the tin and return the tin to the stove. Pour in the stock and boil to reduce the liquid by half again. While the sauce is boiling, add the cream. Bring back to the boil to thicken.

7. Strain the sauce through a sieve into another pan and, off the heat, whisk in the chives, then stir in the mustard. Season with salt and pepper, and a little lemon juice. Pour over the rabbit and serve.

CALF'S KIDNEYS WITH MONTPELLIER BUTTER

Montpellier butter is usually served with grilled fish, but it is equally delicious with kidneys.

Serves 6

3 CALF'S KIDNEYS, ABOUT
    400–450 G EACH, TRIMMED
    OF FAT
SALT AND PEPPER
2 DESSERTSPOONS OLIVE OIL

MONTPELLIER BUTTER
1 BUNCH WATERCRESS
3 SPRIGS EACH OF FRESH
    TARRAGON AND PARSLEY
A HANDFUL OF BABY SPINACH
    LEAVES
1 BUNCH FRESH CHIVES
1 LARGE BUNCH FRESH CHERVIL
250 G UNSALTED BUTTER, DICED
6 ANCHOVY FILLETS
3 EGG YOLKS
1 GARLIC CLOVE, PEELED AND
    FINELY CHOPPED
3 HARD-BOILED EGGS
30 G CAPERS, RINSED AND FINELY
    CHOPPED
30 G GHERKINS, RINSED AND
    FINELY CHOPPED
JUICE OF $^{1}/_{2}$ LEMON
SALT AND CAYENNE PEPPER

1. Cut each kidney into about 10 slices, removing the central core with a sharp knife. Lay the slices on a baking sheet, and season with salt and lots of pepper. Sprinkle them with the oil and set aside. Preheat the grill to its highest setting.

2. Put a large saucepan half filled with water onto the stove and bring to the boil. Pick the leaves from the watercress, tarragon, parsley and spinach, and wash them thoroughly. Put all the above herbs plus the chives into the boiling water and scald them for 30 seconds. Strain the herbs in a sieve and refresh under cold running water. Squeeze the water out of the herbs, place, together with the chervil, in a liquidiser and blend to a smooth paste.

3. Place the diced butter in a mixing bowl and beat it until it is pale and fluffy. Mash the anchovies to a paste, then add them along with the egg yolks, herbs and garlic, hard-boiled eggs, capers and gherkins to the butter. Squeeze in the lemon juice, and season with a little salt and cayenne pepper. Transfer the mixture to a clean bowl.

4. Place the kidneys under the grill for about 5 minutes, then remove from the grill, turn the kidneys over and top each with a generous spoonful of Montpellier butter. Place the kidneys under the grill for a further 5 minutes until browned.

5. Serve immediately with fresh spinach.

Saucisson de Morteau with a Warm Potato Salad and Mustard Sauce

This sausage, from Alsace, is not like the *saucisson sec* which can be found throughout France, but is slightly smoked. It needs to be cooked first, and I love it served on a big bed of choucroute. This recipe makes an excellent supper dish.

Serves 4

1 WHOLE *SAUCISSON DE MORTEAU*, APPROX. 300 G IN WEIGHT

500 ML CHICKEN STOCK (SEE PAGE 293)

1 LARGE SPRIG FRESH THYME

1 BAY LEAF

2 GARLIC CLOVES, PEELED

Potato salad

500 G NEW POTATOES (RATTE ARE BEST), WASHED

SALT AND PEPPER

1 SHALLOT, PEELED AND FINELY CHOPPED

Mustard sauce

1 SPRIG FRESH TARRAGON

1 GARLIC CLOVE, PEELED

200 ML DOUBLE CREAM

1 DESSERTSPOON DIJON MUSTARD

1. To cook the sausage, pour the chicken stock into a saucepan, add the herbs and garlic, and bring to the boil. Turn the heat down to a simmer, lower the sausage in and poach for 15 minutes. Remove the sausage from the stock and allow to cool. When cool enough to handle, remove the skin.

2. Boil the new potatoes in salted water until nearly tender, then strain. Peel the skins off and slice the potatoes thinly, into pieces about 3mm thick. Pour a little of the hot chicken stock (about 100 ml) over the potatoes to keep them warm, and mix in the shallot.

3. For the sauce, boil and reduce the remaining chicken stock in another pan, along with the tarragon and garlic, down to about 100 ml, then add the cream. Bring to the boil, stirring until the sauce thickens. Take off the heat and whisk in the Dijon mustard. Do not re-boil the sauce at this stage or it will curdle and taste bitter. Strain out the herbs.

4. To assemble the dish, lay a bed of sliced warm potatoes on 4 serving plates. Slice the sausage evenly and lay the pieces over the potatoes. Spoon the mustard sauce around the outside and serve immediately. As an optional garnish, you could sprinkle some chopped chives over the dish.

Twice-cooked Cheese Soufflés

The beauty of these soufflés is that you can make them one day and eat them the next, and you can use almost any type of cheese.

Serves 8

9 DESSERTSPOONS BÉCHAMEL
  SAUCE (SEE PAGE 297)
9 DESSERTSPOONS EMMENTAL OR
  GRUYÈRE CHEESE, GRATED
9 EGGS, SEPARATED
SALT AND WHITE PEPPER
UNSALTED BUTTER FOR
  GREASING
PLAIN FLOUR FOR DUSTING

SECOND COOKING
100 G UNSALTED BUTTER
400 ML DOUBLE CREAM
8 DESSERTSPOONS EMMENTAL OR
  GRUYÈRE CHEESE, GRATED

GARNISH (OPTIONAL)
200 G COOKED HAM
300 G BUTTON MUSHROOMS
3 SWISS CHARD OR CELERY
  STICKS, LEAVES REMOVED

1. Put the béchamel sauce into a large bowl and stir in the grated cheese. Stir the egg yolks into the mixture and season to taste. Pour the egg whites into a mixing bowl and whisk to firm peaks.

2. Put a deep roasting tin half filled with water onto the stove to boil, and preheat the oven to 220°C/425°F/Gas 7.

3. Coat 8 x 7.5 x 4cm ramekin dishes with liberal amounts of soft butter, then dust the ramekins with a little flour. Turn the ramekins upside down to get rid of any excess flour.

4. Stir half the egg whites into the soufflé mixture and gently fold in the remaining half, taking care not to knock the air from the mixture. With a ladle, fill the ramekins to the top. Place the ramekins in the roasting tin and put in the oven, for about 15 minutes.

5. Remove the tin from the oven. The soufflés will have risen by twice their original volume and will be a golden colour. Take the soufflés in their ramekins from the water one by one, holding them in a tea-towel. Very carefully turn them out upside down onto a cooling rack. The soufflés will deflate, but don't worry – they will rise again. The soufflés could be served now or refrigerated for serving later, reheated with the optional garnish.

6. Preheat the oven to 220°C/425°F/Gas 7. Cut the ham into strips 2.5cm long and 1cm wide, then

wipe, drain and slice the button mushrooms. Peel the fibrous veins from the chard stalks and cut into batons of similar dimensions to the ham. Blanch the chard in boiling, salted water for about 3 minutes, refresh under cold running water and strain. Set aside in a bowl.

7. Grease 8 ovenproof soup dishes with most of the butter and put 1 soufflé in the middle of each. Around the outside, if using, sprinkle a little ham, sliced mushrooms and chard. Coat the soufflés with cream, about 2 tablespoons each. Sprinkle a dessertspoon of grated cheese over the top and 2–3 small knobs of butter. Season and bake in the preheated oven for about 12 minutes. Serve immediately.

ALIGOT

This dish originated in the Auvergne, but everyone in the Aude region eats it too. Some people prefer it without the garlic. It can be served on its own, with a salad, or as an accompaniment to grilled fish or meat. I serve it with sausages and tasty onion gravy known as Sauce Lyonnaise.

Serves 8

2.5 KG FLOURY POTATOES (E.G. KING EDWARD OR CARA)

2 GARLIC CLOVES, PEELED

250 ML DOUBLE CREAM

100 G UNSALTED BUTTER

750 G CHEESE (CANTAL OR LAGUIOLE IS BEST), GRATED

SALT AND PEPPER

1. Peel and wash the potatoes, then boil with the garlic until tender.

2. When cooked, strain and mash the potatoes and garlic, and return the pan to the stove over a very low heat.

3. Add the cream, then the butter, and mix well. When the butter has melted, stir in the cheese. Work the mixture until the cheese has blended with the potatoes.

4. Season to taste and serve immediately.

CHEESE BISCUITS

These are delicious – very crumbly, very simple and very home-made. They are ideal with pre-dinner drinks.

Makes about 30

200 G UNSALTED BUTTER,
   SOFTENED
200 G PLAIN FLOUR
200 G EMMENTAL CHEESE,
   FINELY GRATED
1 EGG YOLK
SALT (OPTIONAL)

1. Preheat the oven to 180°C/350°F/Gas 4.

2. Beat the butter in a bowl until soft. Sieve the flour over the butter and gently rub the two together until crumbly. Add the grated cheese.

3. Plop the egg yolk into the mixture, along with a pinch of salt if you want. Mix it together gently, but don't over-mix it or it will become tough.

4. On a work surface lightly dusted with flour, roll the dough out to about 5mm thick. Using a cutter of whatever size and shape you like, cut biscuits from the dough then place them on a greased baking sheet.

5. Bake in the preheated oven for about 10 minutes until just turning golden brown. Cool on a wire rack and then store in an airtight container.

ROASTED FIGS AND WALNUTS

Don't use green figs for this recipe; buy only the small purple ones, as soft and as ripe as possible. This dish is equally delicious hot or cold, and you could serve crème fraîche or vanilla ice-cream with it.

Serves 6

15 G UNSALTED BUTTER

18 SMALL PURPLE FIGS

5 TEASPOONS CASTER SUGAR

50 G SHELLED WALNUTS

2 TABLESPOONS ACACIA HONEY
  (FROM THE PYRENEES IF
  POSSIBLE)

FRESHLY GROUND BLACK PEPPER

JUICE OF 1 LEMON

1. Preheat the oven to 240°C/475°F/Gas 9 and grease a shallow, ovenproof pan with the butter.

2. Wash the figs, add them to the pan, placing them upright and touching each other. Then sprinkle them with most of the sugar. Bake in the preheated oven for about 15 minutes, basting the figs with the sugar syrup halfway through cooking. Turn the oven down to 150°C/300°F/Gas 2.

3. Take the pan out of the oven and add the walnuts (which taste better if skinned first). To skin the walnuts, simply half fill a saucepan with water and bring to the boil. As soon as it's boiling, carefully plunge the walnuts in and boil them for 30 seconds. Strain them in a colander or sieve and while still hot, scrape and peel off all the skin. Sprinkle with the remaining sugar and return to the oven to cook for a further 10 minutes.

4. Arrange the figs in a serving dish. Add the walnuts.

5. Add the honey to the remaining syrup in the pan. Bring to the boil on top of the stove and then pour over the figs and walnuts. Sprinkle with pepper and lemon juice and serve immediately or refrigerate when cool. The figs will keep for up to 3 days in the refrigerator.

PEAR FRITTERS WITH PLUM SAUCE

You can use other fruits in this recipe; it works really well with apples, for instance. If you prefer, the plum sauce can be replaced with a little strawberry coulis.

Serves 4

1 LITRE VEGETABLE OIL

4 RIPE BUT FIRM WILLIAMS
   PEARS

100 G PLAIN FLOUR

50 G GROUND ALMONDS

CASTER SUGAR FOR DUSTING

PLUM SAUCE

10 RIPE PLUMS (PREFERABLY
   RED)

100 G CASTER SUGAR

100 ML WATER

BATTER

150 G PLAIN FLOUR

150 G CORNFLOUR

1 LEVEL TABLESPOON BAKING
   POWDER

350–375 ML COLD WATER

10 G CASTER SUGAR

1. For the plum sauce, first wash the plums in cold water, cut them in half and remove the stones. Place the fruit in a saucepan and sprinkle with the sugar and water. Bring them to the boil as quickly as possible, skimming off any sediment that rises to the surface. Boil for about 2 minutes, then remove from the heat and cool. When they are cold, liquidise them to make the sauce.

2. For the batter, sieve the plain flour, cornflour and baking powder into a stainless-steel or glass bowl. Slowly beat in the cold water to make a smooth batter with absolutely no lumps, then add the sugar. (If you do get a lumpy batter, take time to strain it, because lumps will ruin the dish.)

3. In a deep saucepan, heat the vegetable oil to about 190°C/375°F.

4. Peel the pears, cut them in half and then into quarters. Remove the cores. Mix the flour and ground almonds together on a plate and dip the pear segments into this, dusting all sides. Once they are well coated, dip the segments into the batter. Lower them gently into the boiling oil and fry until golden brown. Remove them from the oil with a slotted spoon, drain on kitchen paper and then dip straight into the caster sugar to coat. Keep them warm in a low oven (160°C/325°F/Gas 3) or serve them straight away on a layer of cold plum sauce.

APPLE CRÊPES

This crêpe or pancake batter is much lighter and fluffier than the traditional recipe.

Serves 4

APPLE COMPOTE

1 KG SHARP DESSERT APPLES
(E.G. GRANNY SMITHS),
CORED, PEELED AND ROUGHLY
DICED

250 G CASTER SUGAR

1 TEASPOON LEMON JUICE

SEEDS FROM 1 VANILLA POD

CRÊPES (PANCAKES)

200 G PLAIN FLOUR

A PINCH EACH OF SALT AND
CASTER SUGAR

2 EGGS

200 ML MILK

150 ML LAGER

FINELY GRATED ZEST OF 1
LEMON OR ORANGE
(OPTIONAL)

30 G UNSALTED BUTTER

VEGETABLE OR SUNFLOWER OIL
FOR FRYING

1. Place all the ingredients for the compote into a large, lidded saucepan, cover with the lid and bring to the boil. Boil for about 5 minutes, adding a little water if the juice from the apples evaporates during cooking. Remove the lid, turn down the heat slightly and cook for a further 5 minutes. The apples should have reduced to a slightly coarse purée. Take off the heat and set aside.

2. To make the crêpe batter, sieve the flour, salt and sugar into a bowl, and beat in the eggs and milk until smooth. Beat in the lager and stir in the lemon or orange zest, if using. In a small frying pan, melt the butter until it turns a nut-brown colour, then whisk it straight into the crêpe batter. Allow the batter to rest for about 10 minutes.

4. Pour a tiny drop of oil into a frying pan, then wipe it away with kitchen paper. Heat the pan on top of the stove until very hot, then turn the heat down. Pour some batter into the pan, just enough to make a very thin layer, and cook until the underside of the crêpe is golden brown.

5. Place a spoonful of apple compote into the centre of the crêpe. With a palette knife, fold the four sides of the crêpe into the middle, covering the apple compote, turn the crêpe over and place it on a serving dish. Repeat this process until all the batter and compote are used, then place the serving dish in a warm oven to reheat. Serve with Crème Anglaise (see page 299).

CRÈME BRÛLÉE

Everybody seems to have a crème brûlée recipe – so here is mine. If you want to jazz it up, you can poach some pears in Sauterne and lay them on the bottom of each dish. In the summer months, placing raspberries underneath makes a delicious alternative.

Serves 4

2 EGG YOLKS

90 G CASTER SUGAR

1 VANILLA POD

70 ML MILK

175 ML DOUBLE CREAM

1. Put the egg yolks and 40 g of the sugar into a bowl.

2. Split the vanilla pod in two and scrape out all the seeds from both halves into the egg yolks. Whisk to a smooth paste.

3. Add the milk, whisk in the cream and pour the liquid into 4 x 6cm ramekins. Refrigerate for an hour before cooking.

4. Preheat the oven to 150°C/300°F/Gas 2.

5. Fill a shallow roasting tin with water to a depth of about 2.5cm, place on the stove and bring to just below the boil. Put the ramekins into the water and then place the tin in the preheated oven. The crèmes brûlées will take about an hour to set.

6. When the crèmes brûlées are cooked, remove them from the oven and the roasting tin, and allow to cool.

7. When the crèmes brûlées are cold, preheat the grill to its highest setting, sprinkle the tops with the remaining sugar and caramelise under the grill. Serve immediately.

CHOCOLATE AND CHESTNUT TARTS

In this modern take on a classic dish, bitter chocolate offsets the sweetness of the chestnuts.

Serves 8

8 SWEET SHORTCRUST PASTRY
   CASES, 10 X 2.5CM IN
   DIAMETER (SEE PAGE 300)
ICING SUGAR FOR DUSTING

CHOCOLATE MOUSSE
125 G CHOCOLATE (AT LEAST
   75 PER CENT COCOA SOLIDS),
   FINELY CHOPPED
25 G CASTER SUGAR
35 ML WATER
4 EGG YOLKS
250 ML DOUBLE CREAM
25 ML ARMAGNAC

CHESTNUT PURÉE
400 G RAW CHESTNUTS
200 G CASTER SUGAR
SEEDS OF 1 VANILLA POD
100 ML WATER

1. To make the chocolate mousse, first place the chocolate in a bowl over a saucepan of gently simmering hot water, and slowly melt, stirring at regular intervals, then remove from the heat.

2. Put the sugar into a saucepan, cover with the 35 ml of water and bring to the boil. In a mixing bowl, beat the egg yolks until pale, then slowly pour the boiling syrup over the yolks. Whisk them until the mixture (or *sabayon*) is cold.

3. Pour the cream into another bowl and whisk it to soft peaks. Stir the Armagnac into the melted chocolate. Gently stir in the *sabayon*, then carefully fold in the cream. Fill each of the tartlets with the chocolate mousse and place in the fridge to set.

4. Peel off the outer shells of the chestnuts and tip them into a pan of boiling water. Boil for 30 seconds, strain and, while hot, peel off the skins.

5. Put the caster sugar and vanilla seeds into another saucepan, together with the empty pod, and cover with the 100 ml of water. Bring to the boil. Reduce the heat so that the syrup is just simmering, add the chestnuts and cook for about 20 minutes until soft. Leave them to cool in the syrup.

6. Carefully remove the chestnuts from the syrup and place on kitchen paper to dry. Press each piece of chestnut through a garlic press, then carefully spoon the chestnut strands on top of the tarts and dust the tops with lots of icing sugar.

ten

DECEMBER STARTED OUT BITTERLY COLD AND WET, and that's how it carried on. The freezing temperatures came as a shock after the glorious weather we'd had for most of the autumn – not least because they came so suddenly. But that was something I would learn about the Aude – the weather could change at the drop of a hat. One minute you were expiring from the heat and throwing off all your bedclothes, and the next you were wearing 15 layers and suffering from chilblains. I think the children, especially, felt cheated. The autumn had been just like a fantastic English summer, so it seemed logical that the winter would be just like a fantastic English autumn. I knew how they felt – we were in the south of France, after all.

As the dark winter evenings took hold, a general feeling of gloominess set in, although for Kim and I at least, sitting round the blazing log fire did have its compensations. And, of course, for the children there was Christmas to look forward to – although, as Kim and I began to do our Christmas shopping, we were surprised at how quiet and low-key the build-up seemed compared to England. I think it was the kids who probably missed out on this. As far as I was concerned, it was such a relief to get away from all that dreadful commercialism.

The last few weeks had made a huge difference to the family. Kim was especially delighted with her new-found friendship with Lesley. The children were happy in their schools, and everyone was generally feeling more positive. Even Eve was beginning to enjoy life again. She had become inseparable from her new friends, Tatjana and Margaud (Jean-Louis and Marie's daughter), and although she was still missing Tom, we had come to a deal. I would try to turn a blind eye to her long-distance phone calls to him in return for her typing my book manuscript. So far, apart from the odd row, it was working well. Olivia and Martha had made new friends, too, and their French was coming on in leaps and bounds – Olivia, especially, delighted us by being top of her class at school. And, joy of joys, the little ones were not only enjoying their French schools, but had actually started to say they never wanted to go back to England. All music to my ears. And me? Well, I was in heaven of course. Back in the country I loved, and surrounded by a fabulous, never-ending array of wonderful food. What could be better? Apart from the weather, of course.

As the weeks passed, Kim and I really got stuck into our Christmas preparations. This was going to be my first Christmas away from home, and I was excited at the prospect. We were having visitors to stay and there was masses to do, so we battled against the rain, interspersing our Christmas shopping expeditions to Toulouse with our regular routine of school runs. But, however busy we were, and whatever the weather, nothing, but nothing got in the way of my trips to the local food markets. I never tired of these weekly visits and had got all the market days down to a tee now: Castelnaudary on Mondays, St-Félix Lauragais (a tiny one, this) on Wednesdays, Castres on Thursdays, and Villefranche on Fridays. Food

markets had, of course, been the main attraction for me from day one, but now they'd taken on a new dimension. My general confidence had increased, my schoolboy French had vastly improved, and I was even getting the hang of the local dialect. Best of all, the locals, these wonderful, fantastic people, had opened up to me. After months of struggling and hesitant 'Bonjours', I was finally getting to talk to the stall-holders properly – the man who sold olives, the baker, the woman selling Auvergne cheeses, and – my favourite of all – Madame Bondouy, an amazing character who ran a vegetable stall at the markets in Villefranche and Revel. I ran into her so often that she joked about me secretly fancying her (she was 70 if she was a day!).

But it was still the Saturday market at Revel that I loved best. Over the months, I'd come to understand the rhythm of the place, and the natural ebbs and flows of the crowds, depending on what was newly in season: the ceps in September, the oysters in October (crates of them, piled up in their hundreds, and sold out within an hour), and the bream, bass and monkfish in November. I especially remembered one specific week in September, when crowds had gathered around one particular stall, drawn by a rumour that the first celeriac of the year was in.

To someone like me, this kind of seasonal buying was fantastic. But even I have to admit that in one case it went too far, to the point of being irritating. The ingredient in question was fresh Foie gras – the wonderfully creamy liver of ducks (Foie gras de canard) or geese (Foie gras d'oie). Now Foie gras happens to be a favourite of Kim's, and I'd spent the whole autumn trying to track it down. You'd think it would have been easy in France, the home of Foie gras, but every time I tried to find it, there was none to be had, and everyone said, 'No, wait till it gets cold – December's the time.' It sounded daft to me. 'Look,' I'd say, 'livers are livers and ducks have them, so why do I have to wait till the weather gets cooler? I can buy Foie gras all year round in London.' And now, here we were, in December, and, sure enough, the stuff was everywhere – on cue for the Foie gras terrine that forms part of the traditional Christmas meal in the Aude.

I had of course broken my own cardinal rule about trying to buy food when it wasn't in season. But this was no time to feel guilty. Having been deprived of Foie gras for so long, I now leapt at it, and for two weeks Kim and I gorged on it every which way – flash-fried with a green peppercorn sauce, on its own with a walnut salad, and – my favourite – in potato pancakes with sweetcorn cooked in a very sweet duck stock flavoured with Banyuls wine… Heaven!

Meanwhile, our thoughts turned to our own Christmas meal and what to serve as a main course. We wanted something typically French, but none of the normal French Christmas options of oysters, salmon or fillet steak seemed Christmassy enough, and, although many French people have turkey at Christmas, it seemed utterly pointless to have the same thing we would have had in England.

And then Lesley came up with what seemed like the perfect answer: capon, or, as it's called in French, *chapon*. Most people in the Aude had capon at Christmas, she explained, and it so happened that there was a farm very near us in Montferrand that had been going for years and was especially known for its *chapons*. She and Michel had bought one the Christmas before – a marvellous bird, it was, with the most fantastic flavour. All I had to do was to turn up, choose one, and they would send it away to be slaughtered and plucked, ready to be picked up in a few days. What's more, the woman who ran the farm was a real character… And so she went on, in her inimitably endearing way.

Just for the record, capons are castrated male chickens. Normal, full-term cockerels (defined as male birds that are over six months old) have very tough, stringy flesh, and the theory is that the changes in hormonal distribution in the bird, once it's castrated, make it grow and develop differently, giving it softer, fattier flesh. It had been years since I'd had a capon – and I'd certainly never had a French one – so I was grateful to Lesley for the idea.

A few days later, at 8.30 in the morning, I set off for the farm, which was, exactly as Lesley had said, just a few kilometres away. Driving into a dip set between two hills that were covered with wind turbines (a characteristic feature of the Aude), I saw the signpost – '*En Boriés: Produits de Ferme*' – and drove into a yard, where I was greeted by an old, wellie-clad chap with a ruddy, weather-beaten face. I explained what I wanted and he immediately called to his daughter, who came out and introduced herself to me. Her name was Valérie Mazières, and yes, of course, I could have a capon. All I had to do was choose one – she'd take me round the farm so I could find one that I liked, and I could have a guided tour too if I wanted. That suited me perfectly, as I was keen to find out how these capons were reared and what made their flavour so special. As we walked around, I began to get my bearings. There was a house on one side, and a garage piled up with sweetcorn cobs on the other. And there were tractors everywhere, with chickens and capons on them – in fact, with all manner of wildfowl on them. It seemed a rather eccentric place. Still, the poultry was obviously free range, which was an encouraging sign.

BELOW: *Three-year-old Millie – affectionately known as 'Tyson' – plays the fool to camera, with the Christmas tree pot.*

We eventually came across a bunch of capons that were hanging around in a 'loose-endish' sort of way, so I chose a couple and Valérie separated them into a pen. That done, we continued the tour of the farm as she chatted about the family business. She had about 50 capons a year, she said, all reared specially for Christmas. They were bought as baby chicks from a local breeder, and for the first couple of months were reared by hand and kept inside, where they were fed a mixture of powdered milk and maize. At the age of six weeks, she went on (in what I felt was an inappropriately cheerful way), they were sent off to a place in St-Michel de Laviés to be castrated. Not much of a life being a capon, I thought.

Now castration is not a subject that any man feels comfortable with, and I was no exception. And, as she went onto describe the operation (too horrible to be repeated here), I was starting to feel distinctly queasy. 'Er, their testicles

have to be removed, do they?' I asked, knowing the answer full well. 'Of course,' she said. 'Otherwise their meat would be too tough.' 'Ah,' I said.

Standing there at that precise moment, it didn't really seem a good enough reason to me – even with all my passion for great flavours. She carried on talking, and I began to get more and more uncomfortable. Then, suddenly, for reasons I couldn't quite explain, as well as my general sense of physical discomfort, I began to have this strange, irrational feeling of claustrophobia, of being hemmed in – almost as if someone were standing right behind me, staring at me. I looked over my shoulder, but no one was there.

Valérie purposefully carried on. 'Yes,' she said cheerfully, 'some of them die during the operation.' 'Right,' I said. There was that feeling of being watched again. I looked around but, again, there was no one there. It was all this talk

OPPOSITE: *Olivia, the family correspondent, finds a rare quiet moment to write home to her friends.*

about having testicles removed, no doubt, that was making me feel so peculiar. And then I felt a strange sensation in my trousers.

Well, when I say trousers, it was actually at the bottom of my right trouser leg, and it was more like a tugging sensation than anything else. Then I looked down and saw them – two massive turkeys, standing a few inches away from me. Ugly brutes they were, and they were staring at me in what I felt to be a malevolent way. I think, in other circumstances, the term might have been 'in your face', except that they only came up to my knees. One of them was pecking at the bottom of my trousers and the other one was looking at my crotch. I wasn't happy.

As I stood there looking at them, they both stepped forward simultaneously in a synchronised movement. 'Don't worry about them,' said Valérie, casually. 'They're just curious.' 'Right,' I said, as one of them pecked at my shoes. We moved on. And they followed. 'A mating couple, are they?' I asked, my pace quickening. Valérie laughed, hurrying to keep up with me. 'No,' she said. 'They're both male. I think they're gay.' 'Right,' I said, as one of them eyed my crotch again. The four of us moved swiftly on, Valérie chattering about the capons, and me desperately trying to concentrate on what she was saying. 'After two months we change their diet to a mixture of wheat, maize and peas,' she said. 'It's this special food that makes their meat taste so good.' I stopped for a moment to get my breath, and the turkeys stopped too. This was pathetic, I thought. There was no way two turkeys were going to get the better of me. I turned round and stared at them. Momentarily taken aback, they took a step backwards. Then, as one, they edged forward again, and looked up at me impudently. We all set off again, at a trot this time.

Valérie continued to talk, oblivious to what I was going through. The capons were constantly weighed, she said, the aim being to reach an average weight of 4–5 kg by the time they were six months old, which was timed at around Christmas. And then they were for the chop. Ah, the chop, I thought. I darkly muttered something about changing my Christmas order to turkey, and Valérie overheard me. 'Oh, Monsieur Burton Race,' she squealed, slapping me on the shoulder, 'you are so funny.'

Five minutes later I was back in the car, exhausted and traumatised, and it wasn't a moment too soon. The turkeys had followed me all the way, and I just managed to close the door in time, before they got in the car with me. There was no way I was going back there to pick up those capons, I thought. Kim could do it. Meanwhile, I hoped those damned turkeys ended up on someone's Christmas platter.

Our first visitors – Kim's mother, Patsy, her partner, Geoff, and Kim's niece, Molly – arrived on the 23rd, just in time to help out with last-minute preparations. And the next day, Christmas Eve, in time-honoured tradition, we bought the tree, and Patsy helped the children decorate it while I slaved away in the kitchen. In France, as in many other European countries, it's Christmas Eve that's celebrated, rather than Christmas Day, and families traditionally sit down to a Christmas Eve supper, followed by Midnight Mass, but we were going to be following the English tradition and having our main meal on Christmas Day. I had already spent two whole days cooking in preparation.

Christmas morning was the usual chaos, with the kids ransacking their stockings and tearing at their presents, though I suppose I wasn't much better. I was especially delighted at my present from Kim – a painting by Michel of a John Dory, which I'd been admiring in a gallery in Villefranche for weeks. Then, after attending Mass at the local church in Montferrand, we sat down to lunch. There were 17 of us at the table that day: the eight of us, plus Patsy and her party, then Kim's brother, Philip, his girlfriend, Eve, plus an extra friend, and finally Michel, Lesley and Tatjana. There were two tables groaning with food. To start with, by popular request from the children, we had Cauliflower soup with truffle oil. Then the capons with roast potatoes, roast carrots and parsnips, and baby Brussels sprouts. For dessert there was a chocolate *bûche de Noël* (yule log) and, for the traditionalists, Christmas pudding with, of course, wine and port. The capons were a great success with everyone, except for me. Michel pronounced them the best he'd ever tasted, but when I eat poultry, I like something I can get my teeth into, and I found this capon flesh almost too tender and buttery – unnaturally so but everyone else loved it.

OPPOSITE: *Charles and Amelia decorate the tree on Christmas Eve 2002 – their first Christmas away from home.*

By the time our visitors left, on the 28th, I was utterly exhausted with all the cooking and clearing up, and really felt like a break. Kim and I had discussed endless possibilities in terms of going away for New Year. The beauty of the house's location meant that we could be in Andorra or the Pyrenees in a couple of hours, in Barcelona in three, or Milan in four. We mulled over the options – and decided to stay at home.

It was all Jean-Louis's fault. He had read about a restaurant in Revel that was advertising a jazz band and dinner for New Year. The place itself looked beautiful – it had the atmosphere of a real old country inn, so we thought we'd give it a go. What a disaster! The *patronne* was a sour-looking woman with short, peroxide-blonde hair, who wasn't exactly brimming with seasonal cheer, the drinks were priced beyond the stratosphere, and the food was awful. Ah well, I thought, at least there was the jazz. But the jazz band turned out to be a decrepit old man with an out-of-tune accordion, coupled, metaphorically speaking, with an old crone who sang in a tremulous voice and was about as musical as a plate of chips. That was it. We were off. A few minutes later we were back in the car, and half an hour later were back at the house, where we opened some bottles of champagne, saw the New Year in and had our own excellent private party.

We took our break the following weekend, and made for the Pyrenees with the children and Fendi. Although Kim, I and the older girls had often been skiing, this was the first time Millie had seen the snow, and it was only the second time for Charles. They loved it. We had a wonderful weekend, though, unfortunately, not much skiing because there wasn't enough snow.

This was more than could be said for the Aude. When we got back home there was snow everywhere, more than 15cm thick. It was so deep that even the four-wheel drive almost got stuck. Although I'd heard about the extreme range of temperatures in the Aude, nothing had quite prepared me for this.

Snow? Snow? We were 550 km south of England, for God's sake. Still, it all looked very magical, and it certainly concentrated the mind when writing winter recipes. The snow was so bad that the schools were shut for days. The children were delighted, though the novelty soon wore off when we had to send them out looking for firewood. We'd settled in with a siege mentality by now. We had some poussins and sourdough bread in the freezer, some *saucissons secs* and plenty of other dry stores, so food wasn't a problem. But we only had enough oil to heat the house for three days, and that was a real worry. Even when I phoned the delivery company, I was worried the trucks wouldn't be able to make it up the hill to the house. Fortunately, they turned up the next day at 7 a.m.

By 6 January, the snow had cleared enough for us to take a trip into Revel, to buy some provisions. It was Twelfth Night, or the Epiphany, a commemoration of the day the Three Kings took their gifts to baby Jesus, and is celebrated in a big way in France, where it's sometimes called *Le Petit Noël*. The shops everywhere were full of the *gâteaux des rois*, a seasonal speciality cake made of brioche or pastry and filled with frangipane paste. Inside each cake is a plastic *fève* (bean), or figure, representing the Christ Child, and tradition has it that the finder is king or queen for the day. A lovely idea, though one I could see was bound to cause arguments between the children. I gave it a miss.

A few days later the snow had gone completely, and just as I was wondering what else the weather had in store for us, the wind started. The famous Aude wind. I had been warned about it many times before by the locals, who kept telling me it was something that had to be seen to be believed – hence all the wind farms and wind turbines that were around. But don't worry, they'd all said. It only comes in three-day combinations – *trois jours, six jours* or *neuf jours* – so hopefully it wouldn't last too long.

Three weeks later, it was still there – so wild and furious that we had to walk bent double everywhere. Everyone was mightily fed up; we settled ourselves in for long evenings by the fire, and the older girls went on and on about how much colder it was in the south of France than in England. Bored out of our minds, we spent most of the time eating, and I must say that it was in these cold winter months that the big and bold rustic food of the region really came into its own: cabbage and haricot bean soups, pig's trotters, cassoulet, rabbit casseroles, the daubes of wild boar, and, of course, duck.

If there's one ingredient that defines the cooking of south-west France in general, and the Aude in particular, it's duck. From the humblest of homes to the grandest starred restaurants, this versatile bird reigns supreme. The breasts, or *magrets*, are grilled and eaten like steaks, the necks are stuffed with forcemeat to make *cou farci*, the livers make Foie gras, the legs are slowly cooked in their own fat to make Confit, and the gizzards, or *gésiers*, are fried and eaten in salads. Even the carcass doesn't go to waste, but is an integral part of stocks, and particularly the stock of that most famous of regional dishes, Cassoulet. And then, when the bird is all gone and you think it's all over, there is the fat – the delicious, heavenly fat that is used to cook roasts and casseroles, and which, along with the pink-tinged garlic of Lautrec, pervades all the dishes of the region, giving them their uniquely distinct and superb flavour.

Duck has never really caught on in the UK, where, apart from the odd encounter with Duck à l'orange in more upmarket eating establishments, the nearest most people get to eating it is in Chinese restaurants, where it's cooked to oblivion and eaten with pancakes and lashings of plum sauce. I happen to think that duck is, in fact, one of the few meats that's best served overcooked when roasted, though most French people wouldn't agree. But my own personal favourite is duck legs, cooked slowly for four to five hours in a low oven, and that's something you simply wouldn't come across back home. This is partly a cultural thing. The fact is that, as a nation, we Brits simply don't tend to go in for very long, slow cooking, which is what brings out the full flavour of this kind of meat best. Sure, we'll make the odd casserole, but, in general, our idea of cooking meat is to put a joint (of beef or pork) in the oven at a high temperature to seal it, then reduce the heat, cook it for an hour or two, take it out and serve it.

Many people are also put off by the high fat content in duck, the logic being that anything that fatty can't possibly be good for you. The truth is, however, that, while duck is undeniably fattier than chicken and most other meats, the

type of fat it contains is healthier, being monounsaturated – like olive oil – rather than saturated. So, far from heading you towards the nearest coronary unit, it's likely to protect you from circulatory problems and heart disease. (Well, that's what the locals say, anyway.)

In France duck-rearing goes back a long way. From the earliest times, most families had their own geese or ducks on their smallholdings. This was both practical and economical, since the birds were cheap to keep, and every part could be used. The breasts were cooked and eaten, the feathers used to stuff

pillows, and the neck, legs and liver were slowly cooked in their own fat, then stored in it – a method of preservation known as *confit* – a traditional way of keeping food and protein for the long, lean winter months.

Today, the general rural poverty of the Aude, and the lack of good grazing land for cattle, have maintained the tradition of rearing ducks, which have come to replace not only geese, but beef, as a cheap staple food. But in other ways things have moved on. There's no longer any need to keep the duck by-products for winter, and the use of the term *confit* – once used only to mean 'preserve' – is now rather more confusing, referring both to the method of slow cooking, and the preserved parts of the duck that you're more likely to find ready-prepared in a can or jar. In fact, duck by-products are big business these days and you'll be hard-pushed to find any grocery or food shop in the region that doesn't sell a pâté or confit of some kind.

The duck by-product that most people are interested in is, of course, the most famous one of all – Foie gras – that Rolls-Royce of ingredients that is surpassed only by the Périgord black truffle. And, in all my years as a chef, I've found little to beat it in terms of flavour and its soft, melt-in-the-mouth texture. Creamy, flavourful and subtly delicate, whether served in a cold terrine or freshly fried in a very hot pan with a sweet sauce and eaten with a slice of brioche, this is the stuff that dreams are made of.

OPPOSITE: *Ducks and geese are a mainstay of the diet in south-western France, where they've long replaced beef as a staple food.*

But dreams like this come at a price, and in this case it's one that's paid heavily by the ducks. For this exquisite flavour can only be achieved through the very special way that ducks are reared – namely, *gavage*. This, in case you haven't guessed already, is that controversial and, to many people, repugnant method of force-feeding the duck so that its liver is enlarged by up to ten times its normal size.

Gavage is not carried out in all parts of France – it's a speciality of the Landes, Périgord and the south-west – and, although traditionally carried out on geese, is now almost exclusively performed on ducks (over 85 per cent of Foie gras these days is made from duck liver). I had first come across it indirectly at the end of autumn a few months earlier. I had gone to see the mayor, Jean-Claude Marty, in the tiny hamlet of St-Gauderic about a shooting licence. A short, chubby chap with a huge, gleaming smile, Monsieur Marty was a great talker and, as he stamped my forms, waxed lyrical about the old days. His mother, it turned out used to produce the best Barbary ducks in the area, and had reared geese to make *Foie gras d'oie*. She had won competitions and medals galore, he said wistfully. His mother was dead now and things weren't what they used to be. But there was a Monsieur Douy who had a farm called Domaine de Fajac-la-Selve in Pech Luna, on the Mirepoix road, he said. He reared Foie gras ducks and practised *gavage* – perhaps I'd like to go and see him. Perhaps I might even write about it. What would my British readers think of that, he chuckled.

I'd passed off his comments as a joke at the time, but, now that winter had come, and I'd seen all the Foie gras in the shops for Christmas, I gave it some more thought. Kim and I both adored Foie gras, and had been cooking and eating it for years, yet in all that time I'd never really thought much about how it was produced. I knew all about *gavage*, of course, but I had never had any direct experience of it – never seen it and certainly never done it. Now it was raising some important questions for me. The whole basis of killing animals to eat, is, in a sense, based on cruelty, and yet most people happily accept this concept. What's so different about *gavage*? I was perfectly happy to shoot pigeons and pheasants and eat them, but was I prepared to force-feed a duck (or, indeed, watch one being force-fed) and then eat Foie gras? And would I feel the same afterwards? It seemed to me that the least I could do was to find out, and I'd never have a better opportunity than now. Keeping an open mind, I resolved to see and decide for myself. I looked up Monsieur Douy's details and arranged to see him the next day.

It was a cold Monday morning, and the wind was worse than ever. I think my little Citroën Diane van was feeling a little bit like me – not firing on all cylinders. Each hill had to be climbed in second (or first) gear, and the smell of exhaust fumes began to be overwhelming. Not for the first time, I was beginning to wonder about my choice of car. Perhaps I should have gone for something a little more practical and comfortable – or, at least, safe. But I eventually made it to Monsieur Douy's property.

The farmhouse – a huge, crumbling old mansion – was at the top of a hill, and standing outside waiting for me was Monsieur Douy himself, holding a bucket of maize in one hand and his gloves in the other. His thick beard and woolly hat meant I couldn't see much of his face, but he seemed very friendly. We shook hands and, eager to get on with his task, Monsieur Douy led me to the feeding barn as he talked to me about his ducks. He had 150 ducks altogether, he explained, but only about 50 were at the perfectly right stage at any one time.

The ducks were reared from day-old chicks, he said. Some farmers kept them warm under heat lamps and fed and looked after them till they were six months old, but he preferred to bring them to a desired weight after 13–17 weeks. The ducks we were feeding that day, he went on (I wasn't sure I liked the sound of that 'we') were 15 weeks old, so they were literally only a fortnight away from the chop. I was beginning to feel guilty already. The ducks he used were 'Mulad' ducks – a cross between Barbary and Peking ducks. They were all males, and because of their cross-breeding were sterile. The average size of a duck's liver was around 50 g, Monsieur Douy went on to say, but the optimum weight of the liver he aimed for was between 500 g and 600 g. The ducks were traditionally fed on white maize, which made the livers very pale, but he used yellow maize, which gave the livers a buttery hue.

The first thing that struck me about these ducks was their size. They were huge – more like geese than ducks – and they clearly weren't happy when alone. Whenever Monsieur Douy separated one from a crowd of 20 or so in the pen, as he often did to make some point or other, it seemed to look lost and insecure. Feeding them on a one-to-one basis seemed to be such an intimate thing that I couldn't help thinking I might get attached to them over time, especially when, as in this case, they had to be fed twice a day.

And now for the *gavage* itself. At this point anyone who feels remotely squeamish should skip the next paragraph; if you're really squeamish, perhaps skip the next three.

Monsieur Douy went into a pen full of ducks. Inside the pen was something that looked like a small vaulting horse with a sliding lid. He grabbed one of the ducks, and, holding its wings firmly down to avoid being spiked by the duck's vicious thumb claw at the foot of the wing-bone, he unceremoniously shoved it inside the horse, leaving its head and neck sticking out of a hole at the front. Above the duck's head was a huge plastic funnel with a neck over a foot long containing a skewer made of metal wire that was about as thick as a coat hanger. A handle attached to the side of the funnel feeder electrically operated the skewer, which drove the maize down into the duck's crop. Meanwhile, Monsieur Douy was putting the maize into the feeder and massaging the duck's neck to smooth the food down the gullet. Starting gradually from 100 g of maize per feed, he explained, they would eventually build up to 500 g to 600 g a day. Each duck took a couple of minutes to feed, and I watched him feed about a dozen with complete calm and unemotional efficiency. Being calm was essential, he said, otherwise the ducks would feel it and wouldn't feed properly. Remember, he said, you're putting the funnel into the duck's throat with one hand and holding the neck and putting the maize down with your other hand. 'They will feel your mood,' he said. Given the circumstances, it seemed like a strangely placed sensitivity.

Then he offered me the chance to do it. I wanted to run, but equally didn't want to be seen as a wimp, and besides, that's what I was there for, so, without thinking too much, I jumped into the pen, he handed me a duck, and I had a go. The moment I saw it looking up at me I felt sick, but I just looked away, did the business and got out as soon as I could.

As we walked back to the farmhouse, I was still feeling pretty rattled. I asked Monsieur Douy if his ducks couldn't just be fed normally, but he was adamant. 'Absolutely not,' he said. They simply wouldn't eat enough and the livers wouldn't be large enough. Besides, he went on, rather defensively, this type of feeding isn't new. The Ancient Egyptians force-fed their ducks on milk and figs to fatten them as far back as 2,000 BC. What was more, he continued, worse things than this were happening all over the world – and not just to farm animals.

Gavage is, admittedly, a difficult thing to defend. Many locals argue that force-feeding the ducks is essential – not only for Foie gras, but because the extra fat produces wonderfully flavoured meat. I have to disagree on this one. In my experience, I've never found that fattening the duck does anything beneficial to the meat. The legs in confit are fine – delicious, in fact – but that's more to do with the method of slow cooking, which enables the flavour of the fat to be suffused into the meat. The breasts, as far as I'm concerned, are tough to the point of being inedible, and only good enough for lengthy marinating in olive oil and herbs, then shoving under a grill. The fact is that when it comes to eating duck meat in, say, Duck à l'orange, or magrets in green peppercorn sauce, there's nothing to beat the moist, succulent, tender flesh of a Barbary duck, or a similar breed that's bred for the purpose. And as for the fat, well, there's enough fat in a non-foie gras duck to flavour stews and Sunday roasts. And delicious it is too.

When it comes to justifying Foie gras, itself, that's a tough one. After my gavage experience, I couldn't look at Foie gras for weeks, but it was amazing how quickly the experience faded, and now – incredibly – Monsieur Douy's ducks are just a vague memory. What do I think about gavage now? It's repulsive. Do I still eat Foie gras? Yes. Still love it? Yes. Hypocritical? Maybe, but is it really that much worse than eating an egg produced by a battery hen that has been cooped up for its entire life? And how many people who wouldn't go near an abattoir can happily eat meat, as long as it's bought in the sanitised conditions of a supermarket? For most people, ignorance is bliss. At least I was prepared to force-feed a duck myself, so I feel I've earned my stripes. However much of a cop-out it may sound, decisions like this must ultimately always be left up to the individual. Arguments about the rights and wrongs of *gavage* will no doubt rage for years to come. But in the meantime, like it or not, Foie gras – and *gavage* – are here to stay.

By the middle of February, the wind was blowing as hard as ever. It was beginning to have a very bad effect on me by now, and I felt permanently in the doldrums. Kim and I were so fed up we almost stopped going out altogether, apart from visiting Michel's or Jean-Louis's for supper, and drinking their wonderful wines. It was at one of those drunken evenings at Jean-Louis's that the whole business about cooking the Cassoulet started. We'd been talking about food, of course, when he suddenly said that if I really wanted to be taken seriously by people in the food business, the only thing to do was to become a member of the Grande Confrérie du Cassoulet. To this day, I can't really remember how it happened, but one minute I was laughing and treating it all as a joke, and the next I'd agreed. As I left his house that evening in a drunken haze, I asked, 'What do I have to do?' 'Make a good Cassoulet. That's all.' 'Fine,' I replied. 'See you in three weeks,' Jean-Louis shouted out, as he waved me goodbye. It sounded like a breeze.

It was only when I'd sobered up the next morning that I began to realise what I'd let myself in for. It was all very well for Jean-Louis to talk about making a good Cassoulet. But it wouldn't be enough to make any good Cassoulet, however tasty. It would have to meet all the Confrérie's high standards. And I knew enough about the members of the society to know that they took Cassoulet very seriously indeed. These people were real experts. This wasn't about instinctive cooking, which I've always been good at, but about cooking by the rulebook – something I wasn't used to at all.

OPPOSITE: *Learning how to make cassoulet under the eagle eye of Madame Bondouy. Her recipe was delicious, but not what you'd call orthodox!*

For the next two weeks I read every book I could on the subject, but the more I read, the more I found that when it comes to Cassoulet, there was no such thing as a rulebook. No matter how many books I read, there was no uniformity. Some said you had to use breadcrumbs to achieve the characteristic crunchy topping, others said not; some recommended chicken for the stock, others pork; some insisted on Toulouse sausage, some not. And then there was this business of soaking the beans. According to one book, which purported to offer a truly authentic Cassoulet recipe, you had to push the beans down seven times while they were cooking. I spent my time researching, eating, living and breathing Cassoulet. I'd found a place in Castelnaudary (or 'Castel-laundry' as Millie called it) that did take-away cassoulets, and roped Lesley and Michel into endless Cassoulet-tasting evenings. I ate the stuff till it came out of my ears, and felt permanently bloated, and talked about it to everyone I knew.

I soon came to understand that the very mention of the word 'Cassoulet' round here was enough to arouse the highest emotions. Everyone, it seemed, had their own views on what constituted the perfect Cassoulet. I asked Laurent and Evelyne, some charming neighbours we'd recently met. 'Breadcrumbs, chicken stock and no Toulouse sausage,' Evelyne said. 'I should know. I make the best cassoulet in the region.' Then Michel: 'Toulouse sausage and breadcrumbs,' he said. 'No, no breadcrumbs,' said Lesley. 'How would you know?' said Michel, getting heated. 'You're not even French.' 'What about pushing down the beans?' I said, hoping to defuse the situation. They both looked at me as if I was mad.

My next stop was the Brasserie St-Martin in Sorèze, a small restaurant that had become one of our favourite haunts on Saturday nights, when there was a jazz band. I remembered often having eaten Cassoulet there, and now I quizzed François, the owner, about how it was made. 'Definitely sausage, but no breadcrumbs,' he said. 'You achieve the crust by pushing down the beans.' 'Ah,' I said, latching onto this. 'Seven times?' 'No, five,' he said. 'I should know – we make the best Cassoulet in the region.'

I then tried the stall-holders at Revel market, and it was the same: everyone had a different view. And then I happened to mention it to Madame

Bondouy, who roared with laughter. 'Cassoulet?' she said, her eyes shining under her spectacles. 'There's nothing I don't know about Cassoulet. I make the best Cassoulet in the Aude. Come to my house and I'll show you.'

I took her up on her offer and went over late the next afternoon. She opened the door, a broad smile on her face, and clucked and fussed over me in her reassuring motherly way. Now that I was there, I had to see her vegetables, she insisted proudly, and she whizzed me around her massive vegetable farm. There they all were…asparagus, spinach, broccoli, carrots, potatoes, lettuces, tomatoes, courgettes and marrows, peas, runner beans, all covered in plastic sheeting – a practice she bizarrely extended to the furniture in her house. The sofas and chairs were all covered in it, the table was covered in it…even the bird-house was covered in it. Strange.

And then we got to work. Well, when I say *we* got to work, I really mean I got to work while she gave the orders. Madame Bondouy may have been a lovely, smiling grandmother at her vegetable stall, but once inside that kitchen, she was a real tartar. 'Come on, come on,' she said, clapping her hands, as I ran about chopping, slicing and generally acting as her skivvy. It was exhausting stuff. In terms of sheer hard work, not even working as a *sous-chef* for Raymond Blanc had matched this.

'Watch me,' she said. 'This is le *vrai Cassoulet*.' The garlic and onions went in. Fine. Then tomatoes. Then everything but the kitchen sink: saucisson, black pudding, salami, chicken stock, bits of pork belly, duck…and handfuls of breadcrumbs. It all tasted delicious, but I wondered if the Confrérie would approve, and made the mistake of mentioning it to her jokingly. She drew herself up to her full height of 5 feet and glared at me. Confrérie! What nonsense, she said, wagging her pudgy finger. She had been making Cassoulet for years. Her children and grandchildren all loved her Cassoulet and said she made the best Cassoulet around. What was all this nonsense about the Confrérie? I knew when I was beaten and left. It was back to the drawing board.

It was during those weeks of getting bogged down with my Cassoulet recipe that I attended my first Fête du Cochon, or 'Pig Festival' – a celebration of the annual slaughter of the family pig. It's a tradition that goes back hundreds of years, and, like duck-rearing, is a throwback to the times when small communities relied on home-produced products for self-sufficiency. In regions of traditional poverty, such as this, where cattle-grazing land was scarce, it made perfect economic sense to keep pigs that, when slaughtered, provided charcuterie for the whole village for a year.

Although once an essential part of French rural life, the *Fête du Cochon* is now, sadly, dying out, though there are pockets of France where it is still practised. The one I was heading for was in Bouisse, a tiny hamlet in the heart of the Corbières – traditional wine country – and as I drove across the rugged snow-tipped mountain passes early on that cold winter's morning, I began to get a real sense of the remoteness of this French hinterland that is so often referred to as *la France profonde*.

It was the end of February – the traditional time when the pigs are slaughtered – and of course, the wind was blowing, though it wasn't the damp sea wind of the Aude, but a dry wind from the mountains – offering perfect conditions, I knew, for preserving meat. It was a bitterly cold day, with brooding grey skies, and the Corbières vineyards to the right and left of me were bare stumps covered with frost. Tuscan cypresses dotted the landscape, adding a rather mournful air to the already bleak landscape. It felt like an extremely long drive.

After all the dramatic scenery, Bouisse itself was a bit of a disappointment – a small, tumbledown hamlet of no more than 80 houses, half of which seemed to be abandoned – but I pulled up at the pre-arranged house and was greeted by Pierrette – a slim, pretty, bubbly woman in her fifties, who, with her elegant air, seemed out of place in these remote rural surroundings. I'd deliberately timed my visit for a Monday morning, knowing full well that the pig was traditionally slaughtered on a Sunday, then hung for 24 hours before being cut up for its meat. I didn't particularly relish the thought of watching it being killed, nor of hanging around for 24 hours before the celebrations started. I'd heard that the festival lasted for two or three days, with a good time being had by all. I was simply looking forward to taking part in a really traditional rural family event.

OPPOSITE: *Pierrette, her family, me – and what's left of the pig – prepare for the Fête du Cochon.*

Pierrette was disappointed that I'd arrived after the slaughter. Never mind, she said excitedly, there was still plenty to do, and she led me away from the house to a nearby garage. If I thought I'd got off lightly by missing the slaughter, I was very much mistaken.

In the garage was half of the slaughtered pig hanging on a pulley in front of me. The other half was lying on a metal table. Around the table were Pierrette's husband, Didier, her mother, aunt and several old ladies, all wearing plastic aprons and shower caps and up to their elbows in blood. 'It may be the men who kill the pig,' Pierrette said, grinning, 'but it's the women who take over now,' and she promptly donned plastic cap and apron and got stuck into jointing the pig and clearing out its innards.

I'd heard there was a rural saying in the Tarn – 'Tout est bon dans le cochon' ('Every bit of the pig is good') – and they'd obviously heard it here. Every single part of the pig was used. The neck, liver and sweetbreads were removed and cut up to make a special fricassée called *fréginat*; the brains (Pierrette's favourite) set aside to be fried, seasoned and served with *persillade*; the intestines and shoulder meat used to make sausages; the loins and legs used to make hams; the liver and choice pork meats used for pâtés and confits; and the intestines and blood, head, heart and lungs used to make *boudin noir* (black pudding). Finally, the fat was drained and kept to flavour meat that was spit-roasted over the fire.

Pierrette talked me through the ham-making. The H-bone was removed, the fat cleared and sinews removed, and the ham was put into a wooden chest in sea salt for 40 days. After this, she explained, the salt would be brushed off and the ham wrapped in muslin and left to dry in her cellar (she took me there and showed me the previous year's hams hanging from hooks). After three days, it was transferred in its muslin into another wooden chest – this time full of wood ash which would dry the meat – for one to two years.

But the really big thing seemed to be the sausages and *saucissons sec*. I watched as a mixture of shoulder meat and pork fat from the belly was minced through once, then seasoned, then I had a go myself. The women had already

cleaned out the intestines, left the cleaned skins in tons of sea salt overnight, washed them with liberal amounts of water, then hung them up to dry. Now it was my turn to make the sausages. I stuffed the meat into a large piping nozzle, and proceeded to fill the skins until I ended up with a huge snake-like tube. Finally, the women twisted the thing into segments. The *saucisson sec* was made in exactly the same way, except that it was seasoned with salt and pepper and left to dry for at least a month.

Last of all came the black pudding. The heart and head, with the brain removed, was chopped up into pieces and tossed into a huge cauldron in the garden, along with masses of thyme, a bay leaf, some onions and a whole peeled garlic. A fire was lit underneath and the whole lot boiled for four hours. The meat was then chopped and put into a bucket, where it was mixed with the reserved pig's blood, seasoned and piped into an intestine skin. The stuffed skin was then gently poached in warm liquid, removed and set aside to cool.

Once all this was over, I finally had a chance to talk to Pierrette about the traditions behind the fête. It had happened for as long as she remembered, she explained. Her grandparents had kept a pig, which they'd reared indoors in a pen and fattened up with beets, potatoes and cereal. She preferred to leave the pig in the open air and to let it eat naturally because it made for better-flavoured, less fatty meat. Otherwise, in this particular village everything was as it had always been. And that's the way she and Didier liked it. What was fantastic about it, Pierrette said animatedly, was that the meat was so good. There was no comparison between the meat on her pigs and that on pigs reared and killed industrially. 'Industrial' pigs were killed at around three and a half months of age, before their meat had had a chance to develop: they only weighed about 120 kg. Her pigs were fed on natural food and were killed at a year of age. This last one had weighed 300 kg, and the meat was delicious. And what's more, everything was natural. There were no additives whatsoever in her pork products, she went on, which was more than could be said for what was on offer in the supermarkets.

It was all about rediscovering the taste of food as it should be. Or, as she put it, 'Le plaisir de manger encore de vrais produits.' But it was about tradition too. 'Our grandparents always instilled the importance of values and traditions in us,' she said. 'But it's all dying out now. In France we're losing the desire to create our own foods. And, of course, the younger generation aren't interested.' She warmed to her theme. 'But I think it will all come back. After all, our culture is food – *la culture gastronomique*. If we lose this,' she said passionately, 'we will have nothing else.' I turned to Didier for his views on why he wanted the tradition to continue. A man of few words, he just looked at me and said, 'Parce que c'est bon.'

I couldn't argue with that. Having had first-hand experience of making Pierrette's sausages, I was very impressed. As a rule of thumb, she never lets their fat content go over 30 per cent, which means they are 70 per cent pure meat, taken from the shoulder. In the UK, most supermarket-sold sausages are made from lesser cuts and trimmings, and their fat content is double. The home-made sausages also had more texture. Unlike most UK sausages, which are passed through a mincer twice, these had been minced only once, which gave them a much coarser texture – something to really get your teeth into.

The *Fête du Cochon* is in serious danger of dying out completely. Any charcuterie produced from killing a family pig can no longer be sold commercially as it used to be, unless the pig is killed by a butcher and everything is supervised. And at some point killing the pig this way may be banned altogether, which I think would be a shame. It's undoubtedly a pretty gruesome business – sacrificial, brutish and horrible in parts – but it also has a hell of a lot going for it. The pig is treated well and reared humanely, and it's all very economical. Killing one pig can provide enough charcuterie for family and friends for a year. And the meat is delicious. It's also a way of village life. I loved the fact that it was all about sharing – something all the villagers could participate in and get the benefits of. It was also about fun – as I was shortly to discover.

All the grisly business of killing and cleaning out of the way, villagers and friends turned up to celebrate. There must have been about 40 of us at the table that day, as we sat down to some newly cooked Fréginat, and a vast array of pork products still left from the last time around – pâtés, boudins, hams, fricassée, confits, sausages and saucisson sec – eaten with crusty bread and washed down with some of Didier's hearty Corbières red wine.

Like most small-scale vineyard owners in France, Didier is part of a cooperative, where everyone shares their produce. Individually, they don't yield much, but together they can produce respectable quantities: a great idea. His wines certainly went down well that day. Vast quantities were consumed, and there was a general feeling of mellowness as we all proposed a toast. 'To the Corbières,' I said, holding up my glass. 'The Haut-Corbières,' Pierrette said, correcting me. I tried again. 'Le cochon,' I said. This went down well, and everyone clapped and cheered, and became very emotional, with cries of 'Vive la France!'

Dessert consisted of a fantastic array of local sheeps' cheeses, and there was yet more wine as we drifted into general discussions about everyone's favourite topic: food. I kept feeling that I ought to go, but was having such a great time, I simply couldn't make a move. And then it happened. Pierrette brought up the touchy and controversial subject of Cassoulet. 'It's from round here, you know,' she said, 'not Castelnaudary.' 'Ah, you know something about it, do you?' I asked, hoping to get some tips. 'Me, know about Cassoulet?' she

OPPOSITE: *Hearty red wine – we drank gallons of it at the Fête du Cochon, and it was also a perfect antidote to the punishing Aude gales.*

said, indignantly. 'I'll have you know I make the best Cassoulet in the area.' It was definitely time to go…

There was a week to go now before my Cassoulet tasting at the Confrérie, and I couldn't face looking at any more books, so I rang Jean-Louis, met him in a bar and talked to him about my problems with the recipe. Thankfully, he put me straight. No saucisson and definitely no breadcrumbs. The crunchy crust you saw in all good Cassoulets, he explained, was the fat bubbling up and splitting the outside husk of the beans as they cooked. And, yes, the beans had to be pushed down seven times to get the desired effect. And the stock? Again, he was happy to oblige. It was made from duck fat, pork bones, chicken bones, shin of veal and pig's trotters. That was it. I was away.

The day of my Cassoulet tasting came, and I turned up at the agreed place: a barn belonging to one of the Confrérie members on the road between Castelnaudary and Villasavary that I knew was used for all the Confrérie meetings. There were about 20 people when I got there, all wearing those comical costumes, though they somehow didn't look out of place in those rather medieval-looking surroundings. It was a large candlelit room with an open fire and an old-fashioned stove in the corner. I handed my pot of Cassoulet to an old lady, who poured it into a clay pot and put it on the stove to keep it warm.

There was champagne and Foie gras all round to start with, and then the tasting began, and the Confrérie members started picking away at my Cassoulet. There was absolute silence for about 15 minutes – pretty demoralising after all my hard work. Ah well, I thought, it's obviously going to be rejected. At least I won't have to walk around wearing one of those silly hats. And then, after what seemed like a lifetime, the silence was broken. 'A little bit salty,' someone said. Then another person chipped in. 'The beans are a bit overdone.' Then the breakthrough: 'The pork's nice.' And finally the praise: 'It's superb.'

The hard work had been worth it. After another ten minutes, a meat supplier and leading bigwig of the society, Antonio Spanghero, a huge, genial man (he'd once played rugby for France), stood up and made a speech along the

lines of: 'I'd like to welcome Mr John Burton Race, who, I'm sure we all agree, has made an excellent Cassoulet. I hereby decree that he is a member of our great Cassoulet Confrérie.' There were claps and cheers all round, he signalled for me to walk up to him, and he then put a medal over my head, as if I were an Olympic athlete. I was then presented with a special tile to put any future Cassoulets on.

I heaved a sigh of relief. The business side of things now over, everyone relaxed, more Cassoulet was served and a good time was generally had by all.

OPPOSITE: *Charles and Eliza let off steam on a mild but windy winter's day.*

I was a happy man. The last barrier between me and the locals had been well and truly broken. As I left the barn, the wind was as wild as ever. I was beginning to wonder if I'd ever walk upright again. Still, at least I'd finally cracked that wretched Cassoulet recipe. Now there was nothing for it but to sit out the rest of the winter with some bottles of good red wine. I hoped spring wouldn't be too long in coming.

Winter Recipes

CAULIFLOWER SOUP WITH TRUFFLE OIL

I have included this dish for two reasons: first because we used it as a starter for our Christmas lunch, and secondly because it's Eve's favourite.

The French call cauliflower *chou-fleur* – 'cabbage flower' (did you know that cauliflower is a variety of cabbage?) – and this soup without the truffle oil is known as *crème Dubarry*. All the little markets here sell cauliflowers: they are cheap and, in this form, quite delicious.

Serves 8

1 KG FRESH CAULIFLOWER

150 G UNSALTED BUTTER

1 ONION, PEELED AND CHOPPED

1 GARLIC CLOVE, PEELED AND
   CHOPPED

1 SPRIG FRESH THYME

1 BAY LEAF

800 ML MILK

800 ML CHICKEN STOCK (SEE
   PAGE 293)

SALT AND WHITE PEPPER

75 ML TRUFFLE OIL

1. Trim, wash and break the cauliflower up into pieces or small florets. In a large, lidded saucepan, melt the butter and add the cauliflower pieces, stirring them to coat with the melted butter. Cover with the lid and cook over a low heat for 10 minutes.

2. Add the onion, garlic, thyme and bay leaf to the cauliflower. Stir, then cover and cook for a further 5 minutes.

3. In another pan, heat the milk and chicken stock together. As soon as they have come to the boil, pour them over the cauliflower. Turn up the heat and cook the soup on a rapid simmer for half an hour or until the cauliflower is soft.

4. Check the seasoning of the soup, adding salt and pepper to taste. Take the pan off the stove, pour the soup into a liquidiser and blend until smooth.

5. When smooth, pour the soup back into a saucepan and bring to the boil. Turn off the heat and add the truffle oil. Whisk the soup with a hand blender until it froths. Ladle it into lightly warmed soup bowls and serve immediately.

FRENCH ONION SOUP

This is a classic dish that typifies French regional cooking, although it is done badly in many restaurants – done well though, it is delicious.

Serves 6–8

2 TABLESPOONS VEGETABLE OIL

30 G UNSALTED BUTTER

I KG ONIONS (E.G. RED AND
   SPANISH), PEELED AND FINELY
   SLICED

2 GARLIC CLOVES, PEELED AND
   FINELY SLICED

30 G SMOKED BACON OR BACON
   BONE

100 ML COGNAC

300 ML DRY WHITE WINE

30 G PLAIN FLOUR

1.5 LITRES CHICKEN STOCK
   (SEE PAGE 293)

SALT AND PEPPER

CHEESE AND GARLIC CROÛTONS

18–24 SLICES, ABOUT ICM THICK,

FROM A BAGUETTE

3 TEASPOONS OLIVE OIL

I GARLIC CLOVE, PEELED

30 G EACH OF EMMENTAL AND
   PARMESAN CHEESE, FINELY
   GRATED

1. First prepare the croûtons. Place the slices of bread on a baking sheet, sprinkle with half the olive oil and grill them on one side until golden brown. Turn them over and repeat the process. Make several incisions in the garlic with a kitchen knife and rub each croûton on both sides with the garlic. Set aside.

2. Place a large, thick-bottomed pan on the stove and turn the heat up high. When the pan is very hot, add the vegetable oil, which will immediately start to smoke, then the butter. Add the sliced onion, garlic and bacon. Cook over a medium heat for about 15 minutes until the onions are soft and golden brown.

3. Add the Cognac and set fire to it until all the alcohol has burned off, then pour in the wine and reduce the liquid by about half, stirring constantly. Stir in the flour, then pour in the chicken stock. Bring to the boil, skimming off any scum that rises to the surface. Turn down the heat and simmer for about half an hour.

4. To finish making the croûtons, sprinkle the cheese on top and place under a hot grill until the cheese melts and starts to brown.

5. Add salt and pepper to the soup if necessary and serve topped with the croûtons.

SHAD GRILLED IN ANCHOVY BUTTER

Shad look like large herring but have much wider bodies. Ask your fishmonger to gut and clean the fish and remove the eyes and gills.

Serves 8

2 X 1.5 KG SHAD

100 ML OLIVE OIL

SALT AND PEPPER

ANCHOVY BUTTER

200 G UNSALTED BUTTER, DICED

10 ANCHOVY FILLETS, TINNED
    OR WHOLE BOTTLED ONES

JUICE OF 1 LEMON

5 EGG YOLKS

1 DESSERTSPOON CHOPPED FLAT-
    LEAF PARSLEY

1 TEASPOON FRESH
    CHOPPED TARRAGON,
    BLANCHED
    (SEE PAGE 271)

2–3 DROPS TABASCO SAUCE,
    OR 1 SMALL CHILLI PEPPER,
    DESEEDED AND FINELY
    CHOPPED

1. With a small blunt knife, beginning at the tail and working towards the head, scrape off all the scales. Rinse the fish under cold running water and dry thoroughly on some kitchen paper. With a sharp knife, make a couple of score cuts into the flesh. Repeat this on both sides.

2. Preheat the grill to its maximum setting. Lay the prepared fish in a roasting tin. Pour the olive oil over them and season with salt and pepper inside and out.

3. Now make the anchovy butter. Put the butter in a mixing bowl and beat to soften it until it is very pale. Add the anchovy fillets and beat them into the butter. Beat in the lemon juice, egg yolks, parsley, blanched tarragon and Tabasco sauce or chopped chilli.

4. Place the shad under the grill for about 10 minutes. Remove them from the grill and turn the fish over, smear the anchovy butter all over the fish and return them to the grill for about 5–6 minutes until golden in colour. Serve immediately.

ZANDER IN A HERB BEURRE BLANC

A cross between a perch and a pike in appearance and behaviour, zander is prized in France by amateur and professional cooks alike. Ask your fishmonger to fillet the fish and remove all the fine pin-bones for you.

Serves 4

4 ZANDERS, FILLETED, ABOUT
   150 G EACH
SALT AND PEPPER
100 ML OLIVE OIL
JUICE OF 1 LEMON

BEURRE BLANC

4 SHALLOTS, PEELED AND
   CHOPPED
500 G UNSALTED BUTTER
1 SPRIG FRESH THYME
1 BAY LEAF
1 GARLIC CLOVE, PEELED AND
   FINELY CHOPPED
75 ML WHITE WINE VINEGAR
150 ML WHITE WINE
100 ML DOUBLE CREAM
JUICE OF $\frac{1}{4}$ LEMON
30 G CHOPPED FRESH HERBS
   (E.G. PARSLEY, CHERVIL,
   CHIVES AND BLANCHED
   TARRAGON (SEE PAGE 271))

1. First make the *beurre blanc* or butter sauce. Fry the shallots in a shallow pan in a little of the butter but without browning them.

2. Add the thyme, bay leaf and garlic, and pour in the vinegar. Boil and reduce the vinegar until it has evaporated, then add the wine. Boil and reduce the wine by two-thirds, add the cream and bring to the boil again.

3. Chop all the remaining butter into small cubes and whisk it into the sauce, piece by piece, keeping the sauce just below the boil. (If it boils, the sauce will split and be fit only for the bin.) Strain the sauce through a fine sieve into a sauceboat. Add salt and pepper, if necessary, a little lemon juice to taste and the chopped herbs.

4. Preheat the oven to 220°C/425°F/Gas 7. Season the zander fillets, then heat the olive oil in a large, ovenproof pan and, skin side down, add the fish. Place the pan into the preheated oven and cook for about 4 minutes. Remove the pan from the oven, turn the fish over and sprinkle a little lemon juice over each piece. Serve immediately with a little pool of sauce and some Quick-braised Cabbage (see page 132).

ROASTED MONKFISH TAIL IN CAHORS

The tail of a monkfish is where all the meat is. The flesh is very much like fillet steak and is best grilled or roasted. For this dish I have used a red wine from Provence, but most strong-bodied wines will work just as well.

Serves 6

1 X 2–2.5 KG MONKFISH TAIL

COARSE SEA SALT AND PEPPER

1 TABLESPOON OLIVE OIL

JUICE OF 1 LEMON

RED WINE SAUCE

2 DESSERTSPOONS OLIVE OIL

50 G UNSALTED BUTTER

4 SHALLOTS, PEELED AND
  CHOPPED

3 GARLIC CLOVES, PEELED AND
  CHOPPED

1 FENNEL BULB, TRIMMED AND
  CHOPPED

1 BAY LEAF

2 SPRIGS FRESH THYME

2 STAR ANISE

500 G TOMATOES, DESEEDED
  AND ROUGHLY CHOPPED

1 BOTTLE CAHORS

1.5 LITRES FISH STOCK (SEE
  PAGE 294)

200 G OPEN-CAP MUSHROOMS,
  WIPED AND FINELY SLICED

2 BEEF STOCK CUBES, CRUMBLED

1. With a sharp filleting knife, cut away all the dark outer skin and pink membrane from the monkfish tail. Cut down either side of the backbone, freeing the white tail flesh. Portion each tail piece into three. Keep the bones for the sauce, plus any white skin or membrane, but not the dark skin. Preheat the oven to 220°C/425°F/Gas 7.

2. Now for the sauce. In a large ovenproof pan, heat the oil until it smokes and add the butter. Once the butter has melted, add the shallots, garlic and fennel, followed by the bay leaf, thyme, star anise, monkfish bones and tomatoes. Cover with the Cahors and boil and reduce until it has almost evaporated and the sauce is syrupy.

3. Pour in the stock and, as quickly as possible, bring the sauce to the boil. Skim off any froth or sediment that rises to the surface. Turn down the heat to a rapid simmer, cover with greaseproof paper and place in the preheated oven (or simmer on top of the stove) for 20 minutes.

4. Strain the sauce through a fine sieve into a saucepan. Immediately bring the sauce back to the boil, skimming any sediment all the time, and reduce by half. Add the mushrooms to the sauce together with the stock cubes. Carry on reducing the sauce until it starts to thicken – 600 ml per person is plenty. Strain again and keep warm on a low heat, stirring regularly.

5. Season the monkfish steaks with salt and pepper. In a large, ovenproof pan, heat the olive oil, and just as it starts to smoke, carefully add the monkfish piece by piece. Brown them lightly on each side for a total of about 5 minutes, and then place the pan in the oven (at 220°C/425°F/Gas 7) to roast the fish for 10 minutes.

6. When cooked but still a little pink inside, remove the monkfish. Leave in the pan, as you would a piece of beef, to cool and relax. During this time the fish pieces will give up some of their juices. Pour these through a sieve into the finished sauce.

7. Cut each monkfish steak into 4–5 slices, squeeze over the lemon juice and pour a little of the sauce around the fish. Serve immediately.

TERRINE OF FOIE GRAS WITH THREE PEPPERCORNS

There is something special about buying a whole Foie gras duck. The type of duck most commonly used by the French farmers is a mulad – a cross between a Barbary male and a Peking female. Some French farmers, however, prefer to use a Muscovy duck. You can use the liver to make a terrine or, with a hot knife, just slice it and cook it quickly in a skillet pan. You need to learn the technique of de-nerving Foie gras, but practice makes perfect. The secret is not to make too many incisions into the lobes of the liver because the more you cut into them, the smaller the pieces will be and the more the Foie gras will melt in cooking. It is best to make the terrine some time in advance, for the flavours to mature.

Serves 15

1 TEASPOON WHITE
    PEPPERCORNS, CRUSHED
1 TEASPOON BLACK
    PEPPERCORNS, CRUSHED
1 TEASPOON RED PEPPERCORNS,
    CRUSHED
$\frac{1}{2}$ BOTTLE JURANÇON OR
    SAUTERNES OR BANYULS
1 TEASPOON SEA SALT
1 TEASPOON CASTER SUGAR
2 WHOLE, FRESH FOIE GRAS,
    APPROX. 500–600 G EACH

1. With the exception of the Foie gras, place all the ingredients in a bowl, and mix together.

2. Now to de-nerve the Foie gras. This is important for the flavour of the Foie gras, and a bit tricky, but with experience you will soon get the hang of it. First make an incision with a very sharp knife through the middle of the Foie gras and open it up gently with the back of the knife. You will see some veins exposed, which will be full of blood, and you will see some sinews. Using the knife, gently remove these. Repeat this for all 4 lobes of the Foie gras. When this process is completed, put the Foie gras straight into the marinade, refrigerate for about 12 hours.

3. Preheat the oven to the very lowest it can go – about 70°C/160°F/the lowest gas setting.

4. By contrast, cooking the Foie gras is quite easy. Remove the lobes from the marinade and press them as firmly as possible into your terrine mould or other suitable, lidded dish. Put the lid on. Place a roasting tin half filled with water on the

stove to boil, take off the heat and insert the
terrine. Put the tin in the preheated oven for
about 45 minutes.

5. Remove the terrine from the oven, cool, then
    press the terrine down in its dish, and leave in the
    refrigerator for a minimum of 3 days, preferably
    5, or even a week, for the Foie gras to mature.

A Capon for Christmas

The French have their big celebratory meal on the evening of 24 December. They eat oysters and/or Foie gras and a beef fillet or capon, followed by a *bûche de Noël* or Christmas log.

Serves 6

I CAPON, ABOUT 2.5 KG, WITH ITS
    LIVER, OR 2 X 1.5 KG CORN-FED
    CHICKENS WITH THEIR LIVERS
SEA SALT AND PEPPER
GROUNDNUT OIL
I EGG YOLK, MIXED WITH 2
    DESSERTSPOONS WATER
100 G WHITE BREADCRUMBS

STUFFING
12 FRESH CHESTNUTS
GROUNDNUT OIL
I LARGE ONION, PEELED AND
    FINELY CHOPPED
I DESSERTSPOON CHOPPED FLAT-
    LEAF PARSLEY
I GARLIC CLOVE, PEELED
50 G UNSALTED BUTTER, DICED
3 EGG YOLKS
FRESHLY GRATED NUTMEG
I TABLESPOON COGNAC

SAUCE
50 G UNSALTED BUTTER
3 SHALLOTS, PEELED AND
    CHOPPED
I GARLIC CLOVE, PEELED AND
    CHOPPED
I BAY LEAF
I SPRIG FRESH TARRAGON

1. Preheat the oven to 220°C/425°F/Gas 7. With the point of a sharp knife, nick the skins of the chestnuts and place them on a baking sheet. Sprinkle with a little groundnut oil and roast in the oven for about 10 minutes until they split. While still hot, remove the outer shells and scrape off the skins. Chop roughly, then put in a mixing bowl and add the onion, parsley, garlic, butter and egg yolks. Season with salt, pepper and nutmeg.

2. Remove the liver from the capon (or chickens), cut away any discoloured sections and brown in a little groundnut oil. Sprinkle with the Cognac, set alight and add to the stuffing. Beat all the ingredients together until they are well mixed.

3. Season the capon inside and out with salt and pepper, then fill the cavity with the stuffing. Pour a little groundnut oil over the bird and roast in the preheated oven for about 1 hour 20 minutes, or 1½ hours if you are using chickens.

4. Remove the capon from the oven and its roasting tin and place on a rack to cool for 10 minutes. Cut it (or each of the 2 chickens) into 6 portions (2 legs and 2 breasts, halved) and place them on a serving dish. Brush the pieces with the egg yolk and water, and sprinkle with the breadcrumbs. Spoon the stuffing into the middle of the dish and cover with a sheet of foil to keep warm.

5. For the sauce, chop what remains of the capon or chicken carcasses into small pieces and add them to the same roasting tin. Heat the tin on the stove

1 SPRIG FRESH THYME

1 DESSERTSPOON TOMATO PURÉE

50 ML WHITE WINE VINEGAR

1/2 BOTTLE MUSCADET

1 LITRE CHICKEN STOCK (SEE
  PAGE 293)

2 DESSERTSPOONS CHOPPED
  FRESH HERBS (E.G. CHERVIL,
  CHIVES AND FLAT-LEAF
  PARSLEY)

and add the butter, shallots, garlic, bay leaf and herbs. Fry for a minute then mix in the tomato purée and continue frying for a minute longer.

6. Add the vinegar, bring to the boil and reduce until the vinegar has evaporated. Pour in the wine and boil to reduce the liquid by half. Add the stock and bring the sauce to the boil. Skim off any sediment that rises to the surface. Lower the heat and cook and reduce the sauce at a rapid simmer for 10 minutes. When ready to serve, strain through a fine sieve into a sauceboat. Add the herbs. Meanwhile, remove the foil and reheat the capon in the oven until the breadcrumbs are golden brown. Serve hot with the sauce.

BREASTS OF PARTRIDGE WITH A WHITE WINE SAUCE

This is an alternative way of cooking partridge, which would traditionally be roasted.

Serves 4

SKINNED BREASTS OF 4
   PARTRIDGES
4 CLOVES OF GARLIC, PEELED
   AND ROUGHLY CHOPPED
4 JUNIPER BERRIES, CRUSHED
70 ML CREAM
1 SPRIG OF THYME
1 BAYLEAF
SALT AND PEPPER

SAUCE

90 ML GROUNDNUT OIL
CARCASSES OF THE 4
   PARTRIDGES, FINELY CHOPPED
1 CARROT, PEELED AND CHOPPED
1 ONION, PEELED AND CHOPPED
1 CELERY STICK, TRIMMED AND
   CHOPPED
1 LEEK, WASHED AND CHOPPED
2 CLOVES GARLIC, PEELED AND
   ROUGHLY CHOPPED
1 BAYLEAF
1 SPRIG OF THYME
50 ML WHITE WINE VINEGAR
25 G REDCURRANT JELLY
100 ML MADEIRA
250 ML WHITE WINE
1 LITRE CHICKEN STOCK (SEE
   PAGE 293)
200 G BUTTON MUSHROOMS,
   SLICED

1. Lay the breasts in a small, ovenproof dish and sprinkle with the garlic and juniper berries, pour over the cream and add the bayleaf and thyme. Cover and leave to marinate in the fridge while you prepare the sauce.

2. Heat the oil in a large lidded saucepan on top of the stove and, when it starts to smoke, add the partridge bones and fry for about 5 mintues until golden brown. Tip in the vegetables and fry until golden, then add the garlic, bayleaf and thyme.

3. Pour in the vinegar and boil until totally evaporated, then stir in the redcurrant jelly. Pour in the Madeira and again boil until evaporated. Pour in the wine and boil to reduce the liquid by half, then pour in the chicken stock and bring the sauce to the boil, skimming off any froth. Turn the heat down, cover and simmer for 45 minutes, then add the mushrooms.

4. Strain the sauce through a fine sieve into another pan, bring it to the boil, skimming off any froth, then turn the heat down to a simmer, adding salt and pepper to taste.

5. Preheat the grill to its maximum. Remove the partridge breasts from the fridge, season with a little salt and pepper, and place the dish under the grill for 8 minutes, turning the breasts over from time to time until they are firm but with a bit of 'give' in the middle. Serve the partridge breasts whole or finely sliced, with a little of the sauce around them.

DUCK RILLETTES

There are few better ways of using duck legs than to make Duck rillettes, but you need to incorporate some belly pork as well or the rillettes will be dry.

Serves 8

100 G SEA SALT

3 JUNIPER BERRIES, CRUSHED

1 BAY LEAF

1 SPRIG FRESH THYME, LEAVES
  PICKED FROM THE STALKS

1 DESSERTSPOON BLACK
  PEPPERCORNS, CRUSHED

2 GARLIC CLOVES, PEELED AND
  FINELY CHOPPED

800 G BELLY PORK

2 LARGE DUCK LEGS

SALT AND PEPPER

1. Sprinkle the salt into a roasting tin, then add the juniper berries, bay leaf, thyme, crushed peppercorns and garlic. Put the pork and the duck legs in the salt and roll them around in it. Place in the refrigerator and leave overnight.

2. The next day wash off all the salt from the meat and discard the herbs and aromatics. Preheat the oven to 200°C/400°F/Gas 6. Put the meat back in the tin and roast in the preheated oven for about 3 hours.

3. When cooked, cut the pork into manageable pieces and then cut and finely shred it in a food processor. Turn it out into a mixing bowl. With two forks, shred the duck meat from the leg bones and, with a sharp knife, finely shred the skin. Mix this in thoroughly with the pork, and season with salt and pepper to taste.

4. Turn the finished rillettes out into a serving dish and seal the top with about 5mm of fat strained from the roasting tin to render the rillettes completely airtight. (If you have any Foie gras fat from the cooking of the Foie gras terrine on page 120, that makes a tastier alternative.) Leave the rillettes in the refrigerator for at least 2 days so that a full flavour can develop. Serve with fresh crunchy bread or toast and a glass of Alsace wine.

CONFIT OF DUCK

To make the best confit, you need to leave the duck legs overnight in a mixture of salt, herbs and aromatics. Thereafter, you can cook and serve the duck on the same day, or preserve it in jars, sealed in duck or pork fat.

Serves 8

8 DUCK LEGS

100 G COARSE SEA SALT

3 BAY LEAVES

2 SPRIGS FRESH THYME, LEAVES
   PICKED FROM THE STALKS

4 JUNIPER BERRIES, BRUISED OR
   CRUSHED

$1^{1/2}$ DESSERTSPOONS BLACK
   PEPPERCORNS, CRUSHED

3 GARLIC CLOVES, PEELED AND
   SLICED

1. Place the duck legs in a deep roasting tin, sprinkle with the salt and add the bay leaves, thyme, juniper berries, peppercorns and garlic. Place in the refrigerator and leave overnight.

2. The next day wash off all the salt mixture under plenty of cold running water, and dry the legs with kitchen paper.

3. Preheat the oven to 200°C/400°F/Gas 6.

4. Put the duck legs back in the roasting tin and cook in the preheated oven for 2 hours. If eating hot, serve with Aligot (see page 68) and an escarole salad with a Walnut vinaigrette (see page 295).

DAUBE DE BOEUF

Every region in France has its own version of beef stewed in red wine, the most famous being Boeuf bourguignon, and the Aude is no exception. I have used Buzet, an excellent, inexpensive wine, suitable not only for cooking with but also for drinking. You could equally well use a Minervois, Corbières, Cabardès or Madiran for this dish.

For a traditional boeuf bourguignon, the beef is usually cut into cubes of roughly 4–6cm each and larded with pork fat. In this recipe I use smoked bacon. As with most casserole-type dishes, the secret of a good one lies in the stock, and you will find a recipe for the best beef stock on page 293.

Serves 8

2 KG BEEF TOPSIDE OR RUMP,
   CUT INTO 2CM CUBES
500 G SMOKED BACON, CUT INTO
   5MM STRIPS
50 ML GROUNDNUT OIL
1 LITRE BEEF STOCK
SALT AND PEPPER
2 TABLESPOONS CHOPPED FLAT
   LEAF PARSLEY
CROÛTONS WITHOUT CHEESE
   (SEE PAGE 114)

MARINADE

1 BOTTLE BUZET
2 GARLIC CLOVES, PEELED AND
   CHOPPED
1 BAY LEAF
2 SPRIGS FRESH THYME
2 STRIPS ORANGE RIND

1. First marinate the beef. Pour the wine into a large bowl and add the garlic, herbs and orange peel (ensuring all the bitter pith has been cut away). Put the beef into the marinade along with the bacon. Cover the bowl with clingfilm and leave to marinate for several hours or preferably overnight in the refrigerator.

2. The next day strain the beef, reserving the marinade and the other ingredients. Heat a large frying pan with a little oil. As the oil starts to smoke, tip in about a third of the beef pieces and brown them. When the beef is browned, quickly transfer it to a large earthenware casserole dish or a large, enamel-coated cast-iron one, then fry another third of the beef, followed by the final third, tipping them all into the casserole dish. Cover the top of the beef with the bacon followed by the herbs and garlic strained from the marinade. Reserve the marinade.

3. Meanwhile preheat the oven to 200°C/400°F/ Gas 6.

4. Pour the strained marinade into the frying pan and boil to deglaze it. Reduce the wine by half

and then pour it over the beef in the casserole dish. Pour in the stock and bring to the boil. Cover with the lid and cook in the preheated oven for about 2 hours or until tender.

5. When the beef is cooked, remove the dish from the oven and strain the contents. Pick out and keep the bacon strips. Reduce the strained stock by half to thicken, then pour over the beef. Season to taste with salt and pepper.

6. Sprinkle the beef with the bacon lardons and chopped parsley. Serve immediately with garlic croûtons and steamed potatoes. Drink a large glass of Buzet with this dish.

LOIN OF VEAL WITH PIEDS DE MOUTON

The best veal around the Aude, and, indeed, some of the best in France, comes from Lautrec.

Serves 8

3 SPRIGS FRESH ROSEMARY

I X I.5 KG BONED LOIN OF VEAL,
    ROLLED, WITH A GOOD LAYER
    OF FAT

50 ML GROUNDNUT OIL

2 ONIONS, PEELED AND CHOPPED

500 G BUTTON MUSHROOMS,
    HALVED

500 G *PIEDS DE MOUTON* (OR
    OPEN-CAP OR OYSTER)
    MUSHROOMS, TRIMMED AND
    CLEANED

30 G UNSALTED BUTTER

I DESSERTSPOON VEGETABLE OIL

I SHALLOT, PEELED AND
    CHOPPED

SALT AND PEPPER

I DESSERTSPOON FLAT-LEAF
    PARSLEY, CHOPPED

SAUCE

150 ML DRY WHITE WINE

I LITRE CHICKEN STOCK
    (SEE PAGE 293)

350 ML DOUBLE CREAM

JUICE OF $\frac{1}{2}$ LEMON

1. Tie the rosemary to the top of the veal with string. Preheat the oven to 220°C/425°F/Gas 7.

2. In a roasting tin on top of the stove, heat the oil, then brown the loin on all sides. Add the onions and button mushrooms, lifting the veal so that it sits on top. Roast in the oven for 45 minutes, then lay the veal on a rack over a tray to catch the juices.

3. Heat the roasting tin with the onion and mushrooms on top of the stove, pour in the wine and reduce the liquid until syrupy. Add the stock, boil and strain into a saucepan, discarding the vegetables. Bring to the boil, skimming off any sediment. Turn the heat down, and simmer.

4. Clean the *pieds de mouton* with damp kitchen paper. Pat them dry. Scrape off all the fibrous spines underneath the caps, then fry with the shallot in the butter and oil. Season and sprinkle with parsley.

5. Reheat the veal in a low oven at about 180°C/350°F/Gas 4. Add to the sauce any juices left on the board by the veal and bring it back to the boil. Whisk in the cream, squeeze in the lemon juice and reduce the sauce until it thickens slightly. Add salt and pepper, and a little more rosemary.

6. Remove the veal from the oven. With a carving knife, cut through the strings and cut 2 slices per person. It should be served slightly pink. Spoon some mushrooms over each portion of veal and a little sauce around the outside, then serve.

POT-ROASTED PORK WITH THYME-FLAVOURED BEANS

This is a basic example of a pot-roast. You could replace the butter beans with any other type, such as haricots, and use a cheap cut of lamb such as boned and rolled breast instead of pork.

Serves 6–8

2 X 1 KG LOINS OF PORK, BONED

2 LARGE SPRIGS FRESH THYME,
  LEAVES PICKED FROM THE
  STALKS AND CHOPPED

SALT AND PEPPER

1 LITRE CHICKEN STOCK (SEE
  PAGE 293)

1 TEASPOON POTATO STARCH

1 LARGE SPRIG, FLAT-LEAF
  PARSLEY, ROUGHLY CHOPPED

BEANS

500 G Tarbais beans (DRIED
  WHITE BUTTER BEANS), SOAKED
  OVERNIGHT

100 G SALTED BELLY PORK

2 SPRIGS FRESH THYME

1 LARGE ONION, PEELED AND
  HALVED

1 GARLIC CLOVE, PEELED

1 BAY LEAF

1. First, sprinkle the inside of the loins with thyme and season with salt and pepper. Roll up and tie evenly with string, then set aside.

2. Strain the beans and put them into a saucepan. Cover with fresh cold water, then add the belly pork, thyme, onion, garlic and bay leaf. Bring to the boil and skim off any scum that rises to the surface. Turn the heat down and simmer the beans for about 40 minutes until just underdone. Strain the beans and discard the vegetables. Preheat the oven to 200°C/400°F/Gas 6.

3. Sprinkle the beans into a roasting tin. Lay the pork joints on top in the middle of the tin, and pour on the chicken stock. Cook in the preheated oven for about 1 hour.

4. When the pork looks crisp and is a deep golden brown, remove from the tin and set aside to rest. Dissolve the potato starch in 2 teaspoons water, stir this into the beans and meat juices in the tin, and cook for a minute or two.

5. Carve the pork. With a large serving spoon, place a good helping of beans on each dinner plate. Top each serving with 2 slices of pork, then sprinkle with the parsley and serve.

QUICK-BRAISED CABBAGE

This vegetable dish, goes well with partridge and other game birds and with certain fish, such as Zander (see page 117). You can use a traditional white cabbage for this dish, but I prefer the green, Savoy type, which has more taste.

Serves 8

1 CABBAGE, ABOUT 400 G IN
   WEIGHT
120 G SMOKED BELLY PORK
2 SHALLOTS, PEELED AND FINELY
   CHOPPED
2 GARLIC CLOVES, PEELED AND
   FINELY CHOPPED
40 ML WHITE WINE VINEGAR
80 ML WHITE WINE
   (GEWÜRZTRAMINER IS BEST)
60 G UNSALTED BUTTER, DICED
SALT AND PEPPER
60 G FLAT-LEAF PARSLEY, FINELY
   CHOPPED

1. Peel all the outside leaves from the cabbage, discarding any damaged ones. Cut the cabbage into four, turn each quarter on its side and cut away all the middle stalk and white core.

2. Slice the belly pork, then cut each slice into small pieces (lardons). Blanch these in a pan of boiling water for 2 minutes and then refresh under cold running water. Strain and allow to drain.

3. Three-quarters fill a large, lidded saucepan with water. Bring to the boil, add the cabbage, cover with the lid and return to the boil as quickly as possible. Immediately remove the lid and cook for 3–4 minutes. Strain the cabbage into a colander and refresh under cold running water.

4. Put the shallots and garlic into a saucepan along with the vinegar. Over a high heat, reduce the vinegar until it becomes syrupy. Add the white wine and boil again to reduce the liquid by half. Add the butter and lardons, and cook and reduce the liquid until it becomes syrupy once again.

5. Cut the cabbage into fine shreds, add this to the lardon mixture and stir it thoroughly over a high heat for about 2 minutes. Season to taste, sprinkle with the parsley and serve immediately.

POTATO PANCAKES

These pancakes complement most game birds. With the addition of sweetcorn to the recipe, and substituting the plain flour with maize flour, they are a great accompaniment to pan-fried Foie gras accompanied by a sticky sauce made from Banyuls wine.

Serves 6

2 LARGE POTATOES, WASHED

2 EGGS

50 G PLAIN FLOUR

100 ML MILK

50 G UNSALTED BUTTER, MELTED

SALT AND PEPPER

FRESHLY GRATED NUTMEG

1 TEASPOON CHOPPED FRESH
   CHIVES (OPTIONAL)

CLARIFIED BUTTER (SEE PAGE
   298) FOR FRYING

1. Boil the potatoes in their skins. When cooked, strain off the water and, while still hot, peel them. Mash them by hand with a potato masher to make about 250 g potato.

2. Beat the eggs until smooth and completely blended, then stir into the potato, along with the flour, milk and melted butter. Season with salt and pepper and a little grated nutmeg. I like to put a few chopped chives into the mixture for added flavour and colour.

3. Heat liberal amounts of clarified butter in 2 small pans about 10-12cm wide. Spoon about 2 dessertspoons of the potato mixture into each pan, to about 1cm in depth. Cook the pancakes for 2 minutes per side on a high heat.

PEARS IN HONEY AND THYME

I am sure this dish would work just as well in the summer months, but sometimes you need something light and sweet after a heavy main course. I serve these pears with a really sharp Lemon Sorbet (see page 144) for a refreshing dessert.

Serves 6

6 RIPE WILLIAMS PEARS

STOCK AND SAUCE

I BOTTLE SWEET WHITE WINE
  (E.G. JURANÇON)
I TABLESPOON ARROWROOT OR
  POTATO STARCH
125 G CLEAR HONEY
6–7 SPRIGS FRESH THYME
FINELY GRATED ZEST OF 2
  LEMONS

1. Pour the wine into a lidded saucepan large enough to hold the 6 pears. Remove a couple of spoonfuls and pour into a separate bowl. Stir the arrowroot into the bowl of wine and set aside for thickening the sauce later.

2. Put the pan of wine onto the stove. Add the honey, thyme and lemon zest. Bring the liquid to just below boiling point and allow it to simmer gently for about 3 minutes to allow the flavour of the thyme to infuse the stock. Keep warm.

3. Peel the pears, leaving the stalks on. Lower them carefully into the simmering wine stock, cover with the lid and cook for about 15 minutes or until soft. As soon as they are cooked, remove them from the liquid to a serving dish.

4. Stir the arrowroot and wine together again and add to the stock in the saucepan, stirring it at a simmer until it thickens. Pour the sauce over the pears and leave to cool. The pears will keep in a refrigerator for at least 3 days.

5. Serve the pears in individual bowls with a little puddle of the sauce and a ball of lemon sorbet on the side.

WARM CHOCOLATE TART

This tart can be served cold with cream, but I prefer it warm with a Crème Anglaise (see page 299). When cooking with chocolate, always use the best you can afford.

Serves 6–8

1 QUANTITY SWEET SHORTCRUST
   PASTRY (SEE PAGE 300)
UNSALTED BUTTER FOR
   GREASING
PLAIN FLOUR FOR DUSTING

FILLING AND TOPPING
100 G UNSALTED BUTTER, DICED
100 G GOOD-QUALITY DARK
   CHOCOLATE (AT LEAST
   75 PER CENT COCOA SOLIDS),
   CHOPPED
2 EGGS
100 G MUSCOVADO SUGAR
100 ML MILK
100 G PLAIN FLOUR
10 G BAKING POWDER
A SPRINKLING OF ICING SUGAR
   AND COCOA POWDER

1. Follow steps 1–2 for Sweet Shortcrust Pastry on page 300, rolling out the pastry to roughly 5mm thick to line a 20 × 3cm ring mould placed on a baking sheet lined with greaseproof paper.

2. Preheat the oven to 190°C/ 375°F/Gas 5.

3. Now make the chocolate filling. Place the butter dice and chocolate pieces in a bowl that will fit over a saucepan of simmering water without touching the water. Stir them together until melted and smooth. Remove the bowl from the pan.

4. In another bowl, whisk the eggs and sugar together. Stir in the milk and add this mixture to the chocolate base. Sift the flour and baking powder together and fold into the chocolate base. Pour all the chocolate mixture into the pastry base and bake in the preheated oven for about 40 minutes.

5. When cooked, remove from the oven and dust the top with a little icing sugar and cocoa powder. Leave the tart to cool a little before removing the ring mould.

PRUNE TART

France is the third largest producer of prunes in the world, mostly supplied by Agen. Here in the south-west, prune tart is *de rigueur*, so this is my version.

Serves 8

175 G AGEN OR ANY DRY PRUNES, STONED

50 ML ARMAGNAC

1 QUANTITY SWEET SHORTCRUST PASTRY (SEE PAGE 300)

UNSALTED BUTTER FOR GREASING

PLAIN FLOUR FOR DUSTING

ALMOND FILLING

125 G UNSALTED BUTTER

125 G CASTER SUGAR

125 G GROUND ALMONDS

3 EGGS

1 TEASPOON CORNFLOUR

TO FINISH

2 DESSERTSPOONS PLUM JAM

15 G FLAKED ALMONDS

60 G ICING SUGAR

1. Place the prunes in the Armagnac and leave to soak for 2 hours.

2. Follow steps 1–2 for Sweet Shortcrust Pastry on page 300, rolling out the pastry to roughly 5mm thick to line a 26 × 6cm ring mould placed on a baking sheet lined with greaseproof paper. Place in the refrigerator until needed.

3. To make the almond filling, cream the butter and caster sugar together in a bowl until pale and fluffy. Add the ground almonds, then beat in the eggs and stir in the cornflour. Preheat the oven to 220°C/425°F/Gas 7.

4. Remove the tart case from the refrigerator. Spread a thin layer of plum jam over the base. Spoon in the almond mixture and smooth. Strain the prunes through a sieve, retaining the juice, and carefully press the prunes into the almond mixture. Sprinkle with the almonds and bake for about 40 minutes. When the tart is cooked, remove to cool.

5. Pour the juice from the prunes into a saucepan and reduce with the icing sugar to a thick syrup. Brush the top of the tart with the syrup, remove the mould from the tart and serve.

TARTE TATIN

This is always a good winter dessert. You can substitute the apples with pears but remember that there is a lot more water in pears and this can make the filling more liquid. Quince is another good alternative.

Serves 6

125 G UNSALTED BUTTER

125 G CASTER SUGAR

6 DESSERT APPLES (E.G. COX'S, ORANGE PIPPIN OR GRANNY SMITH)

3 TABLESPOONS CALVADOS

PLAIN FLOUR FOR DUSTING

200 G SHOP-BOUGHT PUFF PASTRY

1. Preheat the oven to 200°C/400°F/Gas 6.

2. With 100 g of the butter, grease a heavy, circular, ovenproof pan measuring about 20cm across, and add 100 g of the caster sugar.

3. Peel and core the apples and cut them in half. Lay them, cut side up, in the pan, packing them tightly together. Fill the whole base of the pan as tightly as possible because the apples will shrink during cooking.

4. Put the pan onto the stove over a medium heat. As the butter and sugar start to caramelise, splash on the Calvados and set light to it. Sprinkle the remaining sugar over the apples and dot the remaining butter, broken into little pieces, around the pan.

5. Turn down the heat a little and allow the apples to cook and caramelise to a golden colour. This takes about 7 minutes.

6. Put the pan in the preheated oven to cook for a further 10 minutes. Remove the pan from the oven and allow to cool.

7. Lightly dust a work surface with flour and roll out the puff pastry into a circle about 1cm thick and slightly larger than the base of the pan. Carefully lay the pastry over the cooled apples, tucking it inside the edge of the pan to encase the fruit.

8. Put the tart back in the oven for about 15 minutes to finish cooking.

9. Remove the tart from the oven and allow to rest for about 5 minutes. To turn it out, place a large serving plate over the pan and, very quickly and carefully, invert the tart onto the plate in one swift movement, pastry side down. Serve immediately with vanilla ice-cream or a big dollop of whipped cream.

Hazelnut Meringues with Chocolate Sauce

In winter there is inevitably less seasonal fruit in the markets and so I turn to caramel, nuts, dried fruits and chocolate for making desserts at this time of year.

Serves 4

MERINGUES

3 EGG WHITES

120 G CASTER SUGAR

75 G GROUND HAZELNUTS

10 G CORNFLOUR

CHOCOLATE FILLING

125 G GOOD-QUALITY DARK
   CHOCOLATE (AT LEAST 75 PER
   CENT COCOA SOLIDS), FINELY
   CHOPPED

100 G WHIPPING CREAM

25 G UNSALTED BUTTER, DICED

CHOCOLATE SAUCE

200 ML WATER

80 G CASTER SUGAR

40 G COCOA POWDER

40 G GOOD-QUALITY DARK
   CHOCOLATE, FINELY CHOPPED

TO SERVE

ICING SUGAR AND COCOA
   POWDER FOR DUSTING

1. Preheat the oven to very low (140–150°C/ 275–300°F/Gas 1–2). Pour the egg whites into a bowl and whisk them into soft peaks. Slowly whisk in 90 g of the caster sugar a little at a time, continuing to beat the mixture until it becomes stiff. Mix together the ground hazelnuts, cornflour and the remaining sugar, and gently fold them into the meringue mixture.

2. Line 2 baking sheets with greaseproof paper. Fill a large piping bag fitted with a 1cm plain nozzle with the meringue mixture and pipe 12 x 7cm discs of the meringue onto the baking sheets. Cook in the preheated oven for about 2 hours or until completely dry, then remove from the oven and allow to cool. When the meringues are cold, store in an airtight plastic container.

3. For the filling, place the chocolate in a bowl. Pour the cream into a saucepan and bring to the boil, then remove from the stove. Add the chocolate. Stir until the chocolate has melted and the mixture is smooth. Add the butter and stir until smooth. Allow to cool.

4. For the sauce, bring the water, sugar and cocoa powder to the boil together in a saucepan, then turn the heat down to a gentle simmer and whisk the sauce for about 2–3 minutes until smooth. Remove from the heat, add the chocolate and whisk until it has melted and the sauce is smooth. Put the pan back on the stove and continue to

whisk the sauce as it comes back up to the boil. Remove the sauce from the heat and strain into a bowl. Cool and then refrigerate.

5. Whisk up the chocolate filling to the consistency of whipped cream. If it has set, stir it in its bowl over a pan of warm water to soften. Fill a piping bag fitted with a 1cm nozzle, and pipe a blob 1cm wide on top of 4 of the meringues. Sandwich another meringue on top, pipe on some more filling, then add a final meringue. Dust the tops with icing sugar and cocoa powder. Place the three-layer meringues on plates and spoon the sauce around each.

LEMON SORBET

Lemon sorbet is a good dish to serve after a really rich main course as it is so light and refreshing. Use it as an accompaniment to a lemon soufflé, for instance, or cold lemon tart.

Serves 8

240 G CASTER SUGAR

150 ML WATER

12 LARGE LEMONS

1 TABLESPOON LIQUID GLUCOSE

1. Place the sugar in a small saucepan along with the water and heat so that the sugar dissolves, then take the pan from the stove to cool.

2. Squeeze and strain the juice from the lemons and stir it into the syrup, followed by the liquid glucose.

3. Pour the lemon syrup into an ice-cream maker and churn it, then transfer to a clean, airtight, plastic container and place in the freezer. Alternatively, pour the syrup into a suitable container and freeze, taking the sorbet out at least twice to mix it, before it becomes fully frozen.

SIMPLE CHOCOLATE TRUFFLES

This recipe is for simple, plain chocolate truffles. Adding something to flavour the chocolate – Cognac, say, or even tea – makes an interesting alternative.

Serves 8

400 G GOOD-QUALITY DARK
  CHOCOLATE (AT LEAST 75 PER
  CENT COCOA SOLIDS)
20 G CLEAR HONEY
25G UNSALTED BUTTER, DICED
200 ML DOUBLE CREAM

COATING

ICING SUGAR, COCOA POWDER OR
  CHOPPED TOASTED NUTS

1. Chop up the chocolate as finely as possible and place 250 g of it in a mixing bowl. Add the honey and diced butter. Pour the cream into a saucepan, bring it to the boil on the stove, then pour it over the chocolate. Whisk until the chocolate has completely melted and the mixture is smooth. Leave to cool.

2. If you prefer to pipe the truffles, you must do so when the chocolate is still fluid. Line a baking sheet with greaseproof paper, then half fill a piping bag fitted with a 2cm nozzle with the truffle mixture. Carefully pipe onto the baking sheet truffles each the size of a large marble. Alternatively, when the truffle mixture is just made, pour it into a glass bowl and put into the refrigerator to set. With a parisienne scoop or melon baller, scoop out the truffles onto the baking sheet.

3. Put the remaining chocolate into a bowl and gently melt over a saucepan of hot water just below the boil, then remove from the heat. Coat the truffles in the melted chocolate, lifting them out with a fork. Then place back on the baking sheet and refrigerate to set. Coat the truffles a second time, refrigerate to set, then roll them in either icing sugar, cocoa powder or chopped nuts. Keep in the refrigerator.

ALMOND BISCUITS

Almonds taste even better in biscuit form. Serve these with coffee at the end of the meal. You can also try melting some plain chocolate and, with the edge of a fork, threading some over each biscuit. You could also dip the top of the biscuits in the chocolate.

Makes about 20 biscuits

250 G UNSALTED BUTTER, DICED

150 G CASTER SUGAR

250 G PLAIN FLOUR, PLUS EXTRA
  FOR DUSTING

A PINCH OF SALT

1 EGG YOLK

ABOUT 20 SALTED ALMONDS
  (SEE OPPOSITE)

1. Cream the butter in a mixing bowl. Add the sugar and beat them together until pale and fluffy. Fold in the flour, add the salt, then bind with the egg yolk. Wrap the dough in clingfilm, then place in the refrigerator for 30 minutes to relax.

2. Preheat the oven to 150°C/300°F/Gas 2.

3. Lightly dust a work surface with flour. Roll out the dough to roughly 5mm thick. Using a small, round or oval pastry cutter, cut the biscuits out of the pastry.

4. Top each biscuit with a salted almond and bake them in the preheated oven for about 12 minutes until just turning golden brown.

SALTED ALMONDS

I love salted almonds, which are perfect to serve to your guests with drinks.

ABOUT 100 SHELLED FRESH
   ALMONDS
1 TABLESPOON SUNFLOWER OIL
15 G UNSALTED BUTTER
FINE SEA SALT

1. Put the almonds into a saucepan half filled with boiling water and cook them on the stove for about a minute. Drain them into a sieve and, while they are still hot, peel off their skins.

2. Place the almonds on a baking sheet and put them in a warm oven (160°C/325°F/Gas 3) for about 15 minutes to dry.

3. Remove the almonds from the oven and tip into a saucepan. Cover them with the sunflower oil and add the butter, then cook on the stove at a high heat, until they turn a light gold in colour. Strain the almonds immediately into a sieve with a bowl underneath.

4. Season the hot almonds with lots of salt, then leave to cool.

THE ARRIVAL OF SPRING WAS LIKE A SHOT IN THE
arm. It was as if everything had been injected with chlorophyll as the
fields went from drab browns and ochres to bright emerald greens, and
everything suddenly burst into life. Daisies, buttercups and cowslips
began to poke through the grass, the cherry blossoms came out in all
their pink glory, and overnight we went from howling winds and grey
skies to bright, blazing sunshine, as if nature had decided to skip a
season and go straight into summer.

It was great to hear birdsong again, and to feel the sun on our skins. By the middle of March it was an amazing 25°C, and we were eating outside all the time. My winter blues now gone, I began to explore food with a new energy and an enthusiasm that was beginning to border on the obsessive.

My current bugbear was bread, probably France's most important national staple, eaten, as it is, morning, noon and night. But even in a country that has always been known for its bread, the last few years have seen a decline in standards. The pressures of market forces have prevailed, and bakers have continued to add cheap chemicals and additives that have worked in their favour by reducing costs, while leaving the consumer to pay the real price. All too often, I found, the bread looked wonderful, but tasted disgusting – floury, pappy and artificial. I'd become increasingly disillusioned and frustrated with it all, and finding a decent baguette or croissant had now become like the Quest for the Holy Grail as, much to Kim – and the children's – irritation, I set off to a different baker's every morning.

I had eventually found a reasonable one in a small village not that far from the house. But there had been several things that had put me off. It wasn't so much that the family cat snoozed on the loaves so that the bread was full of hairs when you got it home, though I have to say that undoubtedly played a part. It was that I'd been sucked into an ongoing ten-year dispute between the village baker and the owner of a tiny hotel next to him. Basically, the baker and his wife, who had been there for 42 years, couldn't understand why the upstart hotel-owner (who had only been there for ten) wasn't more respectful to them. The hotel-owner's take on this was that the baker's wife was always sticking her nose in everything. And so it had gone on, mounting to an ever-increasing fever pitch of emotions.

At this point, enter John Burton Race. I was calmly walking down the street, when the hotelier (a tiny man, no more than 5 feet tall), strutted up to me, shrieking at the top of his voice. My crime, it turned out, was that I had walked past his hotel to get to the bakery (a pretty difficult thing to avoid, as the buildings were adjoining) without asking his permission first. And he was incandescent with rage. No matter how much I tried to pacify him, he wasn't having any of it. I ended up spending two hours having coffee and croissants at his hotel (the croissants were bought from a baker that was miles away, needless to say – anything, rather than use the bakery next door) in an attempt to calm him down.

It had all been a case of French huff and puff, pure and simple, and even though my calming tactics had worked – the hotel-owner was utterly charming and friendly every time I saw him now – the whole incident (plus the cat hairs) meant I simply couldn't face going back to that bakery again. For months now, we'd been buying our bread from a baker in Sorèze. It was the nearest I'd got to a decent loaf, but it was far from perfect. I had lived in hope of finding a good, hearty loaf of bread, made organically in the traditional way, but it didn't look as if it was ever going to happen.

And then I met Barth the baker. It all happened when the road I normally drove down to get to my usual baker was blocked off, and I had to take another turning. It was then that I saw the sign: *'Boulangerie au Pain d'Antan: Pain Cuit au Feu de Bois'*. I was still sceptical – many other bakers made similar claims of baking bread in wood-fired ovens – but it was worth a try, so I went in.

The young man behind the counter didn't inspire me with much confidence. He was barely 30 years old, and with his close-cropped, dyed-blonde hair, cut-off jeans and sandals looked more like an escapee from the surfboards of Biarritz. Obviously not the baker, but someone who worked behind the counter, I thought. I bought a baguette, croissants and pains au chocolat, and left.

An hour later I was back. I'd tasted everything as soon as I got home and it was fantastic. The bread was firm-textured and flavourful, the croissants delicious – layers of butter beautifully combined with light pastry – and the pains au chocolat divine. The chocolate content was higher than in any other pain au chocolat I'd tasted, and, when heated, seemed to melt into the butter to create a taste made in heaven. I had to find out more about the person who made this bread, and why it was so special.

I got the full story from the young man behind the counter – not an employee, as it happened, but the baker himself. His name was Barth

Meskine, and, yes, he did bake in the traditional way, he said, showing me into the adjoining room, where there was a huge 1920s' wrought-iron oven with air vents at the side. Next to it were massive wooden paddles more than 4 metres long that were used to put the bread in the oven. They were made of beechwood – more supple than most other woods, he explained – and had to be that long because of the depth of the oven. He used the oven and paddles every day, he went on, and, as if to prove his point, took me outside and showed me the huge cast-iron cauldron where he deposited the burnt wood ash at the end of each working day. It was 4 p.m. and the cauldron was still hot, while the wall it stood against was grey from the constant proximity to the smouldering ash.

Then it was back inside again to talk about the dough. It was made from type 55 flour – a strong wheat flour – with salt and a starter dough that he mixed by hand, rather than using a machine as other bakers did, then it was churned in a vat with hot water. That was it. No additives, no chemicals, nothing. He dramatically plunged his hands into the huge, cast-iron vat of already-mixed dough in front of us, then took them out, and his hands were completely clean. 'Look, it's not sticky,' he said. I followed suit, and he was right – it wasn't. 'It's wonderful, isn't it?' he said, his eyes shining with excitement. 'I sometimes think it feels alive.' It was a strange thing to say, but I knew what he meant.

I found Barth immensely likeable. Here was a guy who was passionate about his work, and I was moved by the fact that someone so young and hip wanted to preserve an old tradition in this way. I was curious about how he had ended up in this quiet, tiny village. As we sat in his kitchen, drinking a glass of wine, he told me more about his background. Originally from the Dordogne, he'd moved to Sorèze about seven years ago. He had been a baker since his twenties, had never wanted to do anything else, and had always worked with wood-fired ovens. He'd happened to come on holiday to Sorèze some years ago, and walked into the site of the present bakery (then a library) because he'd heard it had been a bakery in the 1930s. (What about that for devotion to a trade?) Then, behind the bookshelves, he'd spotted the oven and that was it. He'd sold up in the Dordogne, bought the new premises with his girlfriend and worked there ever since. It was only when he'd knocked down the shelves

that he'd seen the original cast-iron vat too. He loved it here. It was peaceful and quiet, and he wouldn't dream of being anywhere else. And – as with so many of the people I'd met who produced really fantastic food – he loved his job with a passion.

Barth's enthusiasm was contagious, and I asked if he'd mind if I came back and had a go at baking bread with him. He was delighted that someone else shared his enthusiasm. 'I start at 4 o'clock in the morning,' he said. 'Come at around 4.30. Everything has to be ready for the shop by 7.30 a.m.'

That was fine. Getting up early has never been a problem for me. In fact, early morning has always been my favourite time of day, my special time, and I savoured the sunrise on my way into Sorèze the next day. Now that the wind had gone, it was a pleasure to drive and be able to take in my surroundings again. The fields were sprouting with broccoli and pea shoots, and the acacia trees, with their white blooms hanging like clusters of grapes, were in full blossom. I arrived to find Barth looking very professional in a spotless white coat, his head very hygienically covered in a red pirate scarf – a nice hippy touch, I thought.

He had already started to stoke up the oven with logs of poplar and plane. 'I'm sure it makes a difference to the flavour of the bread,' he said. I was amazed at the quantities: he used 300kg per day, and within 35 minutes it was all reduced to ash that went to the floor of the oven. As the flames in the oven got going, the bricks were turned white, and the temperatures were unbelievable – about 500°C.

We set to work, preparing and shaping the dough into all the different shapes: baguettes, flutes, pain de campagne, croissants and pains au chocolat, then they were put on the paddles and placed in the oven. The paddles were incredibly difficult to manoeuvre, and were so hot I could barely touch them. Then we had to wait until everything was cooked. We kept peering into the oven, although the temperatures were unbearable. Barth was obviously used to it, but after one minute my face looked like a tomato.

We made about 100 loaves that day (the oven had a capacity for 200, Barth said), pain de campagne in the main, though we used the same dough to make baguette-shaped loaves. We also made about 30 croissants with butter, 30 without, and 30 pains au chocolat. All the dough was proved the old-fashioned way, in baskets – not just any old baskets, but original 1920s' reed baskets lined with pure linen cloth. And even when these ran out and he had to use modern cane baskets, he still used linen cloth to line them.

Everything was ready by 7.30 a.m., and at around 8.15 Barth left his girlfriend in charge of the shop as he went on his deliveries. By midday it was all over – perfect timing, he said, for taking his dog for a walk.

As I drove back from Barth's bakery that day, I savoured the beautiful morning. The sky was completely cloudless and I saw a man in a nearby field picking young dandelion shoots (they're very popular in salads here). In all

the gardens I passed, the daffodils were out – a bit of a surprise, as I always associate them so strongly with England. I thought about the wonderful few hours I'd spent with Barth, and how exciting it had been making bread in a traditional bread oven…and about how fantastic the results had been.

In celebration, I decided to make a Walnut bread for the kids – a bad move because it unfortunately coincided with a visit from Kim's mother, Patsy, with whom I was having an ongoing battle in terms of food. It was always the same. I'd spend weeks trying to educate the kids into eating imaginative French food, and then she'd turn up for a weekend laden with bagfuls of English white sliced bread and buns, and that was it. The children would pounce on it all, and my food never got a look-in. The Walnut bread, needless to say, was yet another casualty.

In the middle of March it was Millie's birthday – the first of many spring birthdays in the family. We bought her a bike, which she rode constantly, preferring to ride it indoors because of the bumpy gravel outside. Caution is not a word in Millie's vocabulary, and she'd race around at top speeds, causing

OPPOSITE: *The premises of cheese-maker* extraordinaire – *Maître Xavier in Toulouse. His cheeses are legendary all over the region.*

general mayhem. Occasionally she'd crash into something, then pick herself up and carry on as if nothing had happened. She was so indestructible that Eve nicknamed her 'Tyson'.

Now that the weather was better, we took up family walks again. One of my favourites was a circuit of the Lac de St-Ferreol, a man-made lake in the Black Mountain that gets packed out in summer, when it's a popular boating and picnicking spot. We made use of the relative quiet there when we could.

Around this time too Kim and I found our social lives moved up a gear, and we suddenly began to meet a lot more people. The real turning-point had been meeting Marie-Christine Combes. A descendant of the original Comte Félix de Gineste, Marie-Christine is 15th generation in a long line of blue-blooded French aristos. But due to a strange and, to my mind, rather misogynistic point of French law, the title can be held only by male descendants, so she can't have the title of Comtesse herself. She still, however – along with her husband Claude and her mother, Madame Barand de Gineste – lives in her ancestral home, the Château de Garrevaques, an imposing building originally dating from the 16th century, but rebuilt at the beginning of the 19th century after having been partially burnt down during the French Revolution in 1789.

Today the château is put to practical use, and Marie-Christine and her mother let out part of their family home for 'holidays with a difference', in which guests get to stay in their palatial rooms, drink cocktails in magnificent salons decked with original 18th-century wallpaper and be entertained by genuine French toffs. Charming, helpful and utterly delightful, Marie-Christine proved to be a mine of information about local life, and often invited us to her legendary dinners at the château – fantastic social gatherings. (It was, in fact, through her that we'd met Laurent and Evelyne, the lovely couple from the Château d'Airoux, who, along with virtually the entire neighbourhood, had been sucked into the saga of my Cassoulet-making.) We loved meeting new people and spending time with them, but, of course, our dearest friends here were still the ones we'd met first: Lesley, Michel, Marie and Jean-Louis.

Every time we went to dinner at Jean-Louis's we had the most fantastic cheeses imaginable. One day I asked him, 'How come they're so consistently good?' 'Easy,' he said. 'They all come from *Xavier*, in Toulouse.' Now to any cheese-lover in the south-west of France, this simple statement is enough, for the Xavier in question is Xavier Bourgon, *fromager extraordinaire*. With more than 250 cheeses maturing in his cellars, he is one of the most important cheese producers and suppliers in the region. Everyone round here knows that when it comes to cheese, the very mention of his name is synonymous with quality.

Xavier's name had been cropping up for some time now. In fact, every time we went to a top-quality restaurant, there it was on the menu – just a simple

line, near the desserts: *'Fromages de Maître Xavier'*. That was it. And then, of course, there were the personal recommendations. All of Jean-Louis's circle were great fans, as were Lesley and Michel, as was Marie-Christine Combes…as was virtually everyone else we met. So when Jean-Louis suggested that I meet the great man, I felt almost as if I knew him already.

It was a rainy day at the beginning of April, and I'd decided to make use of the time by working on the book and writing up some recipes. I was getting a bit bogged down with it all, and starting to feel sorry for myself when the phone rang. It was Jean-Louis, sounding very excited, in the way he only ever is when talking about food. He had a couple of spare tickets for one of Xavier's celebrated cheese-tastings: 'It will be an unforgettable experience,' he said, urging me to come. 'Besides, it will do you good to stop working and to get out of the house. I'll pick you up on Friday evening.'

We all met up as planned and drove to Toulouse, where we managed to find a parking space just outside Xavier's establishment. We walked through a doorway with the word *'Xavier'* in lights over it, and went downstairs into a large cellar full of people. We were greeted by a jovial, dapper little man with a goatee beard who, in his navy blue smock and large, blue-rimmed glasses, looked like a cross between a French Impressionist painter and a 1980s' advertising executive. Was this Xavier? I wondered – and then I saw the discreet green 'X' monogrammed on the pocket of his smock and knew I was in the presence of the great man himself.

There was a long, dark wooden table in the room, set for about 20, with wine-glasses, baskets of bread and plates of crudités. Most of the people there were obviously part of Xavier's close-knit circle – the local cheese *cognoscenti* – but there were some I recognised as friends of Jean-Louis. Among them was Antonio Spanghero – the ex-rugby player turned Cassoulet expert who'd initiated me into the Confrérie. Still flushed with success at having mastered the recipe, I smiled, before firmly blending into the background with Kim – and my glass of wine.

After about half an hour of general socialising and chit-chat, Xavier waved his arms and asked us to sit down. He then launched into his favourite subject straight away. The table we were sitting at, he explained solemnly, was taken from a giant slab traditionally used to press cheeses. I'd noticed a groove running all around the edge. This, he pointed out, was to catch the whey as it oozed down the sides. Then, like a general addressing an army going into battle, he prepared us for what was in store. Over the course of the evening, he said gravely, we would be presented with a variety of cheeses accompanied with two white wines, followed by a red wine, and finally a dessert wine.

The first wine to be served was a Vin de Savoie Aprémont. Swirling the wine around the bowl of his glass, Xavier proceeded to sniff it and to explain the importance of *le nez*. It all seemed a bit odd to me – I thought this was meant to be a cheese-tasting, not a wine-tasting – but Xavier carried on regardless. Wine had to be allowed to 'cueillir sur la langue' he explained, the front and back of the palate being the most important places, in terms of taste buds. As we all sat in hushed attention, he banged the table loudly with his hand, explaining that it was exactly the same with cheese. In order for cheese to be properly savoured, he exclaimed, you had to know how to eat it properly.

This was all news to me. I thought that you just, well, put it in your mouth and that was it. Not so, Xavier said. He put some cheese in his mouth and closed his eyes, then, turning to the side so we could get the full benefit of the view, chomped away at the cheese, while making a circular movement with his fingers that was meant to imitate the moving jaws. Cheese needed to be chewed properly, to 'purger l'air' so that the cheese was properly oxygenated – this was 'très important, messieurs,' he proclaimed sweepingly. Only when the cheese was correctly oxygenated would its full flavour and aroma come out.

I was feeling a bit peckish at this point, and reached out to get a piece of bread, as Xavier went onto describe the next important rule of thumb. Never eat too much bread, he warned, wagging his finger. When eating cheese, too much bread will not only fill you up, leaving no room for the cheese, but it will spoil the flavour of the cheese itself. The bread should be placed over the cheese in a thin layer so that it looked like part of the cheese itself. 'Pouf!' he cried, smashing a piece of bread against the cheese in his hand.

With more than 25 years in the cheese business, Xavier clearly knew his stuff, but if the cheese business ever collapsed, he could just as easily have got a job on the stage, I thought. Then Xavier went onto his next point: how to tell what sort of cheese you are eating. He put several cheeses in front of us, describing the three main types, and the differences between them. It was all to do with the colour: there were three main kinds of white in a cheese, he said. Whitest of all were the *chèvres*, or goat cheeses; the *brébis*, or ewe's cheeses, were a mother-of-pearl colour, while cows' cheeses were a more 'natural' creamy-white colour.

We were then all given a soft cheese and asked to guess what type it was. It was certainly white, and could have been either goat's or ewe's. Most people thought goat's – only one other person and I put our hands up to ewe's milk cheese, and we were right. The give-away, Xavier said, was the long, lingering taste – a sure indicator of ewe's milk cheese.

Next we were given a Camembert-type cheese, and Xavier explained the way to eat it. Take off the rind, he said, then eat the central part. This was the *coeur*, the heart of the cheese, and this was the part that should be eaten, and the rind thrown away. The cheese near the rind, he said, had undergone what he called *saponification*. 'Try it and see,' he said. 'It will taste soapy.' We tasted it, and, sure enough, it did. Fascinating stuff.

The next wine was a Côte du Jura, served with a Beaufort cheese, then a Comtè, then a Fribourg. And so it went on, with cheese after cheese being served with wine after wine. Every so often people would ask him questions, and he would answer – sometimes categorically, and at others less so, as when someone asked him what temperature wine should be when served with cheese. 'Ah,' he said slyly, 'it depends on what effect you want to achieve.' But usually he held centre stage, as he excitedly explained the mysteries of his favourite foodstuff. The flavour of cheese was a fragile thing, he said, and could have many subtle variations, according to what the cow had eaten. One farmer he knew had been climbing a tree and slipped, clutching a branch with leaves on it. As he fell, the leaves passed over the cow's back. And lo and behold, you could taste the leaves in the cheese, he said excitedly. (I really wasn't sure about that one!) As he talked, he became more and more animated, often getting up and pirouetting around the room while making a particularly enthusiastic point. Showman he may have been, but cheese was clearly this man's life.

There must have been 20 cheeses in all, finishing with a sublime Brie aux truffes – a soft, creamy cheese with a vein of truffles in the centre. And then, to finish, ice cream – delicious, but too fatty, I couldn't help thinking, after all those cheeses. By the end of the evening, my head was swimming from all the wine, and I felt totally bloated and cheesed out. The virtues of cheese, it seems to me, are best savoured in small quantities. It had all been entertaining, but definitely a case of overkill. It was time to get back to my recipes.

Family matters dominated life for the next few weeks. At the beginning of April, Olivia and Martha fell in love…with the same boy. His name was Fabrice and he was in Olivia's class, so Olivia naturally felt she had first claim. But Martha, though a year younger, had a crush on him too. For days, Kim and I were subjected to regular bulletins on the state of Fabrice's health, the clothes and music he liked, and what he ate for breakfast, lunch and supper. And then he had his hair cut, and for a moment Kim and I thought it was all over. He had a lovely face and lovely eyes, Olivia pointed out, but he didn't look good with his hair short. Still, she continued cheerfully, Martha was welcome to him until his hair grew back again. (Don't you just love teenage girls?) As soon as his hair grew, however, Olivia was back on the case, and insisted that I buy her a pair of high-heeled boots so she could make an impression on him. I wouldn't like to say what she looked like, but if you can imagine a penguin wearing stilettos… . It all came to an end soon afterwards when Kim went to pick up the girls at school one day and Fabrice was there. Charles, sitting in the back of the car, leant out of the window and shouted, 'Are you in love with my sisters?' The poor chap went beetroot and didn't know what to do with himself. Olivia and Martha were furious, and didn't know where to look. And that was the end of that.

Eve had found the whole thing hilarious. She'd had a rather low profile in the last few weeks, busying herself with seeing friends and taking driving lessons, and then suddenly, out of the blue, announced that she wanted Tom to come and stay for a week. It all came as a bit of a surprise because she hadn't

mentioned him for ages, and I'd just assumed the whole thing was off. But there you go.

When the day came, I went with Eve to pick him up at the airport. We waited for ages as everyone came through, and then, just as we were beginning to wonder if he'd missed the plane, there he was – a tall, thin figure with spiked blonde hair and an unmistakable gait. I know I've sometimes been a bit unfair to Tom. I'd met him a few times and he was a nice enough bloke – but I suppose most fathers feel no one is ever good enough for their daughters.

As he ambled amicably through, shoelaces and bag undone, I saw his passport hanging out of his trouser pocket – a sure recipe for disaster – so I grabbed it and put it in the kitchen table drawer as soon as we got home. For the next few days, he and Eve mooched around the place, as I desperately tried to hold in my irritation about the chewing gum on the chairs, the beer cans, the bits of crisps on the floor…but it was all amicable enough. And then one day, about halfway through his stay, I was working upstairs on the book and happened to look out of the window, when I caught sight of him, walking purposefully down the drive, bag in hand. He and Eve had obviously had a row, and either she'd chucked him, or he'd walked out.

The passport, however, was still in the kitchen drawer, and, amusing though it might have been to let him storm off without it, I didn't have the heart, so I called him back, gave him his passport and drove him to Carcassonne to catch the flight home. We sped up the motorway to the airport, only to find that there was no room on the flight, which meant I had to drive him back home. It didn't do my temper any good, and it certainly did nothing for his sense of pride, as he had to spent the next 24 hours with us (the atmosphere was indescribable). The next morning, we set off for Carcassonne again, and as soon as we got to the airport, we discovered that I'd inadvertently given him my passport instead of his own.

I nearly wept with rage and anger, but managed to control myself enough to plead with the man at the airport desk to let him through with his provisional driving licence. He eventually relented, and I went back home to recover.

And so, emotional crises over, the weeks passed, and before long our minds were beginning to turn to Easter – and chocolate.

It was around mid-April that I first met the Cormary brothers. Kim, the children and I had all gone to spend the day in Castres – a small town that's often dubbed 'the Venice of south-west France' (a bit of an ambitious claim, I'd always felt) on the basis of the fact that it has a row of half-timbered, 17th-century weavers' houses built on a waterway.

Castres has a lot to recommend it – attractive buildings and squares, a lovely

OPPOSITE: *Martha and Olivia talk of young love and other weighty matters in the garden.*

flower market, good restaurants and fantastic shops – all of which had combined to make it a good, and closer, alternative to Toulouse for family outings. On this particular day, Kim had sent me off to look for some Easter eggs, while she and all the children went to buy Olivia some new trainers for her birthday.

It hadn't taken much to persuade me, since chocolate happens to be one of my greatest weaknesses. Besides, it was Easter, or *Pâques*, a big event here, which is celebrated by giving gifts and chocolates. Apart from Christmas, this, I knew, was the biggest season for all chocolate-makers, and they would really be pushing the boat out in terms of what they had to offer. Added to which, of course, I was in one of the great chocolate-making countries of the

world. In France chocolate-makers, or *chocolatiers*, are seen as masters of their art and have to undergo a gruelling training – almost as long as a lawyer or doctor. It's a measure of how seriously the whole business is taken that even a fairly small town such as Castres has about half a dozen top-quality chocolate shops.

I had already walked past two, and was wondering which one to opt for, when I saw the sign, '*Cormary – Chocolat Artisanal*'. I don't know what it was that made me choose it, but from the moment I pushed that baguette-shaped door handle, I somehow knew I'd found the right place.

The shop itself was tiny, but the displays of chocolates and pâtisserie were stunning. It was the chocolate I latched onto first, of course. There was something here for everyone: exquisite hand-made chocolates for the sophisticated palate, chocolate churches, chapels and white-clad figures for children celebrating their First Communion, the usual selection of Easter specialities – eggs (plain or marbled, in dark, milk or white chocolate), frogs, mice, rabbits, flowers – Disney characters (Pinocchio, Donald Duck, Snow White, complete with seven dwarfs) – and the rather more kitsch, though exquisitely made, soldiers, skiing snowmen, and men with cigarettes and newspapers. Finally, in a touch of wicked humour, there was a life-sized Tutankhamun mask, which, gold leaf and all, was frankly indistinguishable from the real thing. I had the feeling that everyone who worked here had a good time.

The breads and pâtisserie were equally superb. There were 11 types of bread, including orange and hazelnut-flavoured breads, chestnut bread (delicious with game) and seaweed bread to eat with fish, plus the local sweet specialities of Lou Tarnes (a divine mixture of hazelnut meringue, apples, honey and almonds) and croustade (a soft apple pie).

This was all fantastic stuff. But it wasn't just the goods on display that made this shop so wonderful – it was the great, friendly atmosphere of the place, and the people who worked there: the jolly woman behind the counter, the old lady who helped out and, of course, the Cormary brothers themselves, Roger (*chocolatier*) and Benoît (*pâtissier*). Roger was older and bearded, and

OPPOSITE: *Double trouble: me with Benoît and the other Frère Cormary* – chocolatier *Roger.*

Benoît clean-shaven, but in every other respect these two round, smiling brothers, with their blue-and-white-checked trousers, white T-shirts and shoes, reminded me of Tweedledum and Tweedledee, their pot-bellies sure signs that they had probably eaten too many of their own wares.

After a few minutes of laughing and joking, Roger (12 years Benoît's senior) invited me upstairs to see where he made his chocolate. 'Benoît's always going on about his pâtisserie,' he said, in his impenetrable accent, 'but it's all about chocolate. Chocolate's the really important thing. I've learnt the hard way,' he grumbled. 'Benoît's always had it easy.' To a chocoholic like me, walking into Roger's private den was the closest it gets to being in paradise. I walked around the room in a daze, looking at the massive slabs of raw, unprocessed chocolate with their labels of origin – a list of ever-more exotic places – Guyana, Venezuela, Haiti, Mexico, Far East, Madagascar... . And the other delights in store: trays of luxurious dark chocolates decorated with gold leaf, two-coloured fans (one side dark chocolate, the other white), sumptuous liqueur chocolates, fabulous round and heart-shaped chocolate lacquer-ware boxes in delicate, glossy pinks, blues, lilacs and greens (made from warmed, tinted cocoa butter, he explained – a special favourite for the Fête des Mères or Mother's Day), and of course, more set pieces for Easter – 300 of them, crowned by a stunning centrepiece – a massive 60cm egg made from beautiful, shiny dark chocolate and weighing a staggering 6kg.

Then, just as I felt I couldn't possibly take in any more, Roger moved onto sweets: *croquantes*, made from almonds, sugar and egg whites, and *nougatines Castraises*, a local speciality, first brought to the region, it turned out, by an Englishman. I perked up at this and wanted to know more. 'Hmm, it was the 19th century, I think. I don't remember his name,' he said, off-handedly. (Funny, I thought, how anything English was automatically swept under the carpet.)

Aware that time was running out, I started to make my excuses to leave, but Roger wasn't having any of it. He wanted me to look at more chocolates. This time it was his wonderful ganache fillings: coffee, pistachio, vanilla, orange, caramel, fresh mint... . The list was endless, but he insisted I try them all. 'It's the mark of a good chocolate, the way it works with the filling,' he said. 'You should always taste the filling first,' he said, 'and the chocolate a few seconds later. If you taste the chocolate at exactly the same time as the filling, it's a bad chocolate.'

Before I left, he insisted that I see his current creation: chocolate horses piped with white royal icing, destined to go onto a gorgeous, brightly coloured carousel with a pink nougatine roof. As I looked at it admiringly, I couldn't help noticing that it had a choux pastry base (Benoît's handicraft) and wondered how the overlap between the two brothers worked.

As if on cue, Benoît popped his head round the door – I got the impression he rarely visited Roger's private domain – 'Ah, I see you're admiring my choux

pastry,' he said. 'That's the most important part of the whole thing, of course. The chocolate would be nothing without my magnificent choux pastry.'

And, to Roger's intense irritation, he proceeded to show me an example of his choux pastry at its best – a breathtaking *croquembouche*, that tower of light-as-a-feather choux buns filled with vanilla *crème pâtissière*, which forms the centrepiece at French weddings. The whole thing is held together with a delicate cobweb of white spun sugar – meant to represent the bride's veil, Benoît explained. Of course, he used choux pastry on a smaller scale, too, he went on, in his *religieuses* (chocolate-filled choux buns shaped to look like nuns), and he had so many other things to show me – his *gâteaux opéra* (made from a layer of almond sponge with coffee and chocolate cream), his selection of small pastries, and of course, his superb apple *croustade*, which he insisted on showing me how to make. 'Not as good as my chocolate,' Roger butted in.

They both insisted I come back to find out more, and it didn't take much to make me agree. I couldn't think of anyone better to learn about chocolate- and pastry-making with. These two characters were obviously among the best in the business, and I was sure to have a good time into the bargain, so I agreed to come back. I hurriedly bought some Easter eggs and left. As Benoît led me out, he said, 'You don't want to listen to Roger. He's always going on about chocolate.' There was obviously a lot of rivalry between these two. 'Do you get on with each other?' I asked. 'Fine,' he said, 'absolutely fine.' Then, as he closed the door, Benoît yelled out after me. 'As long as he's always upstairs and I'm downstairs.'

I was back a week later, and I don't think work has ever been so much fun. It was Roger and the chocolates first. He had a very dry sense of humour, which made concentrating difficult at times, but he certainly knew his stuff. We made the chocolate in the usual way from a bitter chocolate base, with cocoa butter, sugar and milk, and he then spent hours tempering it (i.e. slowly heating and cooling the mixture to allow the cocoa butter molecules to solidify in order to achieve the right texture). I'm a bit of a purist when it comes to chocolate textures, but the results were perfect: a rock-hard texture with a shiny, lacquered appearance.

With the exception of vanilla and coffee, I don't go in much for flavoured ganaches, but Roger's real speciality was developing new flavours for his hand-made chocolates, and he was especially proud of his lavender ones. He had bought some pure lavender oil from an apothecary, and when he suggested putting it into the chocolate I was rather sceptical. However, I had already tasted the local speciality of crystallised violets dipped in chocolate, which had worked fine, so I was willing to give it a go, and was very pleasantly surprised with the balance he achieved. Roger was certainly a master of his craft. The whole process was, of course, punctuated by his dry jokes and humour, and endless cups of liqueur-laced chocolate and coffee served by the nice woman behind the counter (Benoît's wife) and the old lady (the boys' mother).

On to Benoît, the pastry-maker, who showed me how to make his famous croustade. And, yet again, as I was to find so often in France, alcohol was involved. Although it was the early morning, Benoît was convinced that we'd make much better pastry if we had some pastis. So he poured generous amounts of the stuff into two glasses, with just a dash of water so that it was barely clouded, and then showed me how to make the croustade dough. This, it turned out, was very similar to croissant dough – a lot of butter and yeast. The apples were cooked like a compote, with lots of sugar and a little vanilla, and then covered with the pastry and cooked in the oven till golden brown with a deliciously smooth textures. All the while, Roger stood in the background making sarcastic comments, until eventually Benoît got so annoyed that he told him to **** off. As soon as Roger was out of the door, he said, 'Making chocolate is a girl's job, of course. It's pastry. That's the thing.'

Several hours – and glasses of pastis – later, I left, laden down with bags full of delicious chocolates and *croustade*. I laughed all the way home. Roger and Benoît were two of the funniest men I'd ever met. But they were also supremely professional. Their products looked and tasted superb, and, what's more, they were completely natural, made by hand with no chemicals or additives. Yet another example of a family business at its best.

I decided to celebrate my time with Benoît and Roger by having a chocolate party and Easter egg hunt. Kim and I made some chocolate choux buns and

chocolate and vanilla mousses, and on the morning of the party, Martha and Olivia spent hours hiding 100 chocolate eggs in the long grass. We invited about 40 people, and the house and garden were full of guests and very excited children – all great fun. Eliza and Millie dressed up as Easter bunnies, and Charles, determined not to be left out, was dressed as an egg. He'd insisted on being an egg, but, as always with Charles, he hadn't really thought about the implications. The egg had so much stuffing in it that it was hot and uncomfortable, making it difficult to walk, and he kept falling over. He then demanded a chick costume instead, and simply could not comprehend that we couldn't just rustle one up then and there.

He got his own back a week later, when it was his birthday. Eve made a wonderful chocolate cake, which he loved, and he then insisted on his favourite dinner – sausages, chips and beans – which we all had, followed by more chocolate cake. A week after that it was my birthday, and we celebrated with a trip down the Canal du Midi, and another of Eve's delicious chocolate cakes, which I ate with some fabulous Banyuls wine – to my mind, not only the best, but the only accompaniment to chocolate.

OPPOSITE: *A celebration of chocolate – our Easter party, involving an Easter egg hunt.*

BELOW: *My birthday tea!*

Even I had become completely sated with chocolate by now, and my mind turned to seasonal produce: the hugely popular local violets used in soaps, crystallised in sweets, and an essential part of a local armagnac-based liqueur; the fantastic selection of newly arrived seafood – gurnard, *dorade* (sea bream), red mullet, trout, sea bass, monkfish, clams and baby scallops – and, of course, the wonderful vegetables that were around everywhere.

Madame Bondouy (all our past differences about Cassoulet now forgotten) and her stall came into their own now, and it was great to see her beaming so proudly at her produce: fresh parsley, spinach, carrots, broccoli, Swiss chard, radishes, massive spring onions, peppers, fat white asparagus, globe artichokes like footballs, and plump pea pods looking fit to burst, and begging for a dash of butter and chervil.

It was great to see food in all its glory again, to get away from the drab browns of the winter dishes, and savour the bright colours of young salad shoots and

light vegetable soups, and taste the seasonal specialities on offer in the restaurants. It was around this time that I went to the Auberge du Poids Public, the local one-Michelin-star restaurant in St-Félix Lauragais, and discovered one of the famous specialities the region has to offer: pigeon.

BELOW: *Memories of our family Easter party*

Pigeon is one of the most highly prized delicacies of south-west France, and is certainly the classiest of birds when it comes to flavour. Now in the UK, the words 'classiest' and 'pigeon' don't often sit happily in the same sentence. But, then, this is not your Trafalgar Square pigeon, or your common or garden wood pigeon, well known for its dark, gamey meat, but the king, or perhaps I should say prince, of all birds destined for the table: the *pigeon de Lauragais* – the squab, or young pigeon whose succulent, buttery flesh graces the tables of the rich and famous, and has a price tag to match.

The most famous local breeder of these young birds, or *pigeonneaux* is Baron Louis-Charles de Roquette, who, as his title implies, is just about as far as you

can get from the traditional British cloth-cap stereotype of a pigeon-fancier. Descended from a long line of aristocrats, and born in the Château of St-Félix Lauragais, he turned his hand to pigeon-breeding in the mid-1970s, and built up the business so successfully that he now supplies the top restaurants in France, including the deluxe Hotel Negresco on the Côte d'Azur and Maxim's in Paris.

I'd already come across the Baron de Roquette's name many times before, of course, but only in connection with his *conserverie* (preserving) business. I say 'of course' because it's a name that's hard to miss round here, emblazoned as it is on the tins of pâte de foie, confits and rillettes that he supplies to all the top-quality food shops. But the first I'd heard of his pigeon-breeding was through Marie-Christine Combes, who, it turned out, was a childhood friend of his. I had been telling her about the fantastic roast pigeon I'd eaten at the *Auberge*, and how struck I was by its tender meat and subtle flavour – so different from that of pigeons I'd cooked and eaten before. So when she happened to mention that it was probably one that had been reared by the Baron, I wanted to find out more. I'd already discovered that a crucial factor in the flavour of both capons and duck lay in their type of feed. Was this also the case for *pigeonneaux*?

As I drove up the long drive to the beautiful farmhouse where the Baron now lived, I noticed the remains of an old *pigeonnier*, or pigeon-house, in his garden. These strange-looking structures are a very common sight in the Aude and the Tarn, where they are relics of a bygone age, when pigeons first acquired their posh associations. Under the *Ancien Régime*, before the French Revolution, pigeons (and particularly squabs) were the favourite food at court, and you could only have a *pigeonnier* with special permission from the king. The only people to have the ear of the king were aristocrats, with the consequence that *pigeonniers* became powerful status symbols and people vied with each other (in a kind of 'Keeping up with the Joneses' way) to build more and more elaborate versions as indicators of their social standing. The Revolution in 1789 changed all that, and under the new democracy everyone had the right to raise pigeons. *Pigeonniers* sprouted everywhere, but because no one really knew how to rear the birds, the practice of pigeon-breeding died out, and didn't come back into fashion for more than 100 years. Meanwhile, the *pigeonniers* remained, in their varying stages of decay and widely ranging shapes, the one in the Baron's garden being the most common – a covered platform supported by four stone pillars (the structures were raised to stop the rats from getting at the birds). Seeing it made me wonder if the structure itself had inspired him to start rearing pigeons.

Married to a British sculptress, who is well known locally, the Baron Louis-Charles spoke excellent English, and it was a great relief not to have to struggle with my limited French again as I sat back and listened to his story. In around 1970 his father had sold the château, he explained, and become a gentleman farmer, working in the fields and rearing pigs. When the bottom subsequently fell out of the pig market, Louis-Charles had to find a new source of income and had opted for pigeons. And, yes, it was the *pigeonnier* in the grounds of the new house that had given him the idea. He got his first pigeons, White Kings and Silver Kings, from a friend. They laid eggs, and *voilà*, the business was born.

Pigeons were wonderful, he enthused… . They loved the wind, and tolerated cold temperatures in winter and hot weather in summer. What's more, he said animatedly, they were fascinating because they were a microcosm of human society. 'Did you know,' he asked me excitedly, 'that pigeon couples like to have the same nest and mate for life?' (I had to admit I didn't.)

He went on, the secret of their wonderful flavour, he explained, was in the totally natural way they were reared. The adult couple were fed on a diet of sunflower seeds and maize. Then, a few days before hatching the eggs, they produced *bouillie*, a milky mixture, which they regurgitated and fed to the chicks. The babies were reared by the parents in the nest till they were about 28 days old, then either killed for the table or left to become new parents. 'You can tell when the time is right,' he said, 'when the chicks make a certain sound we call le cri du nid.' Once killed, the squabs are hung and the feathers removed by waxing, which leaves a totally smooth skin.

As we walked out, I saw the squabs and pigeons in huge covered cages. They couldn't be let outside, the Baron explained, or they might be shot. But they were easy to keep. The cages were fumigated once a year, and the birds'

OPPOSITE: *The elusive*
crayfish – once native to
the streams in the Black
Mountain, but now,
sadly, imported

droppings (known as *columbine* in French – such a nice word for pigeon shit) make a wonderful manure for the flowers if left for a year. This, together with the chicks' natural diet and the lack of antibiotics in their food meant that everything was organic. 'It is the artisanal way,' he said. And that's the way he wanted to keep it. These days he had only around 500 pigeons, rather than the 2,000 he'd had at his peak, but that was because he preferred to go for quality rather than quantity. It was 'une passion', he said, breaking into French, something he liked to keep up as a good balance with his Foie gras and preserving business, which was really taking off.

I'd learnt a couple of important lessons from my visit. First, that, yet again, as with capons and ducks, when it came to flavour, what you got out depended on what you put in. The common thread between all these birds, apart from the way they were reared, was maize. And second, the importance of doing things in the traditional way. I loved all these wonderful cottage industries – traditional but dying ways of life that I hoped would continue. Not for the first time, I wondered how long they would last. But in the Baron's case, knowing how successful his tinned pâtés and confits were becoming, I couldn't help wondering if he might eventually leave his pigeons and go off to make his fortune in Foie gras. I was glad I'd seen him when I had.

In May Charles had caught his first fish – a roach – in one of the freshwater streams in the Black Mountain. To those in the know, the Black Mountain is prime fishing country, a great source of pike and trout, dotted as it is with lakes and rock-pools. This I knew, but I always imagined that you had to go quite high to find them. What I hadn't realised was that the water at the top of the mountain seeped through the rocks and travelled downhill to create fishing streams at the bottom, alongside the main road, leading to the bizarre sight of rows of men with fishing rods standing with their backs to roaring traffic. I puzzled about that one for months…

It was Jean-Louis who first told me about the crayfish. 'You can find them in the Black Mountain rock-pools,' he said. 'They're all over the place. We should go on a fishing expedition some time, in the spring.' That had been months ago. And now it was spring, and nothing had happened. But I hadn't forgotten. And the more that Charles, crowing over his fishing success, kept pestering me to go out fishing again, the more I thought about it. Every time I saw Jean-Louis, I'd tentatively mention it, like a child hinting to his parents that he wants a bike. It wasn't just the fishing I was interested in, of course – it was the thought of eating freshly caught crayfish again.

Once tasted, the *écrevisse*, or crayfish, is never to be forgotten. A freshwater fish, it's often confused with its saltwater counterpart, the *langouste*, but is in fact much smaller – no more than 8 – 10cm inches long. Crayfish don't have much meat, admittedly, and what they do have is mostly in the tail. But it tastes fantastic eaten in a salad with fresh Foie gras.

By the end of May I was beginning to wonder if the whole story of the crayfish in the Black Mountain had just been in my imagination. And then, by chance, I found a newly opened restaurant – in the Black Mountain, as it happened – with baskets of crayfish piled up to the ceiling. I asked the *patronne* where they were from. 'We catch them here, in the Black

Mountain,' she said. Aha, I thought. 'Where?' She suddenly began to look wary, so I didn't push it – she obviously wanted to keep the location secret.

By sheer coincidence, we were going to the Château Garrevaques that night, and I mentioned the story to Marie-Christine and her husband, Claude. 'I'm very surprised,' Marie-Christine said. 'There are no crayfish in the Black Mountain any more. They are all imported from Turkey or Louisiana these days. Of course, there were plenty when I was a child,' she went on. 'I remember them crawling around the baskets in our kitchen.' I felt really disappointed.

The whole idea of finding crayfish in the Black Mountain had assumed magical proportions to me, and now, after having my hopes raised, it was obviously never going to happen. 'There used to be a man who caught crayfish there,' she went on. 'I'm sure he would know… . Of course, he's getting on now, so I don't know how much he'd remember. Now what was his name?' She furrowed her brow. 'Boque, Roque… . No, it was Roche, I think. Yes, that's it, Claude Roche.'

I tracked down Monsieur Roche at his home in Revel, an attractive house set in a wide street with a pedestrianised area lined with plane trees. The moment I mentioned the crayfish, his face lit up. I'd obviously woken a deep, long-held memory. As we sat in his living room – the shade was welcome after the heat outside – he talked, his daughter translating. 'Ah, yes, the crayfish,' he said, dreamily. 'Yes, monsieur, it is true. There were crayfish in the Montagne Noire, but that was a long time ago now…' 'What happened?' I asked him. 'They all died,' he said, 'from a disease passed on by a fungus. It ate their shells, you see. But they were so wonderful.' And then he went onto tell me his story.

'Every year, on a Sunday in the middle of September, there was a festival in my village called the Argent Double, named after the river (a tributary of the River Aude) that ran through the village. Well, that river was absolutely crawling with crayfish. There were thousands of them. On the Sunday afternoon, about half a dozen of us would go down to the river. We knew there was a rock with an enormous hole in it, and we dammed the river so that the hole in the rock was filled with water. There were hundreds of crayfish in it, and the trick was to catch as many as possible, then unblock the river again. The crayfish were then all divided up by size and taken home. Once there, we would make a Court-bouillon, then boil them and leave them to cook in it. The next day we would have them with mayonnaise.'

Now that Monsieur Roche's memories had been awakened, there was no stopping him, as he relived his boyhood exploits. 'Every now and again, two or three of us would go out with a lantern at night and catch them in the Black Mountain. We used to bring them home, put them in a frying pan with Persillade, then flambé them with *eau-de-vie*. Ah, the taste was something I'll never forget,' he said, going into a reverie, then recovered himself. 'It was all illegal, of course, though you could fish them by day with a special licence. People used to hang a thread from a tree, put some worms on the end and the crayfish would come for them – doucement,' he said quietly. 'Some people preferred the balance system – netted baskets with mutton in them. The crayfish would come and eat it. But that was 50 years ago…'

And then, in an ironic twist of fate, he got a job as an official *garde de pêche* for a huge private estate. Poacher had now turned gamekeeper, and Claude Roche's life changed for ever. Eating all that crayfish had clearly given him a special relationship with them, which developed into a lifelong fascination, as Roche began to study them in detail, eventually becoming a world expert. ('He even went to Paris to take special exams,' his daughter said, proudly.)

Far from eating them, he went onto breed them, the first person in France to do so. And then, in around 1970, they all died out…killed by a deadly virus caused by tarmac. 'They were destined never to survive the modern age,' he said sadly. 'No, there are no crayfish left in the Black Mountain now,' he continued. 'Well, maybe some – a few perhaps, but they are very rare.' These days they are mostly imported from Turkey and Louisiana (Marie-Christine had been right, then). People had tried to release Turkish crayfish in the local waters, but he didn't know if it had worked. He had heard rumours that some were being bred in the rivers of private estates, but nothing more.

There were, of course, trout in the Black Mountain, he said animatedly. We embarked on a long discussion about angling, and hatched up a plan to go on a special fishing trip with Charles one weekend. It wasn't the same as catching crayfish, but it would have to do. I thanked him profusely for his help, and took my leave. As he walked me back to the front door, his eyes misted over again. 'I can still remember the taste of those crayfish,' he said dreamily.

I left the old man to his memories and walked out into the dappled sunlight, where boys in jeans were playing boules. It had been a fascinating afternoon, and I'd been touched by Monsieur Roche's charming, innocent stories. As I drove back home, I noticed the patches of yellow in the fields – the first signs of the rapeseed shoots pushing their way through the ground. The banks were already starting to fill with poppies and the mountains in the distance were cloaked in a shimmering heat haze. It was going to be a fantastic summer.

Spring Recipes

DANDELION SALAD

In France it's commonplace to start a spring lunch with some sort of green salad or *salade verte*, and dandelion leaves are excellent for this purpose. At this time of year dandelions can be found growing everywhere. The French for dandelion is *pissenlit* – a reference to its diuretic nature! – and it can be bought from any marketplace and gathered from the garden. When preparing this salad, discard all the bitter-tasting outer leaves, retaining just the smaller, tender inner ones.

Serves 6

180 G DANDELION LEAVES

100 ML TARRAGON VINAIGRETTE
  (SEE PAGE 296)

6 ANCHOVY FILLETS, MASHED TO
  A PASTE

1 GARLIC CLOVE, PEELED AND
  FINELY CHOPPED

SALT AND PEPPER

1. Wash and pick over the dandelion leaves, discarding all the outer ones, and dry them thoroughly in a clean tea-towel.

2. Arrange a large handful of the leaves in the centre of 6 plates.

3. Pour the tarragon vinaigrette into a mixing bowl, adding the anchovy, garlic and salt and pepper to taste, then whisk all the ingredients together.

4. With a teaspoon, spoon some vinaigrette around the leaves and serve immediately.

Asparagus Hollandaise

In the south-west of France the asparagus season starts at least a month earlier than in England. In fact, white asparagus is usually available in March, with the more common green asparagus coming into season from the middle of April. It is always better, wherever possible, to buy locally grown asparagus in season, as it will have the best taste.

You need roughly 200 g of asparagus per person. If you don't like hot asparagus, it is lovely served cold with a Tarragon vinaigrette (see page 296). This dish could be used as the main course for a light lunch or the hors d'oeuvre for a formal dinner.

Serves 4

1 QUANTITY HOLLANDAISE
    SAUCE (SEE PAGE 298)

800 G FRESH ASPARAGUS

SALT AND PEPPER

1. Make the hollandaise sauce (page 298), and keep it warm in a bowl over a saucepan of hot water, while you prepare and cook the asparagus.

2. With a vegetable peeler, carefully peel the outer layer of the asparagus, from below the tip to the end of the stalk, trying not to peel too deep. (It is important to remove this layer because it is extremely fibrous.)

3. Cook the asparagus spears in boiling salted water – preferably with the tips out of the water – for about 4 minutes, depending on size, to the point where they are still a little firm (*al dente*).

4. Place the asparagus spears in a serving dish and serve the warm, newly made hollandaise sauce separately in a sauceboat.

CRAYFISH IN A COURT-BOUILLON WITH MAYONNAISE

In France crayfish are very much a culinary delicacy. There are two main types: the small ones (also native to Britain) are known as *écrevisses à pattes blanches*, and the larger, more aggressive ones as *écrevisses de la Meuse* or *à pattes rouges*.

Before you cook crayfish, it's important to prepare them properly, removing the central portion of the fan-shaped tail and pulling out the intestinal tract. This is an unpleasant thing to have to do, but I think completely necessary, because the crayfish will taste bitter if you don't. You can ask your fishmonger to do this, if you prefer. Some people advocate putting live crayfish in the freezer for a couple of hours before cooking them, and believe that this is the most humane way of killing them. I think a quick plunge into boiling water is best. All this aside, I like to cook crayfish in the simplest possible way to show off their delicate flavour, and here is a good recipe.

Serves 8

2 KG LIVE CRAYFISH

2 LITRES COURT-BOUILLON
   (SEE PAGE 294)

MAYONNAISE (SEE PAGE 297)

1. Hold a crayfish in your hand, gripping it about 1cm below the head. With the thumb and forefinger of your other hand, take hold of the middle section of the fanned tail and twist and pull out, all in one motion, the intestinal tract. Place the crayfish in a large pan under cold running water and repeat this process for the other crayfish.

2. Bring the *bouillon* to the boil in a large saucepan. Strain off the crayfish and, in one swift motion, drop them into the pan. Bring back to the boil and the crayfish are ready. Remove from the heat and strain, retaining the *bouillon* for future use.

3. Divide the crayfish between 2 serving plates or divide into portions and place on 8 serving plates, and sprinkle with all the vegetables and herbs from the *bouillon*. Serve immediately. You will need finger bowls to wash your hands in, a plate or bowl for the shells, some nut-crackers or fish-crackers for the claws, along with the mayonnaise, some crunchy fresh baguette and copious amounts of dry white wine.

Red Mullet Salad

The mullet available in the Aude come from the Mediterranean and are smaller than those you get in Britain which tend to come from Cornwall. Ask the fishmonger to gut the fish, cut off the fins and gills and trim the tails.

Serves 6

6 RED MULLET, ABOUT 200 G
    EACH
2 GARLIC CLOVES, PEELED AND
    VERY FINELY CHOPPED
JUICE OF ¹/₂ LEMON
80 ML OLIVE OIL
SALT AND PEPPER
GARLIC CROÛTONS (BAGUETTE
    SLICES RUBBED WITH GARLIC,
    SPRINKLED WITH OLIVE OIL
    AND BAKED OR GRILLED)

TOMATO VINAIGRETTE
225 ML FISH STOCK
    (SEE PAGE 294)
75 ML TARRAGON VINAIGRETTE
    (SEE PAGE 296)
2 BEEF TOMATOES, SKINNED,
    DESEEDED AND DICED
I SHALLOT, PEELED AND FINELY
    CHOPPED
2 GARLIC CLOVES, PEELED AND
    FINELY CHOPPED
6 FRESH BASIL LEAVES, FINELY
    SHREDDED

1. With a small, blunt knife, scrape off all the scales of the fish from tail to head. Wash the mullet under plenty of cold running water, and dry them on kitchen paper.

2. With a sharp knife, score 2–3 diagonal cuts across the body of each fish. Turn each of them over and repeat the process on the other side, then lay them in a roasting tin.

3. Put the garlic into a small bowl, squeeze in the lemon juice and pour in the oil. Season with salt and plenty of pepper, and pour over the fish.

4. To make the vinaigrette, first pour the fish stock into a shallow pan, bring to the boil and reduce it by two-thirds. Pour the reduced fish stock into a bowl and, while it's still hot, whisk in the tarragon vinaigrette. Add the tomato dice, shallot, garlic and basil leaves. Stir the mixture with a spoon, then season to taste.

5. Wash and trim the salad leaves. Dry them thoroughly in a tea-towel and place in a bowl.

6. To cook the red mullet, preheat the grill to its maximum setting. Place the fish under the grill and cook for about 5 minutes each side. Alternatively the fish can be fried.

SALAD

¹/₂ HEAD CURLY ENDIVE

2 HANDFULS ROCKET LEAVES

I RADICCHIO

7. Lay out 6 dinner plates. Arrange a mixture of leaves in a tall mound on one side of each plate. Scatter with garlic croûtons and place a mullet next to each pile of salad.

8. Pour the vinaigrette back into the saucepan and warm it without letting it boil. Put 2–3 spoonfuls of the vinaigrette over each fish and serve.

Deep-fried Fillets of John Dory

John Dory is a versatile fish and can be cooked in different ways. It has a delicate flavour, so it's best to choose a sauce that won't overpower it. Gribiche sauce (see page 296) is a perfect one. Ask your fishmonger to fillet 3 fish into 12 fillets and remove the skin.

Serves 6

12 JOHN DORY FILLETS

SALT AND FRESHLY GROUND
  BLACK PEPPER

50 G PLAIN FLOUR

GRIBICHE SAUCE (SEE PAGE 296)

750 ML CORN OIL FOR DEEP-
  FRYING

FERMENTATION

1 TABLESPOON WATER

12 G FRESH YEAST

1/2 TEASPOON CLEAR HONEY

1 DESSERTSPOON PLAIN FLOUR

BATTER

250 G PLAIN FLOUR

200 ML MILK

1 EGG

1 TABLESPOON OLIVE OIL

1. Season the 12 fish fillets with salt and pepper and dip them in the flour, patting off any excess, before setting them aside on a plate.

2. For the fermentation, pour the water into a bowl and dissolve the yeast in it. Add the honey and sprinkle over the flour, then put in a warm place, such as an airing cupboard, while you make the batter.

3. Sieve the flour into a mixing bowl. Add the milk, then the egg, and whisk the mixture until smooth. Add the olive oil and whisk again. Season with salt and pepper, then stir in the fermentation. Cover the bowl with a clean, damp cloth and prepare the gribiche sauce.

4. Fill a large saucepan a third full with corn oil, then heat on the stove. Once the oil has reached the required temperature (about 190°C/375°F), dip the large fillets one by one into the batter and then lower them carefully straight into the oil. These larger fillets will take about 5 minutes to cook. With a slotted spoon, remove the fillets from the oil onto kitchen paper to drain. Cook the smaller fillets for about 3 minutes or until the batter is golden. Drain well on kitchen paper and serve the fish immediately.

TROUT WITH CAPERS

On my way to Bayeux, to see the famous Tapestry, I repeatedly saw signs at the roadside advertising '*la pêche ici – truites, écrevisses*'. After about the third sign, I decided to stop. I drove down a long, made-up driveway to a small wooden house, where you could buy a pole and some maggots. An elderly chap led me to a small lake fed by a waterfall from the hills. I baited my hook and within minutes – bingo – I caught one. That afternoon I caught eight small brown trout, the best variety as far as eating goes. Rainbow trout – with characteristics of both a freshwater and a sea trout – are the next best thing, however. Some of them go out to sea as 2-year-olds, returning to the rivers to spawn before heading back to the lakes to get their condition back. Others don't move, staying put like their brown trout brothers in the rivers or lakes all their lives.

Serves 2

2 BROWN OR RAINBOW TROUT

2 DESSERTSPOONS PLAIN FLOUR

SALT AND PEPPER

2 TABLESPOONS GROUNDNUT OIL

1 LEMON, PEELED AND
   SEGMENTED

1 GARLIC CLOVE , PEELED AND
   CHOPPED

2 DESSERTSPOONS BOTTLED
   CAPERS, SQUEEZED DRY

75 G UNSALTED BUTTER, DICED

1 DESSERTSPOON FINELY
   CHOPPED FLAT-LEAF PARSLEY

1. Gut and clean the trout. Cut out the gills with sharp scissors, tail to head, and scrape off all the scales with a blunt knife. If the trout are larger than 400 g, cut through either side of each of their backbones and remove it. Cut away all the small rib or pin bones, then dry the fish on some kitchen paper.

2. Sprinkle the flour onto a plate and season it with salt and lots of pepper. Roll the trout fillets in the flour, shaking off all the excess.

3. Put a large frying pan on the stove, pour in the oil and heat it until it just starts to smoke. Carefully lay the trout in the pan and cook the fish on one side for about 6–7 minutes to brown them, then turn them over and cook on the other side, for a similar length of time.

4. Now tip in the lemon segments, garlic, capers and butter dice. As soon as the butter has melted and starts to froth and colour – but not burn – sprinkle the parsley into the pan. Serve immediately with a glass of dry white Gaillac.

Steamed Trout from the Black Mountain

In Revel market I bought rainbow trout and cooked them *en papillote*, as the French call it ('in paper' or, in this case, a sheet of foil).

Serves 4

4 RAINBOW TROUT, ABOUT 400 G
   EACH, GUTTED
SALT AND WHITE PEPPER
90 G BABY SPINACH LEAVES
8 SORREL LEAVES
I CARROT, PEELED
I FENNEL BULB, TRIMMED
I CELERY STICK, TRIMMED
I LEEK, WASHED AND TRIMMED
2 COURGETTES, TOPPED AND
   TAILED
400 ML FISH STOCK
   (SEE PAGE 294)
JUICE OF ½ LEMON
100 G UNSALTED BUTTER, DICED
I TEASPOON FENNEL SEEDS
4 SPRIGS FRESH YOUNG
   TARRAGON

LEMON AND GARLIC BUTTER
60 G UNSALTED BUTTER
I GARLIC CLOVE, PEELED AND
   CRUSHED
JUICE OF ½ LEMON
SALT AND CAYENNE PEPPER

1. Scrape the scales from the trout with a blunt knife, cut off the fins with a sharp knife and trim off the tail. Wash the trout under plenty of cold running water and place on some kitchen paper to drain. Season.

2. For the lemon and garlic butter, first melt the butter in a small saucepan. Add the garlic and squeeze in the lemon juice, followed by a pinch each of salt and cayenne pepper. When the butter has melted, take off the heat and set aside.

3. Trim and wash the spinach and sorrel leaves and drain in a colander. Cut the remaining vegetables into slices about 9cm long and 3mm thick, then cut them into matchsticks (julienne). On a plate, arrange the vegetables in separate piles in this order: carrots, fennel, celery, leek and courgettes.

4. Pour the fish stock into a saucepan and bring to the boil. First add the carrots, then, at 2-minute intervals, the fennel, celery, leek and courgettes. Immediately strain the julienne through a sieve over a smaller saucepan (to catch the stock). Spread the vegetables out on a plate to cool.

5. Put the saucepan with the stock back onto the stove and bring to the boil, so that the liquid reduces by half. Squeeze in the lemon juice, then whisk in the butter piece by piece, until it has dissolved. Pour the stock into a bowl and set aside.

6. Preheat the oven to 200–220°C/400–425°F/ Gas 6–7. Cut 8 sheets of foil each about 45cm

long and 30cm wide. Place 4 of the sheets of foil on a work surface. In the centre of each, using half the spinach and sorrel, lay down a green base for the trout. Top the piles of greenery with half the vegetable strips. Lay the trout down on top of the vegetables and brush liberal amounts of the lemon and garlic butter over each fish. Put some more spinach and sorrel over the trout and add the remaining vegetable strips.

7. Spoon 4 dessertspoons of the finished fish stock over each of the fish, ensuring none of the stock runs over the edge of the foil. Sprinkle in the fennel seeds and put a sprig of fresh tarragon on top. Put the remaining sheets of foil over each of the fish and carefully fold the edges over three times to seal firmly. Lay the sealed bags in a roasting tin and cook in the oven for about 10 minutes. During cooking, the bags will puff up.

8. Serve the *papillotes* straight from the oven onto dinner plates at the table. Each guest should cut or break open the bag themselves – the mouth-watering aroma of the dish filling the air. Serve with a little Butter sauce (see page 296).

GRILLED LOBSTER IN GARLIC AND CHILLI BUTTER

This is a very simple dish and one that can easily be cooked outside on a barbecue grill or in a roasting tin over the red-hot embers of an open fire.

Serves 4

4 X 450 G LOBSTERS

4 TABLESPOONS OLIVE OIL

SALT AND PEPPER

GARLIC BUTTER

250 G UNSALTED BUTTER, DICED

2 SPRIGS FRESH TARRAGON, BLANCHED AND FINELY CHOPPED

3 SPRIGS FLAT-LEAF PARSLEY, FINELY CHOPPED

1 BUNCH FRESH CHERVIL, FINELY CHOPPED

2 GARLIC CLOVES, PEELED AND FINELY CHOPPED

1 SMALL RED CHILLI, DESEEDED AND FINELY CHOPPED

JUICE OF $\frac{1}{2}$ LEMON

SALT

1. For the garlic butter, put the diced butter in a mixing bowl and beat to soften until it becomes pale in colour. Mix in the herbs, garlic and chilli. Add a little lemon juice and salt to taste.

2. Kill the lobsters by inserting the point of a sharp knife straight into the air vent at the top of the head, and split each in half lengthways. Remove the entrail line and, with a teaspoon, take out the brain sac at the top of the head. With the back of a knife, crack the claws. Place the lobsters in a roasting tin with their claws and pour the olive oil over the lobster. Season with salt and pepper.

3. Put the tin onto the red-hot embers of an open fire or, alternatively, shell side down on a barbecue grill. Cook the lobsters for 5 minutes.

4. Remove from the heat and, while the meat is still pink, pack some garlic butter into the head and over the tail meat, and continue cooking for a further 5 minutes. The butter will melt and the flavour of the herbs will scent the lobster flesh.

5. Serve immediately with chunks of garlic bread fried in a pan over the same fire with what's left of the butter and a little olive oil to help brown it.

Roast Quails with Grapes

If you can't find *verjuice* (the first pressing of white grapes), use a Muscat instead.

Serves 4

8 QUAILS, ABOUT 150 G EACH,
   WISHBONES REMOVED
SALT AND PEPPER
50 ML WALNUT OIL

SAUCE

1 CARROT, PEELED AND CHOPPED
1 ONION, PEELED AND CHOPPED
1 CELERY STICK, TRIMMED AND
   CHOPPED
1 LEEK, WASHED AND CHOPPED
1 BAY LEAF
1 SPRIG FRESH THYME
1 SPRIG FRESH SAGE
1 SPRIG FRESH HYSSOP
2 GARLIC CLOVES, PEELED AND
   CHOPPED
150 ML VERJUICE OR MUSCAT
400 ML CHICKEN STOCK (SEE
   PAGE 293)

GARNISH

300 G MUSCAT GRAPES,
   BLANCHED AND SKINNED
1 DESSERTSPOON CASTER SUGAR
1 DESSERTSPOON WATER
150 G SMOKED BACON CUT INTO
   STRIPS AND BLANCHED
1 TABLESPOON OLIVE OIL

1. Preheat the oven to 220°C/425°F/Gas 7. Season the birds. Heat the walnut oil in a roasting tin and fry the birds on all sides until golden. Put in the oven for 6 minutes, then remove and place on a rack to cool.

2. Cut off the legs and remove the breasts, placing these on a serving dish; they should still be very pink. Chop up the carcasses finely.

3. Reheat the roasting tin, add the vegetables, and fry to brown them. Add the herbs, garlic, and *verjuice*. Boil to reduce the liquid by two-thirds, then add the stock and transfer the liquid to a saucepan. Add the carcasses, bring to the boil and skim off any sediment that rises to the surface. Turn down the heat to a rapid simmer, and cook and reduce the liquid by half for about an hour.

4. Place the skinned grapes in a pan, sprinkle with the sugar and water, and heat through gently to glaze. Fry the bacon in a little olive oil until golden, then set aside.

5. Strain off the sauce into another pan through a sieve. Put it back on the stove and boil and reduce until syrupy.

6. Sprinkle the lardons and the grapes over the quail. Return the dish to the oven (at 220°C/425°F/Gas 7) for about 6 minutes. Remove from the oven and cover the quail pieces with the sauce. Serve.

LAURAGAIS PIGEONS WITH HONEY SAUCE

The pigeons used here are a local speciality, but corn-fed squabs should be obtainable from a high-quality butcher.

Serves 6

6 LAURAGAIS PIGEONS OR QUAIL
   OR GUINEA FOWL, WISHBONES
   REMOVED
4 DESSERTSPOONS CORN OIL
SALT AND PEPPER

HONEY SAUCE

100 ML CORN OIL
250 G CHICKEN PIECES (WINGS
   ARE BEST)
60 ML SHERRY VINEGAR
60 G CLEAR HONEY
3 SHALLOTS, PEELED AND FINELY
   CHOPPED
2 GARLIC CLOVES, PEELED AND
   FINELY CHOPPED
I CELERY STICK, TRIMMED AND
   CHOPPED
I CARROT, PEELED AND CHOPPED
I LEEK, WASHED AND CHOPPED
I BAY LEAF
I SPRIG FRESH THYME
I LITRE CHICKEN STOCK, BOILED
   LONGER FOR A STRONGER
   TASTE (SEE PAGE 293)

1. Preheat the oven to 220°C/425°F/Gas 7. Chop the wings up for the sauce.

2. Heat the oil in a roasting tin. Season the birds and, when the oil starts to smoke, put them into the tin. Brown on all sides, then roast for about 10 minutes. Take them out to rest. When cool enough, put them on a board and carve them by first removing the legs and then the breasts. Put to one side. Then finely chop the carcasses.

3. Now for the sauce. In a large saucepan, heat half the oil until it starts to smoke. Add the chicken and pigeon wings and carcasses to brown them. Pour in the vinegar and bring it to the boil. Add the honey and bring to the boil again.

4. Using the remaining oil, fry the shallots, garlic, celery, carrot and leek until golden, then add them to the wings and honey syrup. Stir and coat all the ingredients until glazed. Add the bay leaf, thyme, stock and bring back to the boil, removing any froth. Simmer rapidly for an hour. Strain through a sieve into another saucepan and boil it again, to reduce it by two-thirds.

5. Reheat the pigeon for 5 minutes in the oven (220°C/425°F/Gas 7), then place on a serving dish. Bring the sauce back to the boil and strain it, then pour over the pigeons. Serve immediately.

ROASTED LAMB CUTLETS WITH A PARSLEY CRUST

Ask your butcher to split 2 'best ends' of lamb into 4, then remove the top skin and the shoulder blades, chine them and trim and clean the tops of the cutlets, retaining 1.5 kg of lamb bones to make the sauce. If the lamb bones don't make up to 1.5 kg ask your butcher for some more.

Serves 8

2 DOUBLE BEST ENDS OF SPRING
  LAMB, ABOUT 5 KG IN TOTAL,
  TRIMMED AS ABOVE
SALT AND PEPPER

SAUCE

30 ML OLIVE OIL
1.5 KG LAMB BONES, CHOPPED
  INTO SMALL PIECES
1 LARGE CARROT, PEELED AND
  CHOPPED
1 LARGE ONION, PEELED AND
  CHOPPED
1 CELERY STICK, TRIMMED AND
  CHOPPED
1 LEEK, WASHED AND CHOPPED
20 G TOMATO PURÉE
300 G TOMATOES, HALVED AND
  DESEEDED
$^{1}/_{2}$ BOTTLE DRY WHITE WINE
2 GARLIC CLOVES, PEELED AND
  ROUGHLY CHOPPED
$^{1}/_{2}$ BAY LEAF
1 SPRIG FRESH ROSEMARY
1.5 LITRES CHICKEN STOCK
  (SEE PAGE 293)

1. For the sauce, in a large saucepan heat the oil until it begins to smoke, then add the lamb bones and fry until golden brown. Tip in the prepared vegetables and cook until they too are golden brown. Add the tomato purée to the pan, followed by the tomatoes. Pour in the wine and bring to the boil immediately, then add the garlic and herbs. Pour in the chicken stock, bring to the boil and remove any sediment that rises to the surface. Turn the heat down and allow the stock to simmer rapidly for approximately 1$^{1}/_{2}$ hours.

2. Strain the sauce through a fine sieve into another saucepan. Again, bring the sauce to the boil, removing any scum that rises to the surface, then turn down the heat and reduce the sauce for about 15 minutes, until it is thick enough to coat the back of a spoon.

3. Preheat the oven to 220°C/425°F/Gas 7. For the herb crust, chop the garlic to a purée, mixing this with a teaspoon each of salt and pepper. Mix together thoroughly in a bowl with the parsley, breadcrumbs and olive oil.

4. Brush both sides of a piece of lamb with the mustard, then dip the lamb, pressing it 'fat' side down first, into the aromatic breadcrumbs, to coat the outside. Press some more breadcrumbs onto

HERB CRUST

2 GARLIC CLOVES, PEELED

SEA SALT AND PEPPER

75 G FLAT-LEAF PARSLEY, FINELY
    CHOPPED

100 G DRIED WHITE
    BREADCRUMBS

3 TABLESPOONS OLIVE OIL

2 TABLESPOONS DIJON MUSTARD

the opposite side. Repeat the process for the other pieces, then roast in the preheated oven for 30 minutes only. Once cooked, the lamb will have a deep, crisp crust around it and will be nicely pink inside. Lay the lamb pieces on a chopping board and cut 2–3 cutlets per person. Arrange the lamb cutlets on dinner plates, spoon around them some of the sauce and serve immediately with new season broad beans.

Snails with Herb and Chilli Butter

In the old days, the snails were left to starve for at least a fortnight in a cool dark place. While this practice is completely unnecessary, it is important to purge them and this can be done by covering them, still alive, with a handful of sea salt and 2 handfuls of flour. Put them in a bucket and leave overnight in your garden shed or garage, during which time they give up all their impurities. In the morning run the bucket under cold water to wash them thoroughly.

Cook the snails in a *court-bouillon* (see page 294) for about 10 minutes and strain through a colander to cool. You then pull them out of their shells easily using a pin or needle.

Serves 2

ABOUT 24 SNAILS

90 G GRATED FRESH WHITE
   BREADCRUMBS

HERB AND CHILLI BUTTER

125 G UNSALTED BUTTER, DICED

2 SPRIGS FRESH TARRAGON,
   LEAVES BLANCHED AND FINELY
   CHOPPED

3 SPRIGS FLAT-LEAF PARSLEY,
   LEAVES FINELY CHOPPED

1 BUNCH FRESH CHERVIL, LEAVES
   FINELY CHOPPED

2 GARLIC CLOVES, PEELED AND
   CRUSHED TO A PASTE

1 FRESH RED CHILLI, DESEEDED
   AND CHOPPED

LEMON JUICE

SALT

1. Prepare the snails as described above.

2. Preheat the oven to 220°C/425°F/Gas 7. Put the butter in a mixing bowl and beat until it becomes soft and pale. Add the chopped herbs, garlic paste and chilli to the butter. Mix all the ingredients together well, squeezing in a few drops of lemon juice and seasoning with a little salt.

3. Put a coffeespoonful of butter into each snail mould or shell. Add a snail to each, and another coffeespoonful of butter on top. Sprinkle a generous teaspoonful of grated breadcrumbs over the butter.

4. Place the snails on a baking sheet and cook in the preheated oven for about 10 minutes or until the breadcrumbs are golden and the butter bubbling. Serve immediately.

POMMES BOULANGÈRE

These potatoes are great with lamb, but they are also delicious with certain fish dishes such as red mullet, sea bass or even roasted turbot.

Serves 4

1 KG FLOURY POTATOES, PEELED

80 G UNSALTED BUTTER

225 G ONIONS, PEELED AND
  SLICED

1 SPRIG FRESH THYME

1/2 BAY LEAF

1 GARLIC CLOVE, PEELED AND
  CHOPPED

2 SPRIGS FLAT-LEAF PARSLEY,
  FINELY CHOPPED

1.5 LITRES CHICKEN STOCK
  (SEE PAGE 293)

1. Preheat the oven to 190°C/375°F/Gas 5.

2. Slice the potatoes finely, either with a sharp knife or a mandolin, into pieces approximately 3mm thick. Place in a bowl and cover with water to prevent them going brown.

3. In a frying pan, melt half the butter and sweat the onions with the thyme, bay leaf and garlic until soft and golden.

4. Sprinkle the parsley onto the onions, then remove the pan from the stove. Drain the potatoes and dry on kitchen paper.

5. In an earthenware dish about 4cm deep, place a layer of potato slices, spread half of the sliced onions over the potatoes and then another layer of potato. Add the remaining onion and the final layer of potato.

6. Bring the chicken stock to the boil and pour it carefully over the potatoes. Cut up the other half of the butter and dot it around the top of the potatoes. Place the potatoes in the preheated oven and bake for one hour or until soft when pierced with a skewer and brown on the top.

Pithiviers of Goat's Cheese

Buy cheese no older than a week, then it won't be necessary to remove the rind.

Serves 4 (makes 2 large pithiviers.)

4 MEDIUM-SIZED SPINACH
LEAVES, WASHED, STALKS
REMOVED AND BLANCHED

100 G SHELLED WALNUTS,
BLANCHED AND SKINNED

2 X 150–200 G ROUND GOAT'S
CHEESES

500 G SHOP-BOUGHT PUFF
PASTRY

PLAIN FLOUR FOR DUSTING

1 EGG MIXED WITH 35 ML MILK
FOR EGG WASH

WALNUT CREAM VINAIGRETTE

120 ML CHICKEN STOCK
(SEE PAGE 293)

1 GARLIC CLOVE, PEELED AND
CHOPPED

60 ML DOUBLE CREAM

60 ML WALNUT VINAIGRETTE
(SEE PAGE 295)

A FEW DROPS OF LEMON JUICE

SALT AND PEPPER

1. Refresh the spinach in cold water, then dry on a clean tea-towel.

2. Push half the skinned walnuts into the cheeses, then wrap the spinach leaves around each cheese.

3. Cut the pastry into quarters. Dust a surface with flour, then roll each quarter out to 3mm thick and 15cm wide. Place a cheese in the centre of one piece of pastry and brush the egg around the edge of the pastry around the cheese. Place another piece of pastry on top and gently press and mould both pieces of pastry together without trapping air.

4. Using a 15cm cutter placed over the *pithivier*, cut away all the excess pastry. With the back of a knife, lightly score the top, but do not puncture the pastry. Repeat the process for the other *pithivier*, leaving both to relax for 20 minutes before cooking. Preheat the oven to 220°C/425°F/Gas 7. Brush the *pithiviers* with egg wash and place in the oven on a baking sheet lined with greaseproof paper to cook for 15 minutes, until golden.

5. To make the walnut cream, pour the stock into a saucepan, add the garlic, then bring to the boil and reduce by half. When the liquid is reduced but still boiling, whisk in the cream. Take the pan off the stove and whisk in the vinaigrette. Season the sauce with a few drops of lemon juice and salt and pepper, then strain into a sauceboat and add the remaining walnuts. Remove the *pithiviers* from the oven, cut each one into 4, spoon a little of the walnut cream around and serve.

GOUGÈRES

Traditionally *gougères* are little choux buns made with grated cheese, usually Gruyère, though you could also try a cheese from the Franche-Comté. Some people pipe a cheese sauce or fondue into the buns, but I prefer them without. They are delicious as an accompaniment to red Burgundy wines, or indeed any aperitif. They always taste better warm.

Serves 8

125 G UNSALTED BUTTER

I LARGE PINCH SEA SALT

PEPPER

300 ML WATER

240 G PLAIN FLOUR

5 EGGS, BEATEN

225 G GRUYÈRE CHEESE, GRATED

OLIVE OIL FOR GREASING

I EGG, BEATEN, FOR EGG WASH

1. Preheat the oven to 220°C/425°F/Gas 7. Cut the butter into rough pieces and place in a saucepan along with the salt, pepper and water, then bring to the boil.

2. As soon as the butter has dissolved and the water begins to froth and bubble, remove the pan from the stove and vigorously beat in the flour until you have a smooth paste. Return the pan to a gentle heat and stir and beat the mixture until it forms a ball that comes clean away from the sides of the saucepan.

3. Remove from the stove and beat the eggs into the paste, a little at a time, then stir in the cheese. The choux paste should look glossy and smooth and come away from the pan.

4. Lightly grease a baking sheet with a little oil. Fill a piping bag fitted with a 1cm nozzle with the choux paste and pipe small, round balls each about 2–3cm across and 2–3cm high. There should be 4 balls per person and the balls should be 4cm apart. Brush the egg wash over the tops of the buns and bake in the preheated oven for 30 minutes until golden and expanded three times their size. Remove from the oven and enjoy!

LEMON CAKE

I saw one of these in the pastry shop in Villefranche and thought I would buy it to try. This cake originates from the Savoie, where it is called *biscuit de Savoie au citron*. It's a virtually fat-free sponge, rather like a lemon sponge finger, and is very easy to make – good to eat with a glass of champagne if you have some friends coming around for afternoon tea.

Serves 8

30 G BUTTER, SOFTENED

250 G CASTER SUGAR

8 EGGS, SEPARATED

A PINCH OF SALT

100 G PLAIN FLOUR

FINELY GRATED ZEST OF 2
   LEMONS

1 DESSERTSPOON ICING SUGAR

1. Preheat the oven to 220°C/425°F/Gas 7, and grease a 20cm cake tin or soufflé mould with the soft butter. Then sprinkle the tin with a little of the caster sugar.

2. Pour the egg whites into a mixing bowl, add the salt and beat them until they stand in soft peaks, then whisk the sugar in gradually to make a meringue mixture.

3. Whisk the eggs yolks in another bowl, then very carefully stir them into the meringue mixture with a spatula. Fold in the flour and lemon zest, and whisk for a further 15 seconds.

4. Spoon the finished cake mixture into the prepared tin or mould, and dust the top with a little icing sugar. Bake in the preheated oven for about 20 minutes.

5. Turn the cake out onto a rack to cool. It will naturally shrink a little and become misshapen. Don't worry, this is how it is supposed to look. Dust it with a little more icing sugar.

LEMON CHIBOUST TARTS

I like to serve these, the Rolls-Royce of tarts, with *Crème anglaise* (see page 299).

Serves 6

200 G SWEET SHORTCRUST
   PASTRY MADE INTO 6 X 8 X 2CM
   TART CASES (SEE PAGE 300)
PLAIN FLOUR FOR DUSTING
UNSALTED BUTTER FOR
   GREASING

LEMON FILLING

FINELY GRATED ZEST AND JUICE
   OF 2 LEMONS
100 G CASTER SUGAR
75 G UNSALTED BUTTER
2 EGGS, BEATEN

CHIBOUST

1 GELATINE LEAF
100 ML DOUBLE CREAM
JUICE OF 3 LEMONS
3 EGGS, SEPARATED
120 G CASTER SUGAR
10 G CORNFLOUR, DISSOLVED IN
   1 DESSERTSPOON WATER
ICING SUGAR FOR DUSTING

1. Preheat the oven to 220°C/425°F/Gas 7 and leave the tart cases in their rings after blind-baking.

2. For the filling, put the lemon zest and juice, sugar and butter into a saucepan, and bring to the boil, then remove from the stove. Add the egg and return the pan to the heat. Whisking all the time, bring back to the boil to thicken. Pour the filling into a bowl to cool. Fill the pastry cases with the lemon curd and remove the tart rings. Cut 6 pieces of greaseproof paper each about 26 x 4cm, and wrap around the tarts. Fasten with tape and refrigerate.

3. Soak the gelatine in water to soften. Bring the cream to the boil, remove from the stove and stir in the lemon juice. Whisk the yolks and half the sugar together until pale, then whisk in the cornflour and water. Pour the boiled cream and lemon juice over the yolks a little at a time and mix. Pour into a pan and bring back to the boil, stirring, until it thickens. Remove from the stove and stir in the drained gelatine to melt.

4. Whisk the egg whites to soft peaks, adding the remaining sugar a little at a time. Fold the whites into the gelatine lemon mixture, then spoon onto the tarts, smoothing the tops with a knife. Dust with icing sugar and place in the freezer. Remove the paper rings and place the tarts under a hot grill. When the tops are golden, put the tarts into the refrigerator to defrost, leaving them for at least 2 hours before serving.

CHOCOLATE AND VANILLA MOUSSES

This recipe makes individual mousses, for which you will need 4 × 5 × 5cm ring moulds.

Serves 4

SPONGE

25 G ICING SUGAR

25 G GROUND ALMONDS

I EGG

I EGG YOLK

3 EGG WHITES

15 G CASTER SUGAR

20 G PLAIN FLOUR

CHOCOLATE MOUSSE

30 ML SUGAR SYRUP
(SEE PAGE 299)

3 EGG YOLKS

65 G GOOD-QUALITY CHOCOLATE
(AT LEAST 75 PERCENT COCOA
SOLIDS), CHOPPED INTO SMALL
PIECES AND MELTED

125 ML DOUBLE CREAM LIGHTLY
WHIPPED

VANILLA MOUSSE

2 EGG YOLKS

I VANILLA POD, SPLIT

35 ML SUGAR SYRUP
(SEE PAGE 299)

$^1/_2$ GELATINE LEAF, SOAKED IN
WATER

120 ML WHIPPING CREAM

GARNISH

COCOA POWDER

1. Preheat the oven to 190°C/375°F/Gas 5. Whisk the icing sugar, almonds, whole egg and egg yolk together until pale. Whisk the whites into peaks. Gradually add the sugar. Fold the meringue into the other mixture and stir till smooth. Sift the flour and fold. Pour the sponge mixture onto a baking sheet covered with greaseproof paper, spreading it to about 5mm thick. Bake for 7 minutes, then remove and cool.

2. To make the chocolate mousse, boil the sugar syrup and pour over the yolks, then whisk until it turns pale and thickens. Pour the chocolate into the mixture and fold in with the cream.

3. Now for the vanilla mousse. Mix the yolks and vanilla seeds. Boil the sugar syrup and pour over the yolks, then whisk as above. Boil 20 ml of the cream, then add the drained gelatine and stir until dissolved. Add to the egg mixture. Lightly whip the remaining cream and fold into the mousse.

4. Using one of the moulds as a stencil, cut out 4 bases from the sponge. Place each mould on a plate and put the sponge bases at the bottom of the moulds. Half fill each with some chocolate mousse. Top with the vanilla mousse and smooth it level. Put the mousses in the refrigerator to set, for 2 hours. To serve, remove from the refrigerator, warm a sharp knife and cut around the edge of the mousses, while lifting the moulds. Dust with cocoa powder.

FLOATING MERINGUES AND VANILLA SAUCE

The French call this dish *oeufs à la neige*, and the meringues are marshmallow-like in texture.

Serves 6 (makes 18 meringues)

MERINGUE

1 VANILLA POD, SPLIT

550 ML MILK

6 EGG WHITES

200 G CASTER SUGAR

TO SERVE

CRÈME ANGLAISE
   (SEE PAGE 299), MADE USING
   THE MERINGUE-POACHING
   MILK

300 G STRAWBERRIES, WASHED
   AND HULLED

2 DESSERTSPOONS ICING SUGAR,
   PLUS EXTRA FOR DUSTING

60 G FLAKED ALMONDS

1. Bring the vanilla pod and milk to the boil. Then remove from the heat.

2. Whisk the egg whites to stiff peaks, then gently whisk in the sugar, a little at a time.

3. Put the milk back onto the stove to simmer. Dip 2 large identical serving spoons into it. Use these to form the meringue into a large egg shape. Place this into the milk and poach it for 2 minutes each side until firm to the touch. Lift out with a slotted spoon and place on a clean tea-towel to drain. Repeat until all the mixture is used up, then refrigerate the meringues.

4. Put half the strawberries into a liquidiser and blend to a purée, then sieve into a saucepan. Add the sugar and boil to reduce until syrupy. Skim off any froth that rises, then set aside. Dice the remaining strawberries into 5mm cubes. When the syrup is cold, stir in the strawberry dice.

5. Preheat the grill to its maximum. Dust the almonds on a baking sheet with icing sugar and carefully toast them until golden. Cool. Spoon 3 dessertspoonfuls of the strawberries into the centre of 6 soup plates. Place the meringues, 3 per person, on top of the strawberries, and pour the sauce over the meringues. Sprinkle a few almonds over and dust the plates with a little icing sugar

CRÊPES SUZETTE

When this classic dish was first devised, it had no alcohol in it whatsoever, but I like it with a good slug of Grand Marnier, though Cointreau makes a good alternative.

Makes 20 crêpes

200 G PLAIN FLOUR

2 EGGS

200 ML MILK

150 ML LAGER

FINELY GRATED ZEST OF 2
    ORANGES (SEGMENT THESE
    FOR THE GARNISH)

A PINCH EACH OF SALT AND
    CASTER SUGAR

30 G UNSALTED BUTTER

30 ML CORN OR SUNFLOWER OIL
    FOR FRYING

ORANGE SAUCE

200 G CASTER SUGAR

75–100 ML GRAND MARNIER

JUICE OF 3 ORANGES AND FINELY
    GRATED ZEST OF 1

100 G UNSALTED BUTTER, DICED

1. Sieve the flour into a mixing bowl, then whisk in the eggs. Immediately add the milk, then, still whisking vigorously, add the lager and beat the batter until smooth. Stir in the grated zest, salt and sugar. In a small frying pan, 25cm in diameter, melt the butter until it starts to turn brown, then whisk it straight into the *crêpe* batter. Allow to rest for about 10 minutes.

2. Heat a frying pan on the stove. When it is hot, add a little oil to the pan and pour in just enough pancake mixture to coat the base of the pan. As soon as the mixture sets on one side turn the *crêpe* over using a palette knife. When the other side is cooked and golden, turn it out onto a serving dish. Fold the pancake in four and keep warm in a low oven (120°C/250°F/Gas ½). Repeat this process until all the mixture is used.

3. Now for the sauce. Heat the sugar in a small frying pan and, just as it starts to melt, add the Grand Marnier and set alight. Pour in the orange juice and bring the sauce to the boil, skimming off any froth that rises to the surface. Boil and reduce the sauce by half. Add the orange zest to the sauce, along with the butter, whisking it in piece by piece until it dissolves.

4. Remove the *crêpes* from the oven. Place the orange segments around the outside of the *crêpes*, then pour over the hot orange butter sauce and serve immediately.

APRICOT SABAYON

The apricots for this dish are marinated in a local sweet wine called Muscat de Rivesaltes, but you can use any sweet wine of your choice if this one is not available.

Serves 8

16 LARGE, RIPE APRICOTS

300 ML MUSCAT DE RIVESALTES
   OR OTHER SWEET WINE

2 DESSERTSPOONS APRICOT
   LIQUEUR OR EAU DE VIE

8 EGG YOLKS

80 G CASTER SUGAR

60 G FLAKED ALMONDS

2 DESSERTSPOONS ICING SUGAR

1. Wash the apricots and cut them in half, put them in a bowl and cover them with the wine. Add a generous couple of spoonfuls of sweet liqueur, or eau de vie if you prefer. Cover the bowl with clingfilm and put in the refrigerator to macerate for several hours or overnight. Remove from the refrigerator and strain the apricots into a sieve placed over a bowl.

2. Pour the egg yolks into a thick glass or stainless-steel mixing bowl. Whisk in the wine and juice from the apricots, then add the sugar. Half fill a large saucepan with water and heat it to simmering point on the stove. Place the bowl containing the egg and wine mixture (*sabayon*) over the hot water and beat it rapidly for at least 5–6 minutes until it thickens and turns pale in colour.

3. Meanwhile, preheat the grill to its maximum setting. Arrange the apricot halves on 8 plates each about 26cm in diameter. Cover them with liberal amounts of the *sabayon*, sprinkle with a few flaked almonds and dust with a little icing sugar.

4. Place the plates under the grill to glaze the apricots, which will take less than 30 seconds. Pull the plates out as soon as the *sabayon* starts to colour. Serve immediately with Almond Biscuits (see page 148) and some of the same sweet wine used in the recipe.

Chocolate Choux Buns

When I made these choux buns they were a huge success. I had to stand back, though, because the kids, all six of them, gobbled them down at top speed!

Makes about 40 buns

Choux pastry

100 g unsalted butter, diced

1 teaspoon caster sugar

a large pinch of salt

270 ml water

120 g plain flour

4 eggs, beaten

corn oil for greasing

To serve

250 ml double or whipping
   cream

1 dessertspoon caster or
   vanilla sugar

125 g good-quality dark
   chocolate (at least 75
   percent cocoa solids),
   broken into pieces

1. Place the butter into a saucepan, add the caster sugar, salt and water and bring to the boil. As soon as the butter has melted and the water begins to froth and bubble, take the pan off the stove. Tip in the flour and stir and beat the mixture on the stove, until it forms a ball that comes clean away from the sides of the pan.

2. Take the pan off the stove, scrape all the dough into a mixer or food processor and start to beat it with a plastic cutter on a slow speed. Gradually add the eggs to the mixture, with the machine still turning, until they are completely worked in and you have a smooth and glossy paste. Stop the machine and, using a spatula, turn the choux dough out into a bowl.

3. Preheat the oven to 220°C/425°F/Gas 7. Whip the cream in a bowl with the sugar until firm, cover the bowl with clingfilm and put in the refrigerator until needed.

4. Fill a piping bag fitted with a 1cm nozzle with the choux paste and pipe small, round balls each 2 cm wide and 1.5cm high onto a lightly greased baking sheet, leaving 4cm between each bun. Put the choux buns into the preheated oven and bake for about 25 minutes. They should expand at least three times in size and be light, airy and just golden in colour. Remove from the oven and baking sheet, and place on a rack to cool.

5. Meanwhile, place the chocolate pieces in a bowl over a pan of water that is just below the boil, and gently melt, stirring occasionally.

6. Make a small hole in the side of each choux bun with a sharp knife. Fill another piping bag with the whipped cream and pipe it into the buns one by one. Dip the top of each bun into the melted chocolate and leave for a few minutes to allow the chocolate to set. Serve as soon as you can before the choux pastry becomes soggy.

Spiced Pears

These chutney-like pears are excellent with goat's cheese, but are also good as a condiment for game terrines and home-cooked hams. You can substitute the pears with apples, or quince makes an excellent alternative when available. Pears cooked this way will keep for a week.

Serves 12

3 LARGE, RIPE WILLIAMS PEARS
250 ML RUBY PORT
250 ML RED WINE
$^1/_2$ GARLIC CLOVE, PEELED
I SPRIG FRESH THYME
I STAR ANISE
$^1/_2$ CINNAMON STICK
I TEASPOON BLACK
  PEPPERCORNS, CRUSHED
I CLOVE
250 G CASTER SUGAR
250 ML WATER

1. Peel, halve and core the pears.

2. Pour the port into a saucepan, bring to the boil and reduce until sticky and syrupy in texture. Add the red wine, garlic and all the spices and herbs, and boil to reduce the liquid by half. Add the sugar and water, bring the liquid to the boil, then remove from the stove to allow to cool and let all the flavours infuse the syrup.

3. Place the pear halves into the cooled syrup, put the pan back on the stove and poach for about 4 minutes until the pears are tender. Remove from the heat and allow the fruit to cool in the syrup. Store in the refrigerator in sterilised jars with good seals.

4. As you need to use a pear, take one half out, dice it, place in a bowl and cover with some of the syrup. This will serve 2 as an accompaniment to other dishes (see above).

WALNUT BREAD

Everybody knows French cheeses are the best, and the French love to eat their cheese with bread as opposed to biscuits. My favourite is walnut bread.

Makes 2 large sticks

750 G STRONG WHITE BREAD
  FLOUR
200 G GRANARY FLOUR
50 G BRAN
25 G FRESH YEAST
I TABLESPOON CLEAR HONEY
I TEASPOON SALT
2 TABLESPOONS WALNUT OIL,
  PLUS EXTRA FOR GREASING
  AND SPRINKLING
300 G SHELLED WALNUTS,
  CHOPPED
600 ML LUKEWARM WATER
PLAIN FLOUR FOR DUSTING

1. Mix the flours and the bran together in a bowl. Add the yeast, honey, salt, walnut oil and half the chopped walnuts. Gradually pour in the lukewarm water and mix all the ingredients together into a smooth dough. This will take at least 10 minutes.

2. Turn the dough out onto a work surface dusted with flour, and stretch and knead it for 5 minutes. Roll the dough into a ball, put it back into the bowl, cover with a clean, wet tea-towel and put in a warm place such as an airing cupboard for at least an hour to prove and increase three times in volume.

3. Carefully turn out the dough and mix in the remaining walnuts. Cut the dough in half and mould it into 2 loaves shaped like fat cigars. Place the loaves on a lightly greased baking sheet. Score the tops with a sharp knife and sprinkle over a little more oil. Put in a warm place to prove for a further 30 minutes. Preheat the oven to 230°C/450°F/Gas 8.

4. Bake the bread in the preheated oven for 30 minutes, pouring more oil over the bread halfway through cooking. When risen and golden, take the loaves out of the oven and put them on a rack to cool. Eat the same day, or wrap in clingfilm and store in the refrigerator to keep for 2–3 days.

Brioche

For breakfast I love a slice of brioche toast with some home-made strawberry jam.

Makes 2 large tin loaves or 3 smaller, 18cm fluted brioches

500 G STRONG WHITE FLOUR, PLUS EXTRA FOR DUSTING

5 EGGS

25 ML MILK

10 G SALT

50 G CASTER SUGAR

20 G FRESH YEAST, CRUMBLED

350 G UNSALTED BUTTER (FROM BRITTANY IS BEST), DICED, PLUS EXTRA FOR GREASING

1. Sieve the flour into the bowl of a mixer fitted with a flour beater or dough hook attachment. Crack the eggs into another bowl, pour in the milk and add the salt and sugar, then whisk together until completely blended.

2. Set the machine on a low speed and gradually add the egg mixture. Add the yeast and continue mixing for at least another 5 minutes. Piece by piece and very slowly, add the butter to the dough. When completely incorporated into the dough, stop the machine. Remove the bowl and lightly dust the surface of the dough with a little flour. Cover the bowl with clingfilm and refrigerate for at least 12 hours.

3. Dust the top of a work surface with a little flour. Remove the brioche dough from the refrigerator and knead it on the floured surface, turning the dough and stretching it for 10 minutes. Divide the dough into 3 equal parts, roughly 300 g per loaf (or divide into 2 for tin loaves).

4. Lightly grease 3 brioche tins or 2 × 26 × 7cm loaf tins with some butter. Roll the dough pieces and place them in the tins, pressing down. Put the loaves in a warm and draught-free part of the kitchen or your airing cupboard for about 3 hours. During this time the dough will prove and increase at least three times in volume. Preheat the oven to 220°C/425°F/Gas 7.

5. Place the brioches in the oven, allowing about 45–50 minutes for the large loaves, 30–35

minutes for the small ones. The brioche will go
dark in colour and look almost burnt, but this
is normal.

6. Remove the brioches from the oven and turn
    them out onto a rack to cool. Any brioche that
    you cannot use will freeze perfectly well as long
    as the loaf is cold and sealed in clingfilm.

Sum

mer

As we drifted into June, the temperatures soared to 40°C, unusually hot even by Aude standards, and we looked for relief from the blazing sun, seeking out the shadiest parts of the garden. The fields surrounding the house were full of wheat and rape now, and the sunflower shoots were beginning to push through the grass, their heads still curled over shyly.

As I took to the road on that hot, early summer day, I noticed that fields of peas and broccoli had given way to asparagus and acres of white bobbing onion heads, and was full of admiration for the way the farmers had planned their planting, with every scrap of land used to its full advantage, and irrigation systems in place to ensure that all the crops received regular water. It was nearing the end of the asparagus season now, and I was on my way to Puylaurens, where rumour had it that a local vegetable farmer was growing white asparagus in the traditional green way. It's generally white asparagus that's favoured for mass production in the Aude, grown on furrows of sandy soil 45cm high, but this man – a Monsieur Imart – was growing it in furrows of clay soil, only 10cm high, and then not blanching it so that it looked green.

A charming man (I'd been in France long enough to expect no less), Monsieur Imart spent some time showing me his farm, given over exclusively to fruit and vegetables, and his lakes of massive catfish before we got down to business. The asparagus variety he grew was called Cardinal, and it was positively thriving with all this hot weather, he said – growing up to 15cm a day. I was amazed – the asparagus actually did look green. Using a small pointed trowel, he spent hours showing me how to cut it almost at the root, 15cm under the soil. Now I've always been a white asparagus man myself, but Monsieur Imart kept insisting that green was better. 'Take some of mine home, and you'll see I'm right,' he said, handing me armfuls of the stuff as I took my leave. Having the asparagus was perfect as I'd planned that night to make a mousseline – a delicious dip made from sieved boiled egg, double cream and fresh chervil.

It was approaching early evening – the end of a beautiful day – and instead of taking the normal road home, via Revel, I thought I'd take the scenic route, driving cross-country… Call it fate, destiny, or whatever you like, but an hour later, hopelessly lost, I stumbled across the tiny village of Poudis, and somewhere that was to play a huge part in my last three months in France: the Café des Beloteurs. I didn't notice it at first, set back as it was off the road, a nondescript sort of place, with a couple of rusty old tables and an iron bench outside, and not much going on. As I pushed open the door, the noise was deafening, and the clouds of smoke so dense that I could barely make out the room inside. With its ironing board and neat pile of clothes in the corner, it looked just like an ordinary living room – except that it was packed with tables and chairs, all occupied by men who were smoking and drinking lashings of pastis as they played cards. The atmosphere was terrific.

Everything stopped when I walked in, but when I asked if I was anywhere near Montferrand, the locals all roared with laughter. As I stood there, feeling a bit of a prat and wondering what to do, a youthful-looking middle-aged man came up to me, introducing himself as the café owner, Michel Chappert. Yes, of course, he'd set me on the right road, he said, but now that I was there I couldn't possibly leave without having a drink – and learning to play *belote*, one of France's most popular card games. The locals all joined in, and the next thing I knew I was sitting down at a table, pack of cards in hand, surrounded by people giving me orders. The rules seemed fiendishly complicated, but it's amazing what a bit of pastis will do, and three hours later I was a complete expert. I ended up being the last to leave, and although Michel (as he insisted I call him) made me endless cups of coffee to sober me up, he eventually asked a friend who was a local cab driver to take me home.

I got a flea in my ear from Kim that night, and the next morning woke up with an appalling hangover. Incredibly, the next day I went back for more, as Jean-Louis dropped me off at the café so I could pick up my car. I found myself sitting at a table with Michel Chappert again (drinking just coffee this time) as he told me the history of the café. In 1893 the present garage had originally been a forge, he said, owned by his great-grandfather, the local blacksmith (he showed me the open grate, the massive bellows above it, and the old horseshoes nailed to the beams). Another room had been an épicerie (grocery shop); his great-grandfather had been given a licence to run it as a reward for serving in the First World War; he had sold tobacco by the weight in those days, and the old scales were still there to prove it. Michel's grandfather and father had both been blacksmiths, but when his father died in 1958, Michel had set up the café as a 'social club' for people to play belote.

And so it went on… Michel Chappert was one of the most entertaining people I'd ever met, and I almost had to force myself to go. But I finally made it to the car, where I saw the sorry spectacle of Monsieur Imart's green asparagus wilting and drooping in the back seat. I never did find out what

Cardinal asparagus was like and my plans to make that mousseline had to be postponed. But I'd made a new friend, and the Café des Beloteurs became a regular watering-hole, second only to Revel market in terms of regular visits.

The market itself had really come into its own now, as the fantastic fresh summer produce flooded in. The smells of herbs and newly arrived fruits would hit me as I walked into the square – sorrel, chervil, lavender, rosemary, basil, thyme and fresh mint mingling with the sweet heady scent of plump apricots and peaches, and fresh green almonds. Even the most ordinary vegetables had new, exciting versions now: red shallots, tiny white sweet onions, strong red onions with long thin bulbs… Snowy-white aubergines (Madame Bondouy was the only stall-holder to have them) sat alongside their ordinary purple counterparts, and lettuces and salad greens took on all manner of colours and textures with the arrival of frisée, escarole, batavia and feuille de chêne (oak leaf), sold separately, or forming part of the bunches of that wonderful French salad mixture, mesclun. But most of all, it was the fruits that caught my eye – the wonderful varieties of peaches I'd seen when I first arrived almost a year before: the melons, sweet raspberries, pears, plums and – my absolute favourites – cherries.

There was a convent called the Monastère de Prouilhe in Fanjeaux that Kim and I used to pass on the way to Andorra, that had a fantastic cherry orchard in its grounds, and I never tired of looking at it as it changed through the seasons. The fruits on the trees were ripe now, and I'd watched a nun picking them only a few days earlier, marvelling, as always, at how they summed up my ideal of total perfection. Everything about the cherry, it seems to me, is perfect: the spectacular tree, the fine cherrywood, the scented pink blossom that fills the air in spring, and, of course, the fruit itself. Delicious eaten straight from the fridge, and sublime when cooked in desserts or eaten with chocolate, this is one of nature's most wonderful miracles.

And while we're on the subject of perfection, everyone in France knows that the world's best cherries come from the foot of the Pyrenees – Céret, to be precise. This fiercely Catalan town, which, with its *sardana* dances and bullfighting, is in many ways more Spanish than French, produces the world's finest specimens: the Bigarreau Noir, plump, dark and juicy, eaten raw or cooked in desserts with no added sugar, and its white counterpart, the Bigarreau Blanc, used to make jams and preserves, and pickled in vinegar as an accompaniment to duck.

Cherries have been produced in Céret for centuries. For years, in an imaginative example of companion gardening, they were grown alongside the grapes for the local *vin de pays*, in the belief that both plants grew well together. But in the 1990s wine-growers began to complain that their wine was suffering under this arrangement. It was impossible to get a good wine from soil where cherries were grown, they maintained, because all the nutrients from the soil went to the cherries rather than the vines. Today this school of thought still prevails, and cherries have been left to go it alone – a sensible decision, since, with the exception of Banyuls wine, which is highly specialised and sought after, cherry-growing is far more profitable.

One of the main joys of cherry production to me is the fact that it's still carried out on a small, non-intensive scale, which has allowed traditional growing methods to be maintained, without the excessive use of pesticides and the other dangers of mass-production. All this is possible thanks to that admirably enterprising institution underlying so much of France's food and wine production – the cooperative, whereby small growers combine their collective produce and share the profits. I was lucky enough to have been given a contact name at the Céret cooperative some time ago, and seeing the fruit being picked at the convent jogged my memory to follow it up.

So, phone calls and arrangements made, I set off one hot June morning, taking the road to Narbonne, then Perpignan, past lush green countryside with wild poppies growing by the roadside. As I took the right turn onto the D115, the road leading to Céret, the first thing I saw was a roadside stall selling cherries – a reminder, if ever I needed it, that I was on the right road. And then, soon afterwards, I reached the cooperative itself – a huge warehouse-type building with its name emblazoned at the front: '*Cooperative Céret Primeurs*'. The slogan next to it said it all: 'La meilleure cerise de France'. And, as if to prove the point, there they were…crates and crates of these exquisite fruits, so shiny that they looked as if they'd been hand-polished, and almost too perfect to be real. The increase in strong winds

blowing from the Jura had led to a decline in cherry production over the last few years, I'd heard, with growers seeing their annual crop drop from 10,000 to 7,000 tonnes. But as I watched the vans pulling up and unloading their produce onto the weighing scales, and the queues of people waiting to buy, it was difficult to believe this was anything other than a thriving industry.

OPPOSITE: *Plump, sweet and juicy, Céret cherries at their finest – one of my all-time favourite fruits.*

The person I'd come to see was Jacques Arnaudiés, the president of the cooperative, no less. He wasn't there when I arrived, but I was assured that he was on his way, so I bought a punnet of cherries and sat outside, watching the endless stream of buyers leaving with their huge 3-kg boxes of fruit. I waited and waited. Monsieur Arnaudiés was very busy, the receptionist at the cooperative explained half an hour later, apologetically. He'd had to make another call on the way. That was fine by me. I bought some more cherries.

Ten minutes later, Jacques Arnaudiés finally turned up, and as I watched him slowly get out of his car, I was struck by his appearance. With his sunglasses, gold medallion, cigar and swaggering walk, this short, stocky man looked as if he would have been more at home in the streets of New York than a French country town. He looked like the kind of man who, in certain Italian circles, might have been called *Il capo di tutti capi*, the Boss. This was the Cherry Don himself. As I watched him slowly stroll towards a chap in a pick-up truck – obviously an old acquaintance – I was amazed at how unhurried his pace was. In fact, when he eventually made his way towards me, I realised this was a man for whom the description 'laid-back' had been invented. I couldn't imagine him ever hurrying over anything.

Perhaps he'd taken his cue from the cherry itself, one of the slowest-growing of all fruits. Cherry trees are very long-lived – some can go on for 40 years – but make no mistake about it, they need time to fruit – at least five years, and ten before you get a decent yield. So what with that, and the fact that all the edible, red fruits are hand-picked (only the white ones are picked by machine), cherry-growing is a pretty slow, labour-intensive business.

As Monsieur Arnaudiés took me (slowly) to his office, he apologised for his lateness. Being president of the cooperative was a very stressful business, he said, looking totally relaxed. Constant pressure and worries… A lot of work.

As if on cue, the phone rang. He took the call curtly, and we carried on chatting, the phone ringing every few minutes or so, as he told me about his job. Cherries were in his blood, he said. His family had been producing them for years. In fact, you had to be a producer to stand any chance of being elected as cooperative president, he drawled, in his thick semi-Catalan dialect. Some producers worked as administrators, and once you'd been an administrator for two years, you got to stand for president. It had been a slower process for Jacques. (Why wasn't I surprised at that?) He'd been an administrator for ten years before he was elected. The president just happened to retire, so he got the job. 'Yes, but what do you actually do?' I asked him, puzzled. He looked at me in amazement. 'Why, I take all the decisions for the cooperative, of course.'

And then we talked about the cherries themselves, and he showed me his cherry gauge, used to measure the size of the fruits, which went from 22mm in size to 32mm, though in practice the largest fruits sold were around 28mm. Which was the best? I asked. Well, the 28mm cherry was the most commercial and the most expensive, he replied guardedly. And the most popular with the consumer, I continued. 'Pah! What does the consumer know?' he said. 'The consumer always goes for the biggest fruits, thinking they're the best,' he went on. 'Absolument faux,' he said, thumping the table, and went on, 'The 24mm and 28mm cherries are pure show-offs... They look fantastic, but they're full of water. The best cherries are the small ones – they just have sugar and fruit. Ah, the small Bigarreau Noir, he said. Now, that was a cherry. It was only 22mm wide, but it was delicious, cooked in Clafoutis (a popular baked fruit dessert).

In the 19th century, when the railways arrived, he went on, there was a special train that transported these tiny cherries to Perpignan and Limoges, from where they were sent all over France to make Clafoutis. But that was then, and now that small cherry had disappeared because of lack of demand. Why had that happened? I asked him. 'Les dames, monsieur,' he said, shrugging his shoulders. 'The new generation of women didn't know how to make Clafoutis. C'est tragique.' He seemed positively moved with emotion.

There didn't seem to be much else to say on the subject, so I got up to leave.

His curtness now gone, Monsieur Arnaudiés was generosity itself, insisting that I take one of his crates of cherries and that I went to see one of his family's cherry orchards – just a few kilometres away, he assured me. He would arrange for me to be met by his daughter Caroline. Twenty minutes later there I was, in a spot made in heaven. A magnificent orchard with cherry trees stretching as far as the eye could see – and a fantastic view of the Pyrenees. Caroline pointed out the younger trees, on the high ground. The ones stretching out below were all older, she explained. They'd been planted by her grandparents, and had always been there, ever since she was a child (she was 27 now).

Meeting Monsieur Arnaudiés had given me all kinds of ideas. Maybe the small cherry had gone, I thought, but that needn't stop me making a Clafoutis. I'd just have to use something else instead…mirabelle plums, say. I made a parfait with some of the cherries that night, and the next day prepared the rest for my ultimate indulgent dessert. I made a melted icing sugar and vanilla fondant, dipped some whole cherries (stalk and all) in it and left them to set for a couple of hours. Then I made some tempered bitter chocolate, dipped the fondant cherries in it and left the flavours to mingle. The idea behind this is simple: as the cherries carry on ripening, the sugar in the fondant draws out the juice of the fruit, and the sugar melts into a liquid cherry juice that's held by the seal of the chocolate. It takes about a month for all this to happen, but there's nothing quite like that sensation as you take your first bite: the hard chocolate cracks and those cherry flavours explode in your mouth. A month may seem a long time…but then the cherry is proof positive that the best things in life are worth waiting for.

Mid-June was taken up with school plays and performances, as the build-up to the end of term – the last the children would be spending in their French schools. First was the Montferrand school play for Charles, Eliza and Millie, which Kim and I had really been looking forward to, though it was unfortunately rather spoilt by the conditions we had to watch it in. The outside temperature was still scorching, and the play was held in the tiny town hall, which, with its blacked-out windows and closed doors, felt like a sealed oven – not helped by the fact that more than 100 people were crammed in there for an hour and a half. The play, based on the theme of *liberté* was a curious but interesting mixture of dance and mime, where the children all wore black shorts and white T-shirts. I'm not sure how much they – or me for that matter – understood about it, but they were, of course, brilliant, though by the end Kim and I were wilting from the heat and went straight for the ice-cold champagne as soon as we got home.

A week later, we were at Olivia's school, in a hall adjoining the church in Revel, where she sang a solo – not in French, as you might expect, but in Spanish. It was fantastic – Kim and I were bursting with pride. She did so well that her music teacher awarded her the music prize and congratulated her in front of the whole school. This will give you some idea of how well she'd settled into French life. It would be especially hard for Olivia, I knew, when we had to leave.

I was painfully aware that we were nearing the end of our stay now and couldn't bear to think about it, so, in typical ostrich-fashion, I stuck my head firmly in the sand and pretended it just wasn't going to happen. The only thing to do was to enjoy the rest of our time here…the fishing trips with Michel Chappert and Monsieur Roche (they were old pals, it turned out), the dinners with our friends, the drinking sessions at the Café des Beloteurs, and sitting in cafés with Kim and the children, watching the world go by.

It was hotter than ever now, and *midi*, that mysterious time of the day when the shops closed for lunch, really took hold, with everything coming to a total standstill. Just a few days before, I had stood impatiently outside a grocer's shop well past the normal re-opening time and a local – an old man – walked past, looking at me sympathetically. 'Patience, monsieur. They will open one day.' How was I ever going to get used to England again?

In the hot summer weather, outdoor eating became the order of the day, and we grazed on light meals and salads. In an attempt to find more imaginative alternatives, my mind turned to light, flavoursome dips and spreads, such as tapenade – the popular French green or black, olive-based paste, that has now found its way to British shores – and its lesser known anchovy equivalents, Anchoïade and crème d'anchois, spread on a hunk of Barth's finest bread. Anchovies are a big thing in France, but have never quite caught on in the

same way in the UK. Although these small fish are essential ingredients of popular British institutions, such as Worcestershire sauce and Gentleman's Relish, many Brits find them too salty, and tend to avoid them other than as an occasional ingredient in pizzas – a shame, because to my mind this sadly underrated fish has a lot going for it. Used correctly, it can add just the right touch of zest and piquancy to a wide range of casseroles and sauces, and in a Pissaladière or a good salade niçoise, can be a taste of pure summer.

What I'm talking about here is, of course, the preserved anchovy – filleted and canned in olive oil or brine, the way most of us know it. Sadly, the fresh anchovy is a rare sight in British fishmongers, and most people in the UK probably don't even know what it looks like. Well, just for the record, it's a smallish fish, 20cm long at the most, silvery blue in colour, and, like the sardine, is a member of the herring family. It looks rather like the sardine, in fact, although when it comes to taste, it's far superior. Less greasy, with a subtle, delicate flavour, the fresh anchovy is a truly wonderful thing – absolutely heavenly when grilled or fried with olive oil and herbs.

Working on my Anchoïade and Pissaladière recipes for the book had re-awakened my memories of that taste. France has always been a good source of fresh anchovies, and I suddenly felt overwhelmed with a desire to find and eat them again. And, it seemed to me, there was only one place to go: Collioure, the fishing village on the French Catalan coast that's traditionally known as 'the anchovy capital of France'.

Anchovies are not Collioure's only claim to fame, of course. In the 1950s this delightfully picturesque village, with its old fishermen's houses and pretty harbour, was a magnet to Fauvist painters, such as Matisse, who went in droves, attracted by the quality of the light and the charms of the Mediterranean. I had fallen in love with it myself on a brief visit more than 15 years ago, and was curious to see if it was as I remembered, so I hopped in the car and set off.

As I took the road to Perpignan, then down to the Côte Vermeille, the heady scent of the rosemary and lavender bushes by the roadside and the palm trees waving in the breeze told me I could only be in the Mediterranean. I passed some terraced vineyards of Banyuls wine on the hillsides, and a few twisty roads later saw the bright orange roofs of the white-painted houses of Banyuls-sur-Mer and the deep blue Med, shimmering in the sunlight. It was great to be by the sea again and I became excited at the thought of eating freshly caught fish. In fact, my excitement began running away with me. Maybe I'd get to talk to an anchovy fisherman. And maybe, just maybe, if I was really lucky, he'd take me out in his boat.

Seeing Collioure again not only lived up to my memories, but exceeded them. The pink- and yellow-washed houses looked brighter than ever, the harbour even more picturesque, and the sea even bluer and more inviting than I had remembered. But when it came to the fresh anchovies, it seemed that I'd missed them. By more than 50 years, to be precise. For although 'Collioure anchovies' are still served in restaurants here, the truth is that the fresh fish are much more likely to be caught in the next village along, Port Vendre, while Collioure itself is more associated with the preserved variety. Anchovy preserving is more important here than virtually anywhere else in France, though even this has declined in the last decade or so. There was a time when this lovely village had about 100 salting and canning factories, but now there are only three of note, of which the most famous, and most visibly prominent, is *Anchois Roque*.

I was a bit disappointed about the fresh anchovies, but now that I was in Collioure, I could hardly leave without paying Monsieur Roque a visit. So, after asking directions from a helpful assistant in one of his shops, I made my way to his factory on the outskirts of the village. The minute I walked in, I was struck by an unmistakable whiff of anchovies, though the staff, obviously used to it, were totally unfazed. A charming woman ushered me into Monsieur Roque's office while she went to fetch him, and, as I sat there waiting, I noticed the advertising posters on the wall – 'Anchois Roque: Saleur à Collioure depuis 1870'. This was very reassuring – I'd clearly walked into an old-established company where things were done in the traditional way. I was looking forward to meeting Monsieur Roque, and feeling totally relaxed – even the anchovy smell didn't seem quite as bad.

But just as the thought came, it instantly went, and the smell became overwhelming – far worse than when I'd first walked in. And then I heard the door close behind me and realised why. There, in all his glory, was Monsieur Léon Roque, wearing a white plastic gown, cap and mask, and white wellies, and looking for all the world as if he'd just walked out of an operating theatre. Spotlessly clean, he had obviously scrubbed up, but that smell of anchovies had evidently been just too much to contend with.

We settled down for a chat and he confirmed what I'd already suspected – that anchovy production was going down, not just in Collioure, but everywhere. The problem was over-fishing, he explained, which had made these tiny fish so scarce that their prices had shot up. In fact, anchovies were so highly prized these days that they had become like caviar. Of course, in the old days things were very different, he went on. At the turn of the 20th century, anchovy fishing had been huge – all around the Catalan coast in the

OPPOSITE: *Anchovies from the region of Collioure. Delicious grilled or fried with the simple addition of olive oil and herbs, the fresh fish are an all-too-rare sight these days.*

Mediterranean, and in the Atlantic too. In his grandfather's day, there had been more than 100 Catalan fishing boats in Collioure alone, but now the few remaining anchovies left were caught by the fishermen at Port Vendre using two main methods – the *opéragique*, where two boats pull a net between them that catches the fish, and the *lamparo*, where a lamp is carried on the end of the boat, with a net underneath. Anchovies love heat and sunlight, he said, and are instantly drawn to the lit lamp.

The fishing season was a fairly short one – May and June at its peak – but Léon was quick to point out that he got the lion's share of the fish. 'How come?' I asked. 'It's all a matter of contacts,' he said slyly. He knew a fisherman with whom he had a special deal, and negotiated a price before the man even set out to sea. Once he received the fish, his real work started. And he took me through the process.

The anchovies, kept in ice, are brought straight to his factory, where they are packed in sea salt within 12 hours of being caught – the true mark of the Collioure anchovy, Léon explained. They are left like this for a few days, then they are gutted and their heads removed, all by hand. Next they are packed in layers of salt in huge 20-kg barrels for 100 days. The high levels of salt really dry out the anchovies, making the grease float to the surface. Once this has happened, they're rinsed in washes of cold water to remove the salt.

It was at this point that he offered to show me around. Within minutes, I'd donned plastic gown, overshoes and cap, and was following him everywhere – feeling a bit of a twerp – but also impressed at the professionalism and hygiene of the set-up. This wonderfully patient man showed me all around his factory, and I saw everything, stage by stage, right up to the point where the anchovies were cleaned. Mesmerised, I watched rows of plastic-gowned women filleting the fish by hand. They were such neat fillets that I could see this was a true skill that came with years of practice.

The fillets were placed on absorbent paper, and some were salted and packed into jars, while others were set aside for canning. And then, the crucial stage of adding the oil. Olive oil, I assumed – wrongly. Non, non, Léon said emphatically. Olive oil is what they add in Spain, but it is too strong. Sunflower

oil is a much better combination for anchovies. This was the *façon Collioure*.

Léon Roque's thriving little business shifts 250 tonnes of anchovies a year – some exported to New York, Switzerland, Germany, the UK and Belgium, though most are sent just down the road to the Costa Brava, in Spanish Catalonia. I suddenly remembered a type of anchovy I'd had in Spain, called a *boqueron* – marinated in salt, I seemed to recall. 'Ah, oui, boquerones,' he said knowledgeably. He had his own version marinated in wine vinegar, called Roquerones (he beamed proudly at the pun), plus his own stuffed olives, anchoïade (anchovies, oil, tomato purée and garlic), and crème d'anchois (a paste made from butter, garlic, almonds and oil).

This was all fantastic, as far as it went, but talking to Monsieur Roque had made me keener than ever to find out about traditional fishing, and Léon gave me the name of a fisherman in Port Vendre who might be able to help…

My venture into sea-water fishing finally materialised a few weeks later, though not in Port Vendre, as it happened, but further up the coast in

BELOW: Mon Plaisir, *the grandly named fisherman's shack near Gruissan, where I spent three days and nights with the local fishermen. Not exactly the Ritz, perhaps, but a vivid reminder of three very special days in my life.*

Gruissan, a fishing village in the Golfe de Lion, where traditional fishing methods have been practised for centuries. The method I tried is called *caluche* – a back-breaking form of shallow-water fishing, whereby several fishermen are connected to each other and a net, which is in turn connected, in a horsehoe shape, to a series of anchor buoys strategically placed about 500 metres out to sea. The fishermen, connected to each other by a series of belts and ropes, then walk backwards, away from the sea. The secret, as I discovered, was to lean back as you walked, letting your calf and lower back muscles do all the work. Punishing stuff.

My companions were six short, stocky and weather-beaten fishermen, who were about as tough – and kind – as it gets. On the first day we went out we caught two red mullets and a plaice – not much to get back for nearly two hours'-worth of agonising pain. It was the pain, I decided, that probably made them drink so much, for these guys lived and played hard. Up at six, they were pickled at seven, and drank rough red wine in quantities you and I can only shudder at, but I was impressed by their camaraderie. This was a close brotherhood of men who worked, sweated and laughed together, and I

had the feeling they'd do anything for each other. I spent three days and nights with them, eating and sleeping rough on bunk beds that were as hard as nails, and felt honoured to have had a glimpse of their lives.

One of the highlights of my stay with them was when they took me to their special hide-out – some ramshackle huts on a strange, wild spit of land south of the village, full of wild fennel and garlic, with samphire growing on the shoreline. One shack stood out as being slightly less shabby than the others. Painted duck-egg blue, it had the rather grand name of '*Mon Plaisir*', and it was here that the fishermen cooked their local catch. In fact, it was here that they showed me how to make their speciality: eel *bourride*. I watched, fascinated, as they caught small green crabs, removed their legs, then fried the bodies in hot olive oil till they turned bright orange. They then added about 5kg of peeled and halved potatoes and fried them in the crab-flavoured oil, with handfuls of wild garlic and coarsely chopped wild parsley. Then the eels, caught in the estuary, went in – about 4kg of them, chopped into 8cm pieces – followed by some fresh thyme, a bay leaf, a handful of local sea salt and some crushed black pepper. Finally, the whole thing was covered in water, brought to the boil, then simmered for about an hour.

It tasted fantastic – just the ticket for a cold winter's evening, but very heavy and filling for the summer. I wanted some cold water to wash it down, and in my middle-class, namby way (I should have known better) asked for a bottle of mineral water – only to be met with a look of utter disbelief. One of the fishermen, Jacques, handed me a half-empty bottle of red wine, saying his doctor had advised him not to drink water because it corroded the system. There was no answer to that. I took a swig of the wine.

Caluche had its heyday in the 1930s, but at the time of writing, is in the throes of being banned by the European parliament on the grounds that it's destroying the sea bed. I don't understand the whys and wherefores of this, but it seems tragic that these fishermen, who are just trying to scratch a simple living from the sea, should lose their livelihoods. They were wonderful guys, who for three days had been willing to share their lives with me, and I'll never forget them.

The middle of July brought the highlight of our summer family fun, with the village *pétanque* tournament at Poudis – an annual affair taken seriously by the locals, and in which, needless to say, Michel Chappert played a leading part.

If ever there were a national game that crossed all French class barriers, it's *pétanque*, which is played in just about every square in France. Allegedly originating in Marseilles in 1900, its name is said to come from *pieds tanques*, meaning 'still feet' – a reference to the fact that players cannot move their feet within a defined circle while playing the game. Volumes have been written about the rules, but the aim of the game, basically, is to throw the *boule* as near as you can to the jack, preferably eliminating your opponent's chances by knocking his *boule* out of the way. The game works on a points system, with the first team to win 13 points being declared the winner.

The sideboard in the Café des Beloteurs was packed with the gleaming cups and trophies of past winners, and, sitting alongside them, was the ultimate booby prize – a large tile bearing a copy of an early 20th-century illustration of 'Fanny', a lady of dubious repute shown bending down to pick up some boules, with her bottom – a huge expanse of pink flesh – exposed, and two men leering at her. What possible relevance could this have to *pétanque*? I hear you ask. Well, the relevance is that the losers of the competition – the team that wins zero points – has to kiss the tile, at the precise point where Fanny's bottom appears – a quaint custom known as 'Embrasser le derrière de Fanny'. And for anyone who thinks the tone of this book has totally degenerated, all I can say is that you can blame it all on the French 19th-century writer and film-maker Marcel Pagnol, best-known for writing the stories on which the films *Jean de Florette* and *Manon des Sources* were based. Fanny was inspired by a character in his films, apparently, and Pagnol, a fanatical *pétanque* player in Marseilles, invented the custom, though Michel Chappert was, admittedly, rather hazy on how exactly it had happened. There must have been about 80 people at the tournament that day, and we were playing in teams of two: Kim and Lesley were in one team against two other women, Eve and Tatjana in another against two young French guys, and Michel Calvet and I had been teamed up against a couple in their seventies – something I couldn't help feeling relieved at, seeing as I was a complete novice at the game. As we started playing, I couldn't help smirking with confidence. This was going to be a doddle. But pride comes before a fall, and after the third round, I began to realise the old couple were rather better than I hoped. It was only when we stopped for lunch that Michel and I discovered the ghastly truth: that the old man in the couple had once been the petanque champion of Marseilles. Disaster! This new knowledge clearly required new tactics, but first I had to take care of the food.

This involved grilling vegetables and steaks on the charcoal brazier once used as the forge, easier said than done when you can't regulate the temperature and you have 80 people coming in saying 'slightly rare', 'extra rare', 'not quite rare, more of a medium' all the time. It was all rather fraught, and what with the heat, and the knowledge that Michel and I still hadn't won a single point, I lost my temper with a large woman who came in with a cigarette in her mouth. 'No smoking in the kitchen, please,' I said. 'It's not a kitchen,' she replied huffily. 'It's a forge.' 'It's a kitchen now, thank you very much,' I said, and she walked off muttering about how temperamental cooks were.

There were Raspberry and pine-nut tarts to follow, then it was back to the fray, and I must say it was fascinating to see how different Michel's take on it all was from mine. Once I realised we had no hope of winning, I had started to feel very British about the whole thing. You know, it doesn't matter whether you win or lose, but how you play the game. Michel, by contrast, was very Gallic about it all, demanding the tape measure every five minutes. The tape measure is, of course, *de rigueur* in any *pétanque* game, but Michel was beginning to ask for it even when it was pathetically obvious we didn't have a hope in hell of winning the point. And then, at last, it was all over, and time for the final results. Kim and Lesley lost with a score of 13–6, and Eve and Tatjana to a score of 13–9 (not bad for beginners). And the ultimate losers – you've got it in one: Michel Calvet and I, who managed to lose 13–0. And yes, we had to kiss the tile in front of the whole village. And no, Michel Chappert was never going to let me forget it. It was a great day… I can't remember when we've had so much fun.

I'd been meaning to visit a cheese-maker ever since we'd come to France, but somehow it had never happened. And now, here we were, approaching the end of our stay, and I was starting to panic. Part of the problem had been my determination to find the right kind of cheese-maker: a small, traditional outfit producing cheeses that were really representative of the region – in other words, sheep or goat cheeses, which hold pride of place in the Aude – but finding a set-up that conformed to my ideals hadn't been that easy. It was ironic, then, that when it happened, it was almost by accident.

It was a blisteringly hot day and I was on my way back from Pech-Luna, where I'd called in on Monsieur Douy about some last-minute queries I had on the *gavage* text for the book. As I drove out of the village, my mind was on the book, and I was so distracted that I nearly missed the sign – '*Ferme de Joutet: Fromages de Chèvres*'. I must have driven past it countless times before without noticing it. Excited and curious, I took the turning. Even if I couldn't find out anything about goat-cheese farming, at least I'd be able to buy some cheese for a tasty salad that evening.

It was a short drive to the farm, a small house with a couple of huge barns attached, and a view to die for – poppy-strewn fields stretching ahead, with the snow-capped Pyrenees at the end. It seemed perfect. As the car pulled up, a tall, bearded man came out of the house, introducing himself as the goat farmer, Monsieur Brosse. I wanted to buy some cheese, I explained, but more than that, I wanted to see how goat cheese was made. Monsieur Brosse was totally unfazed, as if it was the sort of question people asked him every day.

If I wanted to see how the milking and cheese-making was done, I'd have to come back early in the morning, he said, 7.30 a.m. – that's when he started, but I could come and see the goats right now. I followed him into the adjoining huge barns filled with straw and goats – 120 of them to be precise. They were beautiful creatures – Alpine chamoix, he said proudly, as he affectionately tickled their chins. It was unusual to find a farmer who so clearly loved his animals

The next day I was back, bright and early, and we started the milking – done by machine now, Monsieur Brosse explained, though it was all done by hand in the old days. Well, of course, once I was there, I had to give it a go, and the next thing I knew I was sitting on a stool with my face inches away from a goat's bottom and two goat's teats in my hand. The first thing that struck me about the whole business was the pong, which I can best describe as being like sitting in the middle of a pile of sweaty socks. As Monsieur Brosse gently talked me through the technique – alternately pulling and squeezing – I eventually got the hang of it, and even got a good rhythm going. The only problem then was aiming the teat so that the milk went into the bucket instead of splashing all over me. After ten minutes I was drenched, and Monsieur Brosse gently suggested that we move onto the machine.

I was impressed by the way he lined up the goats and gently coaxed them one by one to the machine. There were two suction tubes that had to be attached to the udders, but the teats had to be pressed gently before they could be put in place. 'Doucement,' said Monsieur Brosse anxiously, at my first awkward attempt. It took two hours to milk them all (1–3 litres per goat), then Monsieur Brosse talked me through what happened afterwards.

The warm milk taken from the goat is chilled to a temperature of 20°C. A special culture is added, then rennet, and the milk is left to coagulate in a muslin bag. After 24 hours it's transferred to another muslin bag, and the whey is separated out to leave a cottage cheese, or *fromage blanc*. The whole thing is then put into a mould – a tube, in the case of the cheese I made – and salt is added. The cheese is left to mature in a *cave d'affinage* under controlled humidity and a temperature of 12–13°C. And that, basically, is it. The rest, he said, depended on personal choice.

First, you had to decide on the shape, he said (he was particularly proud of his *écu* – a shield shape representing the shield of Castelnaudary), then the type of cheese you wanted. This would vary, depending on how long you left it to ripen: a cheese left for a day would be *frais*, if left for a week, *demi-fait*, and when left for a month, mature, though this would be pretty strong, he warned, pointing to a rather whiffy specimen his wife had just put in the larder. The flavour also depended on the size, he said, because of the way the bacteria affected it. A large cheese would taste more strongly than a small one, because its centre was more thinly spread out and therefore more affected by the bacteria as it hit the air.

It is, of course, bacteria that gives French cheeses their unique flavour – all down to the fact that they are made from unpasteurised, or unsterilised, milk. The selling of unpasteurised products in the UK has long been declared illegal because of the health risks the resulting bacteria pose. But to the French, nothing, but nothing stands in their way of the pursuit of excellence, and when it comes to cheese, I have to agree with them. The pasteurisation versus unpasteurisation debate will no doubt go on for years, but I have yet to find a pasteurised cheese that can compare with the wonderful flavour of, say, a really good Camembert.

Such considerations are, of course, irrelevant to people like Monsieur Brosse, who simply continue to produce cheese in the time-honoured tradition, in the certain knowledge that this is the right and only way. The cheeses I made with his help that day were among the best I'd ever tasted. I took them home that evening, rolled one in crushed red shallots, another in cracked pepper, and saved the rest for our salad. Superb.

It was the middle of August – just a few weeks to go before coming back to England, and it was a time for tying up loose ends. These weeks were tinged with sadness for me, and I spent my days working on the last recipes for the book, and going, with Kim and the children, to endless farewell dinners organised by our friends, Jean-Louis and Marie, Michel Calvet and Lesley, Marie-Christine Combes, and Michel Chappert. It was round about then that I ran into my old friends Claude and Moustique again, and we went back to Monsieur Rive's estate to do some more truffle-hunting, though this time there was an added bonus. When we were done, Claude suggested I might like to visit a garlic farm in Lautrec, now officially designated one of the most beautiful villages in France, and the home of rose pink garlic, a stronger, more pungent variation of its ordinary white relative.

As we drove through this picture-postcard hilltop village, with its ancient windmill, narrow streets and appositely coloured rose-pink, half-timbered houses, bunches of the stuff graced every food-shop window. None of your anaemic, papery-looking bulbs, these, but magnificent fat, grape-like clusters of rose-tinged flavour bombs, ready to explode at the merest touch. I couldn't wait to try one. Not long now, Claude said. We were very nearly at the farm.

Following his directions, we stopped off at a tiny hamlet just outside a village called Le Bertrandié. It all looked pretty unprepossessing as we passed a run-down-looking old barn with cows in it (milk-fed veal is Lautrec's other main claim to fame), then reached another two outbuildings. Was this really it? The garlic farm? We walked into the huge old barn nearest us, and there it was – a small, thriving cottage industry, right before our eyes.

Head of operations was Serge Montels, a 40-something man with a thick thatch of brown hair and strange, bushy eyebrows that met in the middle. Charm personified, he welcomed us in and introduced us to his mother, a woman in her seventies, who sat on a stool individually grading and peeling

BELOW: *Happy memories en famille – one of the last of our many family picnics by the Canal du Midi.*

the garlic heads. On the floor around her were the papery outer skins of the heads she'd worked on, lying like discarded moth's wings. Behind her, piled high in the corner, were boxes of garlic heads – all hand-picked and all waiting their turn to be graded and peeled. Père Montels, meanwhile, was in the other barn, pulling down the last of the drying ropes. It all ran like a smoothly oiled machine. As Mère Montels peeled the heads, she handed them to Serge, who deftly tied the long, stiff stems together in decreasing lengths to make a perfect arrangement that looked almost like a posy. Tied, you notice, not plaited – tying in bunches is a feature of Lautrec garlic.

As I watched Mère Montels at work, Serge was anxious to explain. There were six or seven different types of pink garlic, and the peeling was crucial. Unlike in the white variety, each possible outer layer of these heads was removed in order to reveal the pink translucency of the bulbs inside. Lautrec garlic was particularly delicious eaten raw in salads, he went onto say. It was stronger than white garlic, but you could lessen the pungency by taking out the heart in the middle of each clove. 'Try some,' he said, handing me one of the bulbs. I took a tiny bite and felt my head was going to explode. 'Delicious,' I spluttered back. 'Of course it is,' he said confidently. 'This is no ordinary garlic. It's Lautrec garlic.'

Why Lautrec? According to legend, pink garlic and Lautrec have been

inextricably linked since the Middle Ages, when a Spanish travelling merchant stayed at an inn there. He had no money to pay for his room, the story goes, but instead handed the owner a handful of pink bulbs. The owner planted them, and within no time at all the area was positively covered with the stuff. Today, garlic-growing in Lautrec is strictly regulated and is grown from certified seed sown on specially approved clay and limestone soils. It is so highly regarded that in 1966 it gained the accolade of Label Rouge (Red Label), a kind of garlic Appellation Contrôlée – as special recognition of its superior quality.

The Montels' garlic farm sums up everything I think is wonderful about French cottage industries – individual members of a family all working together, with total commitment and pride in their contribution. And what a contribution! This tiny outfit managed to produce 3 tonnes of garlic per hectare. As we talked about it on the way home, Claude told me he thought the days of these one-man businesses were pretty much numbered, and I felt sad at the thought; meeting these small, traditional food producers was something I'd particularly loved about my stay in the Aude.

The family and I spent the rest of the month savouring all the things we loved best: the restaurants, the picnics by the Canal du Midi, fishing in the Black Mountain, card-playing at the Café des Beloteurs, and enjoying the

many local food and musical festivals that seemed to spontaneously combust at this time of year. Everything suddenly came to life now, and the rural peace was shattered by the sound of bands playing loud music in the squares, watched by young people in cafés drinking ice-cold beers, and elegant-looking women drinking out of long-stemmed glasses full of lilac bubbles – that irresistibly summery combination of the local violet liqueur and Crémant de Limoux, the local sparkling wine.

No book about the Aude would be complete without at least a brief mention of its local wines. For although generally shunned in favour of Burgundy and the Loire, this is an up-and-coming region that has a great deal to offer in terms of both quality and price: Corbières, Malpère, Gaillac, Fitou, Fronton, Rivesaltes, Minervois… The list of well-established names is getting ever-longer, and has recently been enriched with the addition of Cabardès – an innovative wine that beautifully combines the very best of Atlantic and Mediterranean grapes.

It was a Cabardès vineyard that I opted to visit in that last week of my stay – intrigued, I suppose, by the fact that its flagship reds are made from a mixture of four different grapes grown in the same soil – unique in terms of wine-growing. The grapes in question are Merlot and Cabernet (Franc or Sauvignon) from the Atlantic, and Grenache and Shiraz from the Mediterranean – and it is their masterful combination that gives Cabardès its uniquely rounded flavour. Each grape imparts its own subtle nuance to the wine: liquorice (Shiraz), pear (Cabernet), berry (Merlot) and fruit (Grenache), and so finely tuned is the blend that using a dash more of any one of the grapes over the others will dramatically alter its taste.

The vineyard I'd chosen came under the umbrella of the Château Auzias, near the *bastide* (fortified town) of Pennautier. It was called Paretlongue, which in the ancient *langue d'oc* means 'long wall', and, as I approached the entrance, I could see why. There, surrounding the vineyards in a perfect circle, was a long stone wall – built by the Romans, who, along with bringing vines to France thousands of years ago, have also left their mark in many architectural features of the region. I was greeted by the estate manager, Alain Bernard, who showed me around the vineyard as he talked to me about the wine.

In a process unique to Cabardès, each grape variety or *cépage* is picked separately, destalked within ten minutes to prevent oxidation, then left under carefully controlled conditions till, say, the following March, when they are tasted. If the fermentation is then judged to be complete, the separate cépages are then mixed together and left to mature in wooden barrels for between a year and 18 months.

I asked Alain what made a good vintage. It depended partly on the quality of the grape, he said, but there were other factors too – the weather, the soil and, most crucially, when the grapes were picked. That would be fairly soon now, he said, but the timing had to be absolutely right – one week too early or too late could make all the difference. Alain would be spending all his time between now and October studying the maturity of the grapes, weighing them, and measuring their proportions of sugar and acidity. 'How can you tell when they're ready?' I asked. 'When they taste right,' he said cryptically. He always knew exactly when that special moment had come, though he couldn't explain why. This instinctiveness is so much a part of all good wines.

Alain Bernard's perfectionism has clearly paid off, and in 1998 Cabardès – originally dismissed as plonk – won the much-coveted designation of Appellation d'Origine Contrôlée (AOC). AOC qualifications, awarded by the Institut National des Appellations d'Origine Contrôlée, are not easy to get, Alain explained. 'In order for the soil to qualify, you have to prove that you have produced consistently good wines for a period of ten years.' Today Paretlongue has 18 hectares of the AOC wine, and another 40 of vins de pays.

As I looked at the plump red grapes, bursting with flavour, I knew the *vendange* wouldn't be far away. Autumn is the culmination of the year for all wine-growers, second only to spring, which, curiously for Paretlongue, was the time given over to celebrating the harvest, in a festival known in the local *patois* as *Dios à Bol* (literally, 'thanking God for good fortune, or wine'). This was the time, Alain explained, when everyone who'd worked on the land (up to as many as 400 people) came to bring their produce, drink the wine and sing and dance in a celebration of good fortune and nature. As with so many other French people I'd met, nature was crucial to Alain Bernard's philosophy. 'If you work with her,' he said, 'you get so much back. Once you

understand that, you understand everything.' As I thanked him and took my leave, I couldn't help noticing the Paretlongue motto hanging on the wall:
• *Faites de bons produits* (Make good products).
• *Ne trichez jamais sur la qualité* (Never cheat when it comes to quality).
• *Ayez des idées simples et appliquez-les scrupuleusement* (Have simple ideas and carry them out honestly).

I couldn't have summed it up better myself. Alain's words and the motto of his vineyard seemed to me to be a perfect point to end this book, and a great illustration of how, when it comes to food, France wins out. The ingredients are second to none, fruits and vegetables are grown seasonally, and the food is produced with simplicity, commitment and passion. This is a country where cooking is valued, where everyone is proud of their culinary heritage, and where food is not only a constant topic of conversation, but a part of life itself.

As I reach the end of this final chapter, I'm thinking about this year and what it's taught me. I've travelled more than 35,000 miles doing my research, but what I've learnt, it seems to me, is that I've just scratched the surface. If only the book had been longer, or I'd had more time… It's been an exciting, wonderful experience, more rewarding than I could ever have imagined, and one of the things that's impressed me most is the wonderful people – all so giving, friendly and proud of what they do. Like champagne being uncorked, their information, overflowing with effervescence and enthusiasm.

But perhaps the most important thing I've learnt is that food is a process of constant learning. And my passion for it is not only back, but stronger than ever. I'm looking out of the window now, and the sunflowers are out, as they were on the day we arrived. The end of another perfect day – and a journey I'll never forget. I shall miss the old farmhouse, the space and the views, and this precious time I've spent with my family – and right now, as I'm writing these final words, I'm wondering what on earth I'll do when I get back to England.

Plan my next book – that's what.

Summer Recipes

ANCHOÏADE

Anchoïade can be served hot, or at least warm, and used as a fishy dip for *crudités*, but I prefer mine cold and just spread on some thin garlic croûtons.

Serves 8

10 SALTED ANCHOVIES OR 2 X
    50 G TINS ANCHOVIES IN OIL
100 ML OLIVE OIL, PLUS EXTRA
    FOR COATING
1 TABLESPOON RED WINE
    VINEGAR
2 GARLIC CLOVES, PEELED AND
    CHOPPED
PEPPER

1. If you're using anchovies that have been preserved in salt, wash them under cold running water and, with a sharp knife, cut and fillet the fish. Drain well on kitchen paper, then place in a large saucepan. If you are using tinned anchovy fillets, pour the entire content of the tin, oil and all, into the pan.

2. Add the olive oil and vinegar, along with the garlic. Over a low heat, warm but do not boil the anchovies, cooking them very gently for about 15 minutes. Stir occasionally.

3. Season with lots of freshly ground pepper, then pour the contents of the pan into a food processor and chop it to a smooth paste.

4. When the anchoïade is completely smooth, pour it into a preserving jar. Pour a little more oil over it, sealing it from the air, and close the lid – it can be kept like this in the refrigerator for at least a week.

TAPENADE

There are two types of tapenade, one made with black olives and the other with green. I favour the one made with green olives simply because I prefer green olives to black ones! Spread liberal amounts on some croûtons made with dry French bread.

Serves 4

250 G PITTED GREEN OLIVES

100 G FRESHLY GROUND
   ALMONDS

40 G CAPERS, RINSED OR
   DRAINED

10 ANCHOVY FILLETS, RINSED OR
   DRAINED

1 GARLIC CLOVE, PEELED

50 ML OLIVE OIL

PEPPER

1. Put the olives and the ground almonds into a food processor and cut and chop them to a fine paste.

2. Stop the machine and add the capers, anchovy fillets and garlic. Start the machine and chop and blend these into the olive mixture until you have a smooth paste.

3. Mix in the olive oil, then season with pepper to taste.

4. Pour the finished tapenade into a preserving jar. Pour a little more olive oil over the top and store in a refrigerator until required.

BABY ARTICHOKE SALAD

In French regional cooking these artichokes are often stuffed and used as a garnish. My favourites are creamy mushroom duxelles as a garnish for veal, or with baby peas (*à la française*) and little lardons of smoked bacon, as a garnish for lamb.

Serves 4

600 ML COLD WATER

2 LEMONS, HALVED

2 DESSERTSPOONS PLAIN FLOUR

1 BAY LEAF

1 SPRIG FRESH THYME

2 DESSERTSPOONS OLIVE OIL

1 ONION, PEELED AND HALVED

2 GARLIC CLOVES, PEELED

SALT

$^1/_2$ TEASPOON BLACK
    PEPPERCORNS

12 BABY ARTICHOKES

TARRAGON VINAIGRETTE
    (SEE PAGE 296), TO SERVE

1. Pour the cold water into a saucepan and squeeze in the lemon juice, reserving the lemon halves. Whisk in the flour, add the bay leaf and thyme, then stir in the olive oil.

2. Stuff each onion half with a garlic clove and add these to the liquid. Season with salt and the black peppercorns.

3. Bring the liquid (a *blanc* in French) to the boil and then turn down to a gentle simmer.

4. To prepare the artichokes, place one on its side and, using a sharp knife, cut off the stalk at its base, quickly rubbing the base with a squeezed lemon half to prevent discoloration. Halfway down the artichoke, saw horizontally through the leaves nearest the base. Peel off and discard any more outer leaves that can easily be pulled off.

5. Put the artichoke, leafy side down, into the *blanc*. (Any remaining leaves and the fibrous 'choke' can be removed after the cooking process, leaving the heart.) Repeat this process with all the remaining artichokes.

6. Cook for about 15 minutes until tender, then drain. Serve warm or cold with a little vinaigrette, or use as a garnish (see above).

BROAD BEAN RAGOÛT

Broad beans are popular in these parts of France. In fact, about 100 years ago, before the haricot bean came along, broad beans were used to make the first cassoulets. I have had this ragoût on numerous occasions, always cooked a different way. This is the version I prefer. In the traditional recipes goose fat is used, but as this might be hard to get, I have used butter.

Serves 6

2 KG SMALL, YOUNG BROAD
   BEANS IN THE POD

60 G BUTTER

300 G BAYONNE, OR ANY DRIED,
   CURED, RAW HAM, CHOPPED
   INTO LARDONS ½CM THICK,
   2CM LONG

2 BABY WHITE ONIONS (SALAD
   ONIONS ARE BEST), PEELED
   AND FINELY CHOPPED

1 TABLESPOON PLAIN FLOUR

300 ML CHICKEN STOCK (SEE
   PAGE 293)

2 GARLIC CLOVES, PEELED AND
   FINELY CHOPPED

1 SPRIG FRESH THYME

1 BAY LEAF

2–3 SAVORY LEAVES, FINELY
   CHOPPED, OR 1 TABLESPOON
   CHOPPED FLAT-LEAF PARSLEY

SALT AND PEPPER

1 PINCH SUGAR

1. Pod the beans and place them in a bowl, then half fill a large, lidded saucepan with water and place it on the stove to boil. Add the beans and cover with the lid to get the water back up to temperature as quickly as possible. Cook the beans in boiling water for 2 minutes, strain them in a colander and refresh under cold running water. Strain once more and peel off the bitter-tasting outer skins to reveal the bright green kernels underneath.

2. In a large, lidded frying pan, melt the butter over a low heat. Add the ham and cook for about 5 minutes.

3. Add the beans, then the onions and stir in the flour. Pour in the chicken stock and turn up the heat. Stir the ragoût until it comes to the boil and then turn the heat down to a gentle simmer.

4. Add the garlic and herbs, and season with salt, lots of pepper and a pinch of sugar. Cover with the lid and cook for a further 10 minutes.

BEANS À LA BORDELAISE

This dish is known in French as *haricots verts à la bordelaise*. It is an ideal summer dish because, at this time of the year, green French beans are so plentiful, although the recipe works just as well with yellow French beans. Whatever type of bean you are using, select only the finest ones for this dish. In the classic recipe, flour can be used to thicken the sauce, but I find this is not necessary as the egg yolks and cream do the job equally well.

Serves 6

1.25 KG FRENCH BEANS

SALT

2 EGG YOLKS

60 ML RED WINE VINEGAR

90 ML DOUBLE CREAM

50 G UNSALTED BUTTER

1 SMALL GARLIC CLOVE, PEELED
   AND FINELY CHOPPED

1 DESSERTSPOON FRESH PARSLEY,
   CHOPPED

PEPPER

1. Top and tail the beans and remove the 'strings' running down the sides. If the beans are young and tender enough, they will not have any strings.

2. Fill a large, lidded saucepan three-quarters full with water seasoned with a teaspoon of salt and bring to the boil. Add the beans and cover with the lid to bring the water back up to the boil as quickly as possible, then remove the lid. Continue cooking the beans for about 5 minutes or until they are tender but still a little firm (*al dente*).

3. Strain the beans into a colander and cool immediately in cold running water. Strain again and set the beans aside in a bowl while you prepare the sauce.

4. Place the egg yolks in a small bowl and pour in the vinegar. Add the cream and whisk until smooth. Melt the butter in a large shallow pan, then add the garlic and fry briefly. Add the beans, then stir in the sauce until it has thoroughly coated the beans. Sprinkle on the chopped parsley and season with a little salt and lots of pepper. Serve immediately.

POTAGE DE PETITS POIS

With the addition of little poached quail's eggs, this dish makes a complete meal on its own – perfect for lunch. If you are using your own home-grown peas, pick some pea shoots as well, as these can be added to the soup bowls as a tasty garnish.

Serves 4

2 KG FRESH PEAS IN THE POD

50 G UNSALTED BUTTER

I SHALLOT, PEELED AND
  CHOPPED

I GARLIC CLOVE, PEELED AND
  CHOPPED

I SPRIG FRESH THYME

I BAY LEAF

450 ML CHICKEN STOCK (SEE
  PAGE 293)

450 ML MILK

SALT AND PEPPER

JUICE OF ½ LEMON

GARNISH

I TABLESPOON MALT VINEGAR

12 QUAIL'S EGGS

20 G PEA SHOOTS OR PODS
  COOKED IN UNSALTED BUTTER

I DESSERTSPOON WHITE
  TRUFFLE OIL (OPTIONAL)

4 SPRIGS FRESH CHERVIL

1. First shell the peas. Then, melt the butter in a saucepan, add the shallot and garlic, and sweat these in the pan to soften them a little.

2. Stir in the thyme, bay leaf and peas, then pour in the chicken stock and milk. Bring the liquid to the boil as quickly as possible and simmer for about 20 minutes.

3. Pour the mixture into a liquidiser and blend until smooth. Season with salt and pepper and add lemon juice to taste. Strain the soup into another saucepan, bring it to the boil and leave to simmer, while you prepare the garnish.

4. Fill a saucepan with a litre of water, add the vinegar and bring to the boil. With the tip of a small, sharp knife, make a hole in the tip of a quail's egg and carefully break the egg into the water. Repeat the process quickly as possible with the other eggs, keeping the water always just below the boil.

5. As soon as the eggs are set but the yolks are still soft – which takes about 2 minutes – very quickly and gently, using a slotted spoon, remove the eggs from the pan. Place them straight into a bowl of iced water to refresh them and stop them cooking any further.

6. To serve, place 3 poached quail's eggs in the bottom of each warmed soup bowl.

7. Bring the pea soup back up to the boil, add the white truffle oil and blend the soup with a hand blender until light and frothy. Ladle the soup over the quail's eggs. Garnish with the shoots or pods (if using) and chervil. Serve immediately.

A LIGHT VEGETABLE BROTH

Many different ingredients can be added to this classic dish – known in French as *soupe au pistou* – but in my view it should be kept relatively simple.

Serves 8

1 LARGE POTATO, PEELED AND
    DICED (KEPT COVERED IN COLD
    WATER, TO PREVENT
    DISCOLORATION)

1 SMALL FENNEL BULB, TRIMMED
    AND DICED

1 CARROT, PEELED AND DICED

1 CELERY STICK, TRIMMED AND
    DICED

2 SMALL BABY LEEKS, WASHED,
    TRIMMED AND DICED

4 LARGE MUSHROOMS, TRIMMED
    AND DICED

1 COURGETTE, TRIMMED AND
    DICED

SALT AND PEPPER

12 ASPARAGUS SPEARS, TRIMMED
    AND PEELED (SEE PAGE 186)

120 G FRENCH BEANS, TOPPED
    AND TAILED

2 PLUM TOMATOES OR 1 BEEF
    TOMATO

110 G UNSALTED BUTTER

1 SHALLOT, PEELED AND VERY
    FINELY CHOPPED

1 GARLIC CLOVE, PEELED AND
    CRUSHED TO A PASTE

1. First prepare and finely dice the vegetables, from potato to courgette, keeping the vegetables in separate bowls so that you can add them to the pan in order of their cooking times.

2. Place a small saucepan half filled with salted water on the stove to boil. Cook the asparagus spears in the boiling salted water – preferably with the tips out of the water – for about 3 minutes so that they are cooked but still a bit firm (al dente). Strain and refresh these under cold running water, then strain and cut each of the spears in half lengthways. Set aside.

3. Cook the beans until al dente in the asparagus water, then strain them and refresh in cold water. Strain again and dice as for the other vegetables. Blanch the tomatoes for 10 seconds in the same water in order to skin them, then deseed and dice.

4. In a large saucepan, melt the butter over a moderate heat. Add the shallot and garlic and gently fry for 2 minutes without browning them.

5. Strain the potato dice and add them to the pan, stirring from time to time. Add first the fennel dice then, at 1-minute intervals, the carrot, celery, leeks, mushrooms and courgette. Stir the vegetables and cook for 1–2 minutes.

6. Add the chicken stock and bring to the boil as quickly as possible, removing any froth or

1 LITRE CHICKEN STOCK (SEE
    PAGE 293)
4 FRESH BASIL LEAVES
1 SMALL BUNCH FRESH CHIVES,
    FINELY CHOPPED
JUICE OF $\frac{1}{2}$ LEMON
2 EGG YOLKS
150 ML DOUBLE CREAM

sediment that rises to the surface, then turn down
the heat to a gentle simmer.

7. Stir the diced French beans, cooked asparagus
    spears, tomatoes, basil and chives into the soup,
    along with the lemon juice.

8. Pour the egg yolks and cream into a bowl and
    whisk them together until smooth, then season.
    With a whisk, stir the egg yolk and cream
    mixture into the soup. Whisk for about 30
    seconds over a moderate heat, without letting the
    liquid boil. Pour the soup into a terrine and serve.

F R E S H G A R L I C S O U P

A parsley coulis (see page 298), swirled into each soup bowl, will help tone down the garlic.

Serves 8

6 WHOLE GARLIC BULBS

125 G GOOSE FAT OR PORK
  DRIPPING

150 G SMOKED BELLY OF PORK OR
  BACON, FINELY DICED

3 POTATOES, PEELED AND FINELY
  DICED

1 SPRIG FRESH THYME

1 BAY LEAF

2 LITRES CHICKEN STOCK (SEE
  PAGE 293)

4 EGG YOLKS

85 ML OLIVE OIL

SALT AND PEPPER

1. With the palm of your hand, push down on the garlic bulbs, freeing the garlic cloves. Repeat this for all the garlic. Fill a large saucepan with water and bring to the boil on the stove, then tip in the garlic cloves and boil for about 7 minutes. Strain the garlic and, while they are still hot, peel the cloves and place them in a bowl.

2. In another, lidded saucepan, melt the goose fat or pork dripping. Add the garlic cloves and pork or bacon dice (lardons) and fry for about 5 minutes on a gentle heat without browning. Dry the potato dice on kitchen paper and add to the lardons. Cover with the lid and cook for a further 5 minutes, then add the thyme, bay leaf and chicken stock. Bring the soup to the boil, skimming off any scum that rises to the surface, turn down the heat and simmer gently for about 45 minutes.

4. Remove the herbs from the pan, then pour the soup into a liquidiser and blend until smooth. Return it to the pan and leave to simmer gently on a low heat.

5. Place the egg yolks in a bowl, then whisk in the olive oil until the mixture is smooth. Still whisking, gradually pour the eggs into the soup without letting it boil. Season and serve.

GRILLED TURBOT WITH HOLLANDAISE SAUCE

This dish is an excellent one for grilling outside on a barbecue – the smell of the fish cooking will make everyone feel hungry. Make the sauce just before you grill the fish, as it should be served warm. Ask your fishmonger to clean and gut the fish, cutting away the gills.

Serves 8

1 X 3 KG TURBOT

1 QUANTITY HOLLANDAISE SAUCE
   (SEE PAGE 298)

1 DESSERTSPOON EACH OF
   CHOPPED FRESH CHERVIL,
   BLANCHED TARRAGON, CHIVES
   AND FLAT-LEAF PARSLEY

MARINADE

500 ML OLIVE OIL

3 GARLIC CLOVES, PEELED AND
   SLICED

1 LARGE SPRIG FRESH THYME

2 BAY LEAVES

50 G FENNEL STICKS (APPROX.
   1 PACKET) OR 1 DESSERTSPOON
   FENNEL SEEDS

1. Cut the tails off the turbot using sharp fish scissors and snip off the fins on both sides. Wash the fish under cold running water and dry thoroughly with kitchen paper.

2. Put all the marinade ingredients into a roasting tin. Place the fish in the tin, cover with clingfilm and store in the refrigerator overnight.

3. When ready to cook, preheat the grill to its highest setting.

4. Make the Hollandaise sauce (see page 298) and add the fresh chopped herbs. Set the sauce to one side, keeping it warm over a pan of hot water until the fish is ready.

5. Remove the fish from the marinade and grill for about 10 minutes on each side. Good accompaniments to this dish, besides the sauce, are steamed new potatoes in their skins and a curly endive salad.

Sea Bream Baked in Salt with a Chive Butter Sauce

Sea bream can be found all year round in the markets of Provence, but is always at its best in the early summer.

Serves 4

2 RED SEA BREAM, APPROX. 750 G
   EACH

2 KG COARSE SEA SALT

50 G DRIED SEAWEED, SHREDDED
   OR FRESH DILL, CHOPPED
   ROUGHLY

150 G EGG WHITES

To serve

1 QUANTITY BUTTER SAUCE
   (SEE PAGE 296)

1 TABLESPOON CHOPPED FRESH
   CHIVES (OR ANY OTHER FRESH
   HERB) FOR THE MIXED HERBS

1. Preheat the oven to 230°C/450°F/Gas 8.

2. To prepare the sea bream, gut them, cut out the gills, cut off the fins and remove the eyes.

3. In a large bowl, mix the sea salt, seaweed and egg whites together. Place half the aromatic salt in a baking dish, lay the fish on top and cover with the remaining salt. Place in the preheated oven and bake for 20–25 minutes.

4. Meanwhile, make the butter sauce. Just before serving, mix in the chopped chives.

5. One of the best things about this dish is that it can be brought straight to the table and served in front of your dinner guests. The salt will have set hard like a white mountain. Break open the crust in front of your diners, and the salt will pull away the skin of the fish. Divide into portions and place carefully on dinner plates, brushing off as much of the salt as you can and serving with the butter sauce.

SALMON STEAKS GRILLED WITH TARRAGON BUTTER

Ask your fishmonger to cut you 6 steaks, each about 2–3cm thick, from the middle of a large salmon that has already been scaled.

Serves 6

6 SALMON STEAKS, TOTAL
WEIGHT 1.25 KG
100 ML OLIVE OIL
SALT AND PEPPER
JUICE OF 1 LEMON

TARRAGON BUTTER
250 G UNSALTED BUTTER
4 SHALLOTS, PEELED AND VERY
FINELY CHOPPED
1 GARLIC CLOVE, PEELED AND
VERY FINELY CHOPPED
100 ML WHITE WINE VINEGAR
75 G CRÈME FRAÎCHE
JUICE OF $\frac{1}{4}$ LEMON
2 SPRIGS FRESH TARRAGON,
LEAVES PICKED FROM THE
STALKS
SALT AND CAYENNE PEPPER

1. For the tarragon butter, melt a small knob of the butter in a frying pan and add the shallots and garlic. Fry them to soften, without letting them brown. Pour in the vinegar and boil and reduce until it has evaporated. Take the pan off the stove and stir in the crème fraîche. In a mixing bowl, beat the remaining butter until pale and fluffy. Add the lemon juice and the cooled shallot mixture, and continue to beat.

2. In a saucepan of boiling water, blanch the tarragon leaves for 3 minutes, strain, refresh under cold running water, then strain again and squeeze dry in kitchen paper. Chop the tarragon very finely and add to the butter. Season with a little salt and a pinch of cayenne pepper. Refrigerate until ready to use.

3. Preheat the grill to its maximum setting. Lay the salmon steaks out on a baking sheet and sprinkle with a little olive oil. Season with salt and pepper, and place under the grill. After 4 minutes, carefully turn the steaks over, sprinkle with lemon juice, spoon tarragon butter over each, and grill for a further 3 minutes. Remove from the grill, carefully pull away the centre bone of each steak and serve immediately.

CRAWFISH FROM SÈTE

In the Languedoc this dish is almost as well known as Cassoulet. Although it's called *langouste à la Sétoise* in these parts, when I was training it was referred to as *langouste à l'americaine*. In England *langoustes* are what we know as spring lobsters or crawfish.

Serves 6

3 X 800 G LIVE CRAWFISH

100 ML OLIVE OIL

100 ML COGNAC

1 ONION, PEELED AND CHOPPED

1 CARROT, PEELED AND DICED

1 CELERY STICK, DICED

1 SMALL FENNEL BULB, TRIMMED
 AND FINELY DICED

1 RED PEPPER, DESEEDED AND
 FINELY DICED

6 TOMATOES, QUARTERED AND
 DESEEDED

3 GARLIC CLOVES, PEELED AND
 FINELY CHOPPED

2 SPRIGS FRESH THYME

1 BAY LEAF

750 ML WHITE WINE

500 ML FISH STOCK
 (SEE PAGE 294)

75 G UNSALTED BUTTER

1 BEEF STOCK CUBE, CRUMBLED

JUICE OF 1 LEMON

SALT AND CAYENNE PEPPER

1 TEASPOON FRESH PARSLEY,
 FINELY CHOPPED

3 SPRIGS FRESH TARRAGON,
 BLANCHED AND FINELY
 CHOPPED

1. The first thing to do is kill the crawfish. Insert a sharp knife quickly into the air vent of each crawfish to make an incision about 2.5cm deep. Pull the tail from the head. Cut the tail meat into 6 pieces and set aside in a bowl. Cut the heads in half. With a teaspoon, remove any coral or orange roe from inside the heads and keep for the sauce.

2. Heat a large frying pan on the stove until it is very hot, pour in the oil and immediately add the crawfish, heads and all, for maximum flavour. Fry for 2 minutes, then pour in the Cognac and set it alight. The alcohol will stay alight for a few seconds and then the flames will extinguish.

3. Add the vegetables, the tomatoes, garlic, thyme and bay leaf, then pour in the wine. Boil and reduce the wine until it has almost evaporated and the tomato quarters are soft.

4. With a slotted spoon, remove the crawfish, then discard the head shells. Place the crawfish tailpieces in a serving dish.

5. Pour the fish stock into the pan with the vegetables, and boil to reduce the liquid by half.

6. Cut the butter into small pieces and whisk them into the sauce. Stir the stock cube into the sauce. Any roe that you reserved should be stirred in, too, to enrich the sauce.

7. Add the lemon juice. Season with salt and a large
    pinch of cayenne pepper. Sprinkle in the parsley
    and tarragon. Remove the crawfish heads from
    the sauce, then pour the sauce over the crawfish.
    Serve immediately with plain boiled rice and a
    glass of Clairette du Languedoc.

GOAT'S CHEESE SALAD

In this recipe I use *Crottins de Chavignol*, but there are so many small regional goat's cheeses that you can take your pick. I like to use a cheese that is quite fresh and soft rather than dry and mature. It is important to dry the leaves thoroughly after washing them so that they 'take' the vinaigrette; you simply will not taste the oils you are using if the lettuce is wet.

Serves 4

4 X 100 G CROTTINS DE
  CHAVIGNOL OR A SIMILAR
  GOAT'S CHEESE, NOT MORE
  THAN 5 DAYS OLD
I TABLESPOON PLAIN FLOUR
I EGG, BEATEN
150 G FRESH WHITE
  BREADCRUMBS
50 G GROUND ALMONDS
SALT AND FRESHLY GROUND
  BLACK PEPPER
500 ML CORN OIL FOR DEEP-
  FRYING

SALAD AND DRESSING

4 DESSERTSPOONS WALNUT
  VINAIGRETTE (SEE PAGE 295)
4 TEASPOONS ROUGHLY BROKEN,
  SHELLED WALNUTS
50 G MIXED SALAD LEAVES
  (E.G. BATAVIA, OAK LEAF,
  LAMB'S LETTUCE, FRISÉE)
I TEASPOON CHOPPED SHALLOT
I TEASPOON CHOPPED FRESH
  CHIVES

1. Preheat the oven to 180°C/350°F/Gas 4.

2. Have the cheeses ready for coating. Tip the flour into a shallow bowl, and the beaten egg into another. Mix the breadcrumbs, ground almonds and some salt and pepper together in a third bowl.

3. Roll the goat's cheeses one by one in the flour and pat off the excess. Roll them in the egg and straight into the breadcrumbs, pressing these on very firmly.

4. Place the cheeses on a plate and refrigerate them while you prepare the vinaigrette. Mix as described on page 295, then add the walnuts.

5. Wash and pick over the salad leaves.

6. Next cook the goat's cheeses. Place a large saucepan on the stove and fill it one-third full with corn oil. Heat the oil, and when it reaches the correct temperature (170°C/340°F), lower the cheeses in with a slotted spoon and fry them for about 2 minutes, until golden brown.

7. Remove the cheeses from the oil, drain on kitchen paper and lay them on a baking sheet. Place in the preheated oven for a further 3 minutes.

8. Place the salad leaves in a large bowl and sprinkle with the walnut vinaigrette, shallot and chives.

9. Arrange the salad on individual plates, place a cooked goat's cheese alongside and serve immediately. A good garnish is Spiced pears (see page 220).

Pissaladière

Pissaladière is a simple dish from the south of France. It is always a good idea to freeze the leftover dough for future use.

Serves 8–10

650 G STRONG WHITE FLOUR

10 G SALT

12 G FRESH YEAST, FINELY
　CRUMBLED

1 TEASPOON MALT EXTRACT

390 ML LUKEWARM WATER

OLIVE OIL FOR GREASING

TOPPING

6 TABLESPOONS OLIVE OIL

25 G UNSALTED BUTTER

1.25 KG ONIONS, PEELED AND
　FINELY SLICED

3 GARLIC CLOVES, PEELED AND
　FINELY CHOPPED

1 BAY LEAF

3 SPRIGS FRESH THYME

SALT AND PEPPER

1 X 50 G TIN ANCHOVIES

30 SMALL BLACK OLIVES

1. To make the dough, sieve the flour into the bowl of a food mixer fitted with a dough hook attachment and add the salt, yeast and malt extract. Turn the machine onto a low speed and gradually pour in the water. Mix all the ingredients together until smooth. This will take about 5 minutes.

2. Stop the machine and remove the dough from the bowl. Place it on a lightly floured work surface and knead, pulling and stretching it, for about 10 minutes. Place the dough back into the bowl, cover with a clean, damp tea-towel and put it somewhere warm to prove for about $1^{1}/_{2}$ hours. During this time the dough will double in size.

3. Turn the dough out onto a floured surface once again and knead it for a further 5 minutes. Cut off a third and roll it out to about 5mm thick, 22cm wide and 30cm long. Lay it down onto a baking sheet lightly greased with olive oil and refrigerate until the topping is ready.

4. For the topping, heat the olive oil and butter in a large, lidded saucepan. Add the onions and garlic, bay leaf and thyme leaves, and season. Cover with the lid, turn the heat up high and cook for about 15 minutes. Lift the lid, give the onions a good stir and carry on cooking them for a further 10 minutes until they are golden in colour and all the liquid has evaporated. Turn the cooked onions out into a bowl to cool.

5. Preheat the oven to 200°C/400°F/Gas 6. Spread all the onion mix over the bread dough, leaving a strip about 2cm wide around the edges. Arrange the anchovy fillets in a criss-cross pattern over the onions and place the olives in the gaps between the anchovies. Drizzle with the remaining oil and cook the *pissaladière* in the oven for about 20 minutes. Serve hot.

Catalan Guineafowl

This is delicious for a summer dinner party, when it can be made in advance and just reheated.

Serves 8

2 GUINEAFOWL

100 ML OLIVE OIL

2 LARGE ONIONS, PEELED AND
    CHOPPED

2 LARGE CARROTS, PEELED AND
    CHOPPED

1 LEEK, WASHED AND CHOPPED

1 CELERY STICK, TRIMMED AND
    CHOPPED

1 GARLIC CLOVE, PEELED AND
    CHOPPED

2 SPRIGS EACH OF FRESH THYME
    AND OREGANO

1 BAY LEAF

1 SPRIG EACH OF FRESH SAGE
    AND PARSLEY

1 KG TOMATOES, QUARTERED
    AND DESEEDED

330 ML BANYULS WINE

750 ML CHICKEN STOCK, COOKED
    LONGER FOR A STRONGER
    FLAVOUR (SEE PAGE 293)

200 G PARMA HAM, CUT INTO
    SMALL STRIPS (LARDONS)

UNSALTED BUTTER, DICED

JUICE OF 1 LEMON

SALT AND FRESHLY GROUND
    BLACK PEPPER

1. Cut each guineafowl into 8 pieces. In a large frying pan, heat the olive oil. When it is hot, add half the guineafowl pieces and brown them on all sides. Remove to a large, lidded casserole dish and brown the remaining pieces in the same way.

2. Add the vegetables and garlic to the oil in the pan and fry until golden. Add the herbs and continue frying, then add the tomatoes and wine. Stirring continuously, boil to reduce the wine until it has fully evaporated. This takes about 15 minutes. Preheat the oven to 220°C/425°F/Gas 7.

3. When the tomatoes have turned brownish and become a syrupy pulp, pour in the chicken stock and bring to the boil, then carefully pour the contents of the frying pan over the guineafowl in the casserole. Cover with the lid and place it in the oven to cook for about 40 minutes.

4. Next, heat more oil in a frying pan and fry the lardons until crisp. Remove from the pan with a slotted spoon and place on kitchen paper to drain.

5. Remove the dish from the oven and, with the slotted spoon, transfer the guineafowl to a serving dish.

6. Pour the sauce remaining in the casserole through a sieve into a saucepan, pushing it through to capture all the flavour from the vegetables. Bring the sauce to the boil, removing any sediment. Turn down the heat and, piece by piece, add the butter, whisking it to dissolve. Add the lemon juice, then season. Pour the sauce over, sprinkle with the lardons and serve.

FOIE GRAS, HAZELNUT AND APPLE SALAD

Made with fresh Foie gras de canard, this salad is exquisite.

Serves 8

1 X 500 G DUCK FOIE GRAS, CUT
    INTO 8 SLICES 1CM THICK
SALT AND PEPPER

SALAD

4 FIRM APPLES, (E.G. GRANNY
    SMITH), PEELED, CORED AND
    VERY FINELY SLICED
100 ML SUGAR SYRUP
    (SEE PAGE 299)
1 VANILLA POD, SPLIT
90 G SHELLED HAZELNUTS
1 KG YOUNG, FINE FRENCH
    BEANS, TOPPED AND TAILED
2 CELERY STICKS, TRIMMED AND
    CUT INTO FINE MATCHSTICKS
JUICE OF $\frac{1}{4}$ LEMON
1 COFFEESPOON CASTER SUGAR
90 G YELLOW FRISÉE OR CURLY
    ENDIVE
30 G LAMB'S LETTUCE
60 ML HAZELNUT VINAIGRETTE
    (SEE PAGE 295)
1 SHALLOT, PEELED AND FINELY
    CHOPPED

1. Preheat the oven to 220°C/425°F/Gas 7. For the salad, place the apple slices in a large bowl, then bring the sugar syrup to the boil in a saucepan. Scrape the vanilla seeds into the syrup, stir and then pour the syrup over the apple. Leave to cool.

2. Place the hazelnuts on a baking sheet and roast for 10 minutes. Tip onto a clean, dry tea-towel, rub them together to remove the skins, then place in a bowl.

3. Cook the beans in boiling, salted water for 5 minutes, refresh under cold running water, then strain and dry. Put the celery in a bowl, squeeze in the lemon juice and sprinkle in the sugar. Mix together. Then wash, trim and dry the leaves.

4. Put 2 large frying pans on the stove to heat: they must be as hot as possible for frying the foie gras. Place the foie gras slices on a plate and season.

5. Lay out 8 plates about 23cm in diameter. In the middle place the apple to form a circular base. Add half the vinaigrette to the beans, mix and season. Place some beans on top of the apple, with some shallot. Pour the remaining vinaigrette over the leaves and mix. Arrange a few leaves over the beans.

6. Fry the foie gras slices for 2 minutes on one side, then turn them over and fry again for 2 minutes on the other side. Lay pieces of the liver on top of each mound of leaves. Add the hazelnuts to the foie gras fat in the pans. Take the pan off the heat and stir them together. Spoon a couple of dessertspoons of the fat and nuts around the salads. Serve.

POULET BASQUAISE

I first ate this dish in Biarritz, and although it is of Spanish origin, it is quite common in the southern part of France – ideal for the summer. This recipe is quick to prepare and tasty to eat, and is better with rice than potatoes.

Serves 8

2 CHICKENS, APPROX. 1.5 KG EACH

100 ML OLIVE OIL

3 SHALLOTS, PEELED AND
  CHOPPED

3 GARLIC CLOVES, PEELED AND
  CHOPPED

3 RED PEPPERS, DESEEDED AND
  CHOPPED

1 GREEN PEPPER, DESEEDED AND
  CHOPPED

1 LARGE RED CHILLI PEPPER,
  HALVED, DESEEDED AND
  CHOPPED

1 SPRIG FRESH THYME

1 BAY LEAF

250 ML DRY WHITE WINE

150 G TOMATO PURÉE

2 PLUM TOMATOES, SKINNED,
  QUARTERED AND DESEEDED

750 ML CHICKEN STOCK
  (SEE PAGE 293)

100 G PITTED BLACK OLIVES

1. Preheat the oven to 220°C/425°F/Gas 7, then cut each chicken into 8 pieces.

2. In a deep saucepan, heat the olive oil and fry the chicken pieces until golden brown. Remove them from the pan and set aside.

3. Add the shallots, garlic, red, green and chilli peppers to the pan, along with the thyme, bay leaf and white wine. Bring to the boil and reduce by half. Transfer to a casserole.

4. Add the tomato purée and chopped tomatoes to the pan. Pour in the chicken stock, bring the liquid to the boil once again, removing any froth or scum that rises to the surface.

5. Turn the heat down to a gentle simmer, then add the chicken pieces and the black olives. Cover with the lid and place in the preheated oven for 45 minutes. Serve immediately.

TRUFFLED CHICKEN

This makes a deliciously light main course for a summer's day. It is very important to poach the chicken as slowly as possible, for about 2 1/2 hours. Cooked too quickly, the bird will be tough; poached for too short a time, it will be underdone and unsafe to eat.

Serves 4

I X 2–2.5 KG CHICKEN (POULET
   DES LANDES OR CORN-FED)
SALT AND PEPPER
I X 50 G TRUFFLE (BLACK OR
SUMMER TRUFFLE, SEE PAGE 41),
FINELY SLICED
I LARGE CARROT, PEELED
2 CELERY STICKS, TRIMMED
I ONION, PEELED
2 LEEKS, WASHED
I GARLIC CLOVE, PEELED AND
CRUSHED
I SPRIG FRESH THYME
I/2 BAY LEAF
2 SPRIGS FRESH TARRAGON
100 G UNSALTED BUTTER
150 ML TAWNY PORT
150 ML TINNED TRUFFLE JUICE
2 LITRES STRONG CHICKEN
   STOCK,COOKED LONGER FOR
   A STRONGER FLAVOUR
   (SEE PAGE 293)
500 ML DOUBLE CREAM, LIGHTLY
   WHIPPED
LEMON JUICE
GRATED TRUFFLE (OPTIONAL)

1. Season the chicken with salt and pepper, then make cuts in the skin and push the truffle slices between the skin and the flesh of the breast and thighs. Roughly chop the vegetables into large chunks.

2. In a large, lidded casserole dish, fry the garlic along with all the herbs in half of the butter but without browning them. Add the port and truffle juice and boil to reduce the liquid by half, then pour in the chicken stock and bring to the boil again, skimming off any froth or sediment that rises to the surface.

3. Turn down the heat to a gentle simmer and add the chicken to the stock. Cover with the lid and poach for about 2 1/2 hours. Check regularly, to ensure that there is enough stock in the pan during the poaching process. Then remove the chicken and place on a wire rack to cool.

4. Strain the stock through a fine sieve into a saucepan, and boil and reduce it by two-thirds. Dice the remaining butter, add the cream to the sauce and whisk in the butter dice, piece by piece. Add a little lemon juice to taste, plus some grated truffle if using. Turn off the heat and the sauce is ready.

5. Cut the chicken into 4 pieces and place in a serving dish. Cover with the sauce and serve immediately. Seasonal young vegetables go well with this dish – baby carrots, turnips, broad beans or baby leeks – along with pasta or new potatoes and a white Châteauneuf-du-Pape.

CALF'S LIVER WITH PARSLEY AND VINEGAR

Serve this dish for a light summer lunch. A purée of potato and celeriac works well with it, but for the summer a salad is a much lighter accompaniment.

Serves 4

4 SLICES CALF'S LIVER, EACH
   SLICE WEIGHING APPROX. 150 G
SALT AND PEPPER
2 DESSERTSPOONS OLIVE OIL
2 SHALLOTS, PEELED AND FINELY
   CHOPPED
2 GARLIC CLOVES, PEELED AND
   FINELY CHOPPED
4 DESSERTSPOONS RED WINE
   VINEGAR
60 G UNSALTED BUTTER, DICED
4 TABLESPOONS FRESH PARSLEY,
   FINELY CHOPPED

1. Lay the liver slices out on a plate and season with a little salt and lots of black pepper.

2. Heat a large frying pan, pour in the olive oil and, just as it starts to smoke, add the liver. Cook each piece for about 3 minutes on one side and then turn it over and cook for a further 3 minutes. Remove the liver, still just pink inside, to a serving dish.

3. To the same frying pan add the shallots, garlic and red wine vinegar. Bring to the boil and reduce the vinegar by half.

4. Add the butter and, just as it begins to bubble and froth, tip in the parsley. Pour the sauce over the liver and serve immediately with a rocket salad and a few new potatoes. Give your guests a glass each of red Frontonnais, or try a red Gaillac, Cahors or Saint-Chinian.

Strawberry Ice-cream with Strawberry Sauce

In the summer, when red fruits are at their best, ice-cream makes a quick and tasty dessert.

Serves 4

Ice-cream

200 ML FULL-FAT MILK

200 ML DOUBLE CREAM

6 EGG YOLKS

125 G CASTER SUGAR

150 G STRAWBERRIES, WASHED,
   HULLED AND CHOPPED

Strawberry sauce

150 G STRAWBERRIES, WASHED,
   HULLED AND CUT IN HALF

50 G CASTER SUGAR

100 ML WATER

1. Bring the milk and the cream to the boil in a large saucepan, then remove from the heat. Put the egg yolks into a food processor with the sugar and blend until pale in colour. Pour in half the hot milk and cream mixture, then turn off the machine. Pour back into the milk/cream saucepan, return to the heat and, with a whisk, stir until the liquid thickens. Keep stirring and do not boil the liquid or the eggs will scramble and the ice-cream mixture will be ruined.

2. Once the mixture has thickened enough to coat the back of a spoon, remove it from the heat once again. Pour the mixture into an ice-cream machine and churn it for about 20 minutes until on the point of setting, then tip in the strawberries. Churn it for a further 2 minutes and stop the machine. Turn the ice-cream out into a plastic container, cover with an airtight lid and place in the freezer to set completely.

3. To make the strawberry sauce, place the fruit in a saucepan, add the sugar and water and bring to the boil, cooking for 3 minutes. Remove from the heat, pour into a liquidiser and blend until smooth. Pour into a sauceboat to cool, then store in the refrigerator until needed.

4. Take the ice-cream out of the refrigerator 5 minutes before serving and serve 2 scoops per person. Pour on some strawberry sauce and serve.

MIRABELLE CLAFOUTIS

The traditional recipe for *clafoutis* uses cherries, but I prefer to substitute these with little yellow mirabelle plums, which are absolutely delicious when ripe.

Serves 4

PASTRY

60 G UNSALTED BUTTER, PLUS
   EXTRA FOR GREASING

60 G ICING SUGAR

2 EGGS

130 G PLAIN FLOUR, PLUS EXTRA
   FOR DUSTING

CLAFOUTIS FILLING

525 G MIRABELLE PLUMS,
   WASHED, HALVED AND STONED

75 G CASTER SUGAR

250 ML FULL-FAT MILK

1 VANILLA POD, SPLIT

2 EGGS

1 EGG YOLK

15 G PLAIN FLOUR

1. Beat the butter and sugar together in a mixing bowl until pale and fluffy. Beat in the eggs and then gently fold in the flour. Roll the pastry into a ball, wrap in clingfilm and leave to rest in the refrigerator for about an hour. Meanwhile, preheat the oven to 200°C/400°F/Gas 6.

2. On a work surface dusted with flour, roll out the pastry to about 3mm thick. Cut out to fit into 4 x 7cm greased ring moulds. Cover the pastry with some greaseproof paper and dried beans and bake 'blind' in the preheated oven for about 10 minutes or until golden. Remove from the oven to cool and lift out the beans and paper. Turn the oven down to 160°C/325°F/Gas 3.

3. Now for the *clafoutis*. First sprinkle the plums with 25 g of the sugar and lay them, cut side down, in the pastry cases.

4. Pour the milk into a saucepan, add the vanilla pod and bring to the boil. In a bowl, whisk together the remaining sugar and the eggs and egg yolk. Add the flour and beat to a smooth paste. Gradually add the hot milk, stirring continuously. Pour this custard mixture over the plums in the tart cases and bake the tarts in the preheated oven for 35 minutes. They are best served warm.

RASPBERRY AND PINE-KERNEL TART

This is, I suppose, like a French Bakewell tart. The contrast of flavour and texture between the soft raspberries and crunchy pine kernels works really well.

Serves 4

UNSALTED BUTTER FOR
  GREASING

PLAIN FLOUR FOR DUSTING

200 G SWEET SHORTCRUST
  PASTRY (SEE PAGE 300)

FILLING

100 G GROUND ALMONDS

100 G CASTER SUGAR

100 G UNSALTED BUTTER, DICED

3 LARGE EGGS, BEATEN

3 DESSERTSPOONS DARK RUM

100 G RASPBERRIES

100 G PINE KERNELS

1. Grease a 20cm flan tin with butter, then dust with flour, shaking out the excess. Follow steps 1–2 for Sweet Shortcrust Pastry on page 300. Roll out the pastry and use to line the prepared flan tin. Refrigerate until needed.

2. For the filling: place the ground almonds and sugar in a large bowl, and add the diced butter. Beat the mixture to a smooth paste, then gradually add the eggs and rum.

3. Preheat the oven to 200°C/400°F/Gas 6.

4. Take the tart base out of the refrigerator and fill it with the almond mixture. Sprinkle the raspberries and pine kernels evenly over the top, pushing them down into the mixture. Bake in the preheated oven for about 30 minutes.

5. Remove the tart from the oven and allow to cool before cutting it. Serve with vanilla ice-cream.

PEACHES IN SAUTERNE

In summer here in France, the fruit for sale in the open markets is just beautiful. Three types of peach are available: the normal yellow ones (I say 'normal', but they're huge), then white peaches, my favourite, and finally the grey-purple 'blood' peaches (*pêche de vigne*), which I've never seen in England. All the peaches picked for the markets around Montferrand come from Eyrieux, near the chestnut town of Privas. If you love peaches as I do, the least you do to them the better, in my view. Choose only ripe ones and use white peaches, if available, although the yellow ones will do equally well for this recipe.

Serves 8

8 RIPE PEACHES

1 BOTTLE SAUTERNES

500 ML WATER

500 G CASTER SUGAR

2 VANILLA PODS

2 TABLESPOONS EAU DE VIE DE PÊCHE OR A SWEET PEACH LIQUEUR

1. Rinse the peaches under cold water. Bring a saucepan of water to the boil. Gently lower the peaches into the boiling water, then immediately take the pan from the stove. With a slotted spoon, carefully remove the peaches and place in a bowl of iced water to cool.

2. Take the peaches out of the water and place on some kitchen paper. With a sharp knife, peel the fruit. Cut through to the stone and gently twist the peaches in half. Discard the stones and put the peach halves into a large, glass serving bowl. Pour the Sauternes over the fruit.

3. Pour the 500 ml of water into a saucepan and add the sugar and vanilla seeds scraped from the pods. Bring to the boil and remove from the stove. Pour the syrup over the peaches and add the peach liqueur. Allow to cool, then refrigerate.

4. I like to eat these cold straight from the refrigerator and drink some of the syrup with them. You can serve fromage frais with them if you wish.

VANILLA PARFAITS WITH WARM CHERRIES

Cherries can be seen in every French market during the summer. Several varieties are available, but my favourites are the sweet, pointed ones known as *guignes*.

Serves 6

VANILLA PARFAITS

50 G CASTER SUGAR

2 DESSERTSPOONS WATER

3 EGG YOLKS

150 ML DOUBLE CREAM

2 VANILLA PODS, SPLIT

CHERRIES

600 G CHERRIES, WASHED AND
   STONED

50 G CASTER SUGAR

100 ML WATER

20 ML KIRSCH OR SWEET
   CHERRY BRANDY

15 G CORNFLOUR

I DESSERTSPOON ICING SUGAR
   FOR DUSTING

1. Place the sugar and water in a saucepan and bring to the boil. Boil the syrup for 2 minutes to melt the sugar, then remove the pan from the stove. Pour the egg yolks into the bowl of a food mixer with a whisk attachment and whisk. Add the syrup and continue whisking for about 10 minutes until the mixture has thickened and increased by about three times in volume.

2. Pour the cream into a bowl. Scrape the vanilla seeds from the pods into the cream, reserving the pods. Whisk the cream until thick and firm, then fold into the egg mixture. Pour the mixture into 6 × 8cm ramekins, and place these in the freezer for about 4 hours to set.

3. Put the cherries in a saucepan with the reserved vanilla pods. Add the sugar and water and bring to the boil. Turn the heat down to a simmer and cook for a further 5 minutes, removing any froth that rises to the surface. Mix the Kirsch and cornflour to a smooth paste and stir into the cherries. Bring the cherries back to the boil and then turn them out into a bowl. Remove the vanilla pods.

4. Take the parfaits out of the freezer, dip each ramekin in hot water and, using a knife, run the tip around the top of each dish. Turn the parfaits out onto 6 dessert plates. Spoon some of the cherries around the outside of each parfait, placing 2–3 cherries on top. Dust the plates with icing sugar and serve immediately.

Basics

CHICKEN STOCK

Makes 3 litres

2 KG CHICKEN BONES OR WINGS

2 CARROTS, PEELED

2 CELERY STICKS, TRIMMED

1 ONION, PEELED

1 LEEK, HALVED

2 SPRIGS FRESH THYME

1 BAY LEAF

A HANDFUL OF PARSLEY STALKS

2 LARGE GARLIC CLOVES, PEELED

1 TEASPOON WHITE PEPPERCORNS, CRUSHED

1. Put the chicken bones or wings in a large lidded saucepan and cover with cold water. Add the remaining ingredients.

2. Bring to the boil, skimming off any scum that rises to the surface, then cover with the lid and simmer for about 2 hours. Remove from the heat and strain through a sieve, discarding the bones and cooked vegetables.

3. Cool and store in the refrigerator for up to 2 days. If you want a more intense flavour, boil to reduce. Season only when about to use.

BEEF STOCK

Makes about 1 litre

90 ML GROUNDNUT OIL

2 KG GOOD BEEF BONES (SHIN OR LOIN ARE BEST)

2 PIG'S TROTTERS, ROUGHLY 225 G EACH, WASHED
  AND CHOPPED

2 ONIONS, PEELED AND CHOPPED

1 LEEK, WASHED AND CHOPPED

2 CELERY STICKS, WASHED AND CHOPPED

2 CARROTS, PEELED AND CHOPPED

4 GARLIC CLOVES, PEELED

1 BAY LEAF

2 SPRIGS FRESH THYME

2 PARSLEY STALKS

1 TEASPOON CRACKED BLACK PEPPERCORNS

1. Heat a little vegetable oil in a large frying pan and fry the bones. (This is important as it will determine the colour of your stock.) When they are a nice dark brown colour, transfer the bones to a large saucepan or stock pot. Add the pig's trotters, along with the onions, leek, celery, carrots, garlic, herbs and peppercorns.

2. Cover the ingredients with water and bring the stock to the boil. As it comes to the boil, a lot of froth or scum will rise to the surface and this needs to be removed. Turn down the stock to a rapid simmer and cook for at least 4 hours.

3. Remove from the heat and strain the stock first through a colander and then through a sieve. Pour the stock into another saucepan, bring it to the boil once again and reduce it by half. Allow it to cool, then refrigerate for up to 2 days or freeze for future use. Season only when about to use.

FISH STOCK

Makes 1.5 litres

2 KG WHITE FISH BONES AND SKINS
60 ML OLIVE OIL
50 G UNSALTED BUTTER
2 ONIONS, PEELED AND FINELY SLICED
4 GARLIC CLOVES, PEELED AND CHOPPED
1 BAY LEAF

2 SPRIGS FRESH THYME
2 SPRIGS FRESH TARRAGON, BLANCHED
3 PARSLEY STALKS
$^{1}/_{2}$ TEASPOON DRIED FENNEL SEEDS
$^{1}/_{2}$ BOTTLE NOILLY PRAT
350 ML DRY WHITE WINE
350 ML WATER

1. Preheat the oven to 190°C/375°F/Gas 5.

2. Wash the fish bones and skins and strain.

3. In a large casserole heat the olive oil and butter together, and quickly add the onion and garlic. Stir and cook for about 2 minutes, but do not colour.

4. Add all the herbs and spices, then pour in the Noilly Prat. Boil to reduce the liquid until it becomes sticky and syrupy.

5. Add the white wine and boil to reduce by half. Add the bones and cover them with water. Bring the stock to the boil as quickly as possible, skimming off all the surfacing sediment. Cover the stock with greaseproof paper and a lid and place in the oven to cook for 15 minutes.

6. When the fish stock is cooked, remove it from the oven and take off the lid and paper. Strain the stock into a colander with a large bowl underneath to catch the liquid.

7. Pour the stock through a muslin cloth to trap all the sediments: this will ensure a clear fish stock. When cold refrigerate for 2 days or freeze until you need it.

COURT-BOUILLON

Makes 2 litres

1 ONION, PEELED
1 CARROT, PEELED
2 CELERY STICKS, TRIMMED
1 FENNEL BULB, TRIMMED
1 LEEK, WASHED AND TRIMMED
6 GARLIC CLOVES
1 SPRIG FRESH THYME
2 SPRIGS FLAT-LEAF PARSLEY

1 BAY LEAF
1 SPRIG FRESH TARRAGON
1 TEASPOON FENNEL SEEDS
2 STAR ANISE
1 TEASPOON BLACK PEPPERCORNS, CRUSHED
1 BOTTLE DRY WHITE WINE
2 LITRES WATER
SALT

1. Cut the onion into large dice and the carrot, celery, fennel and leek into small dice. There's no need to peel the garlic cloves.

2. Put the diced vegetables, garlic, herbs and spices in a large saucepan, then pour in the white wine and boil to reduce by half.

3. Add the water, bring to the boil and, with a ladle, skim off any fat or scum that rises to the surface. Cook for a further 5 minutes, again skimming if necessary. Turn down the heat and simmer for 10 minutes.

4. Add some salt to taste and remove the *court-bouillon* from the stove to cool. When cold, refrigerate and use within 2 days.

ALMOND AÏOLI

Serves 6

200 G BLANCHED ALMONDS

1 WHOLE HEAD GARLIC, PEELED

25 ML WATER

50 ML OLIVE OIL

1. Crush and chop the blanched almonds together with the peeled garlic to make a smooth and very thick paste.

2. Add the water to thin the paste a little and, stirring continuously, slowly add the olive oil.

3. Pour into a preserving jar, top with a little olive oil to seal it from the air, close the lid and refrigerate. Consume within a week.

AILLADE

Serves 6

150 G BEST-QUALITY DRIED WALNUTS

2 GARLIC CLOVES, PEELED

SALT AND PEPPER

200 ML WALNUT OIL

1 TABLESPOON CHOPPED FRESH PARSLEY

1. In a food processor, combine the walnuts and garlic together to a smooth paste.

2. Add dessertspoons of cold water to thin the paste a little. Process again and add the seasoning. Turn down the machine to the slowest speed and very slowly trickle in the walnut oil as if you were making mayonnaise. Add the chopped parsley and stop the machine.

3. Pour the aillade into a preserving jar, pour a little more walnut oil over the top to seal it from the air, close the lid and refrigerate. Consume within a week.

BASIC VINAIGRETTE

Makes 600ml

1 GARLIC CLOVE

JUICE OF $^{1}/4$ LEMON

120 ML WHITE VINE VINEGAR

A PINCH OF SALT

A PINCH OF SUGAR

BLACK PEPPER

500 ML OLIVE OIL

1. Peel the garlic, chop it in two and place in a bowl.

2. Add the lemon juice, vinegar, salt, sugar and pepper to the bowl.

3. Whisk in the oil.

4. Pour the vinaigrette into a bottle with a lid. It will keep for weeks.

NUT VINAIGRETTE

Makes about 200 ml

50 ML SHERRY VINEGAR

SALT AND PEPPER

CASTER SUGAR

100 ML GROUNDNUT OIL

100 ML NUT OIL (E.G. WALNUT OR HAZELNUT)

$^{1}/2$ GARLIC CLOVE, PEELED AND FINELY CHOPPED

1. Mix the vinegar with some salt, pepper and sugar to taste, then whisk in both the oils.

2. Stir in the garlic. Whisk again before use.

TARRAGON VINAIGRETTE

Makes 300 ml

I GARLIC CLOVE, PEELED AND HALVED

JUICE OF $^{1}/4$ LEMON

60 ML WHITE WINE VINEGAR

SALT AND PEPPER

A PINCH OF CASTER SUGAR

125 ML BEST-QUALITY EXTRA VIRGIN OLIVE OIL

125 ML SUNFLOWER OIL

2 SPRIGS FRESH TARRAGON

1. Put the garlic in a bowl with the lemon juice, vinegar, a pinch of salt, 2–3 turns of black pepper and the sugar.

2. Whisk in both the oils.

3. Using a small funnel, pour the vinaigrette, including the garlic, into a suitably sized bottle. Add the tarragon and seal with a lid or cork. Shake the bottle thoroughly before use.

BUTTER SAUCE

Serves 4–6

250 G UNSALTED BUTTER

2 SHALLOTS, PEELED AND CHOPPED

I GARLIC CLOVE, PEELED AND CHOPPED

I SPRIG FRESH THYME

$^{1}/2$ BAY LEAF

I SPRIG FRESH TARRAGON

2 TABLESPOONS WHITE WINE VINEGAR

75 ML DRY WHITE WINE

4 TABLESPOONS DOUBLE CREAM

JUICE OF $^{1}/4$ LEMON

SALT AND PEPPER

1. In a saucepan, melt about 25 g of the butter and add the chopped shallots and garlic, the thyme, bay leaf and tarragon. Fry the ingredients for about 3 minutes but without browning them.

2. Add the vinegar, bring to the boil and reduce the liquid until it has almost evaporated, then add the white wine, and boil and reduce until syrupy. Pour in the cream and bring to the boil once again.

3. Dice the remaining butter and, while the sauce is still boiling, whisk in the butter, piece by piece, until it has completely dissolved.

4. Add the lemon juice, and season with salt and pepper. Heat the sauce to the point of boiling, whisking all the time, then strain into another saucepan. At this stage, you may add some chopped fresh herbs if you wish.

GRIBICHE SAUCE

Serves 6

I TEASPOON CASTER SUGAR

I TABLESPOON WATER

I TABLESPOON TARRAGON VINEGAR

3 EGG YOLKS

I TEASPOON DIJON MUSTARD

125 ML OLIVE OIL

125 ML SUNFLOWER OIL

JUICE OF $^{1}/4$ LEMON

I DESSERTSPOON FINELY CHOPPED FLAT-LEAF
    PARSLEY,

25 G CAPERS, RINSED AND FINELY CHOPPED

25 G GHERKINS, RINSED AND FINELY CHOPPED

SALT AND PEPPER

1. Put the sugar, water and vinegar into a small saucepan and bring to the boil, just to melt the sugar, then take the pan off the stove. Add the egg yolks and mustard to the pan and whisk to a smooth consistency.

2. Mix both the oils together, making sure they are at room temperature. (Cold oil will 'split' or curdle the sauce.) Very carefully pour a little of the oil into the sauce base and, with a whisk, beat and mix in the oil vigorously. Continue this process until half the oil is incorporated into the sauce, which should now be quite thick. Thin it by adding a little hot water from the kettle and then continue whisking in the remaining oil.

3. Squeeze in the lemon juice and add the parsley, capers and gherkins. Season with salt and pepper, then pour into a sauceboat for immediate use.

MAYONNAISE

Makes about 300 ml
2 EGG YOLKS
30 G DIJON MUSTARD
60 ML TARRAGON VINEGAR
20 G CASTER SUGAR

150 ML OLIVE OR SUNFLOWER OIL
150 ML GROUNDNUT OR VEGETABLE OIL
SALT AND PEPPER TO TASTE
LEMON JUICE

1. Pour the egg yolks into a thick glass or stainless-steel bowl and add the mustard.

2. Pour the vinegar into a small saucepan, add the sugar, and boil to reduce the liquid until it becomes syrupy. Remove the pan from the stove and set aside to cool.

3. Mix the two oils together and very slowly trickle them into the egg yolks, whisking vigorously all the while.

4. Once half the oil has been added to the yolks, pour in the syrupy vinegar. Still whisking all the time, slowly pour in the remainder of the oil. Season with salt and pepper and some lemon juice to taste.

BÉCHAMEL SAUCE

Serves about 4
1/4 BAY LEAF
I CLOVE
I SMALL ONION, PEELED
450 ML MILK

A PINCH OF FRESHLY GRATED NUTMEG
60 G UNSALTED BUTTER, PLUS A LITTLE EXTRA
       FOR LATER
60 G PLAIN FLOUR

1. Press the clove into the peeled onion and place in a small saucepan, along with the bay leaf and milk. Add the nutmeg and bring to the boil, then turn the heat down to a gentle simmer.

2. Meanwhile, in another saucepan, melt the butter, then stir in the flour. Mix this roux together thoroughly until it starts to go brown.

3. Gradually, a little at a time, stir in the hot, aromatic milk, straining out the onion as you do so through a fine sieve. Cook the sauce over a very low heat for about half an hour.

4. Strain the sauce through a fine sieve into a bowl. To prevent the sauce from forming a skin, if not using immediately, place a little piece of cold butter on top of the hot sauce.

Hollandaise Sauce

Serves 8

30 G UNSALTED BUTTER

2 SHALLOTS, PEELED AND FINELY CHOPPED

I GARLIC CLOVE, PEELED AND FINELY CHOPPED

I TEASPOON BLACK PEPPERCORNS, CRACKED

2 SPRIGS FRESH TARRAGON

I SPRIG FRESH THYME

I BAY LEAF

2 PARSLEY STALKS

40 ML WHITE WINE VINEGAR

40 ML DRY WHITE WINE

3 EGG YOLKS

I DESSERTSPOON COLD WATER

250 ML WARM CLARIFIED BUTTER

  (SEE BELOW)

SALT AND PEPPER

1. Melt the butter in a saucepan, then add the shallots, garlic, peppercorns and herbs. Be careful not to let the shallots go brown or burn.

2. Pour in the white wine vinegar, and boil and reduce until it has completely evaporated. Add the wine and again boil and reduce the liquid until it becomes syrupy. Remove the pan from the stove and lift out the herbs with a slotted spoon.

3. Put a saucepan of water on the stove to boil. Pour the egg yolks into a bowl that will fit over the saucepan, add the cold water and whisk the yolks over the hot water until they thicken into soft peaks.

4. Gradually pour in the warm clarified butter, whisking all the time until a smooth sauce is obtained. Now add the reduced wine sauce to the yolk and butter mixture, and beat vigorously over the hot water. Season with salt and pepper and a little lemon juice. The sauce is ready, and you should serve it while it is still warm. If making a Béarnaise sauce, add the herbs just before serving.

Clarified Butter

Makes 250 ml

500 G (2 PACKETS) GOOD-QUALITY

  UNSALTED BUTTER

1. Cut the butter into pieces and gently melt in a saucepan. With a ladle, remove any scum or froth that rises to the surface.

2. Very carefully pour off the clear, golden liquid, leaving the sediment at the bottom of the pan. Discard this. Allow the clarified butter to set and use as needed.

Parsley Coulis

Serves 8

200 G FLAT-LEAF PARSLEY, WASHED AND LEAVES

  PICKED FROM THE STALKS

250 ML HOT CHICKEN STOCK (SEE PAGE 293)

50 G UNSALTED BUTTER

SALT AND WHITE PEPPER

1. Bring a large saucepan of water to the boil, add the parsley leaves and boil for 5 minutes or until tender.

2. Strain the parsley then place in a liquidiser with the hot chicken stock and the butter, a pinch of salt and a few turns of white pepper. Blend the parsley to a fine purée, like a dark green sauce.

3. If garnishing soup, carefully swirl the purée with a dessertspoon garnishing from the middle and making a spiral outwards from the centre.

CRÈME PÂTISSIÈRE

Makes about 800 g

1 VANILLA POD
600 ML MILK

6 EGG YOLKS
120 G CASTER SUGAR
60 G PLAIN FLOUR, SIEVED

1. Split the vanilla pod, place it in a saucepan, cover with the milk and bring to the boil.

2. Put the egg yolks and sugar into the bowl of a food processor. Whisk them together until they go pale in colour, then whisk in the flour.

3. As the milk comes to the boil, pour half of it into the food processor as it whisks the egg mixture. Stop the machine and pour the mixture into the remaining milk in the saucepan on the stove.

4. Heat up again, stirring as quickly as possible all the time and trying not to let the liquid boil, as you don't want to cook the egg yolks.

5. When the mixture has thickened, pour and scrape it into a bowl using a plastic spatula. Cover with clingfilm and refrigerate for up to 3 days.

CRÈME ANGLAISE

Serves 6–8

500 ML MILK
1 VANILLA POD, SPLIT

6 EGG YOLKS
100 G CASTER SUGAR
200 ML DOUBLE CREAM

1. Pour the milk into a saucepan and add the vanilla pod. Bring the milk to the boil and then turn the heat down to a gentle simmer.

2. Place the egg yolks in a bowl, add the sugar and mix them together. Remove the vanilla pod. Pour the hot milk over the egg yolks and sugar, whisking all the time so that the yolks don't cook.

3. Pour the mixture back into the milk pan. Place the pan back on the stove and very gently, over a low heat, stir the sauce until it thickens sufficiently to coat the back of a spoon. At no time must the sauce boil or it will be ruined.

4. Strain the sauce through a fine sieve into another bowl, then whisk in the cream.

SUGAR SYRUP

300 ML WATER
100 G CASTER SUGAR

1. Pour the water into a saucepan, add the sugar and boil them together for 5 minutes.

2. When the sugar has completely dissolved, pour the syrup into a container to cool. Refrigerate when cold – it will keep for several weeks.

SWEET SHORTCRUST PASTRY

*Makes enough for 8x10x2.5cm tartlet moulds
or 1 x 28cm flan tin*
100 G UNSALTED BUTTER, CHOPPED INTO 1CM
CUBES, PLUS EXTRA FOR GREASING

100 G ICING SUGAR
1 EGG
200 G PLAIN FLOUR, SIFTED, PLUS EXTRA
FOR DUSTING

1. Place the butter and icing sugar in a mixing bowl and beat together until soft and pale in colour. Add the egg and beat the mixture until smooth, before folding in the flour. Roll the dough into a ball, wrap in clingfilm and allow to rest in the refrigerator for about 2 hours.

2. Dust a work surface with a little flour, unwrap the dough and, if making tartlets, cut it into 8 pieces. Grease 8 × 10 x 2.5cm tart moulds or 1 x 28cm flan tin with a little butter. For the tartlets, roll out the pastry into 8 discs about 3mm thick; for the flan tin, roll out the pastry to about 5mm thick. Line the moulds, trimming off any excess pastry with a sharp knife and lightly pricking the base of each mould with a fork. Put the lined tart moulds or flan tin into the refrigerator to rest again, this time for about 15 minutes. Meanwhile, preheat the oven to 200°C/400°F/Gas 6.

3. To cook the pastry cases 'blind', cover each one with a circle of greaseproof paper and fill it with some dry beans, then bake in the preheated oven for 15 minutes.

4. Take them out of the oven and remove the baking beans and paper, then place the tarts back in the oven for another 5 minutes to turn golden. Remove from the oven, leave to cool once again and then gently lever them out of their moulds using the tip of a knife.

INDEX

For my darling Kim. For coming with me and helping me fulfill some of my dreams. For holding the whole thing together and just for being Kim. For getting my enthusiasm back. I love you.

To all the people that helped me on this incredible journey.

To Pat Llewellyn, 'the goddess', for believing in me, for making it possible. For her effervescent charm, support and encouragement. To Mr Ben Frow for his faith and expertise.

To Eve for typing the book. Olivia, Martha, Eliza, Charles and Amelia for trying their best and for being great. To Patsy, the best mother-in-law, for her love and support, and to Geoff for his hard work in holding the fort. Thank you to my Mum. Thanks to Brian Hladnick for his friendship and for being a real man in a time of crisis. To Mr Francis Green for his support. To Tracy Fanning for being mad!

To Martha Delap who made the unbearable bearable and for her kindness and love towards our children. To Jim Funnell, the superstar director. To Luke Cardiff and Patrick Acum, the camera boys. To Stuart Thompson and Steve Bowden for surround sound. Joanna Hayes. Valerie Messersi. Nathalie Vancauwenberghe. Caroline Bacle. Lesley Gardner. Mark Haliley. Tim Bridges. Anthony Hayes. Jo Hook in the office. Ginny Rolfe and Kate Habershon, the food stylists of the year. For me anyway! To Adam Lawrence and Kimble Watson for their photos and very bad jokes.

Lesley and Michel Calvet, very good friends

To Bonne Maman. Grande Confrérie du Cassoulet. Messieurs Roger and Benoît Cormary.

Monsieur & Madame Chappert – Café des Beloteurs, Poudis. Pierrette Lacombe-Canizares. Jean-François Daviaud. Laurent and Evelyne at the Chateau d'Airoux. Monsieur Bernard. Dominic Auzias. Monsieur Cavaillés. Françoise Gerrco. Baron de Roquette. Carol Cambolive, Head Mistress of the Montferrand School. Christian Brosse. Marie Christine Combes at the Château Garrevaque. Barth Meskine. Madame Catherine de Lassus and Monsieur Charles de Lassus. Monsieur Jacques Arnaudiés. Monsieur Roche. Claude Bescombe and Moustique. Sister Claire at the Monastère de Prouilhe in Fanjeaux Monsieur Imart from Puylaurens. The fishermen at Gruissan: Jean-Paul Alric, Marceau Martin, Denis Bes, Andre and Bernard. Serge Douy. And to the hundreds of people in the south-west of France especially the people of Revel market without whom I couldn't have written this book.

To Miren Lopategui for all your hard work, patience and dedication. Pia Tryde – photographer *extraordinaire* and to Stephan Bold her assistant. To Susan Fleming for all your help on the book. For the Power Rangers – Fiona MacIntyre and Lesley McOwan – Real Professionals! Sarah Bennie. David Eldridge, the designer of the book. All the people at Ebury.

Daniel Pemberton who composed the music for the television series.

Managing Editor: Lesley McOwan; Editorial Consultant: Miren Lopategui; Consultant Recipe Editor: Susan Fleming; Copy Editors: Trish Burgess and Kate Parker; Design: Two Associates; Production Manager: Henrietta Scott-Gall; Photographer: Pia Tryde; Props stylist: Pippin Britz; Food stylist: Eve Dendle.